LESSON ONE

'Fiction is an outdated means of expression, Marco, ripe for innovation.'

'What do you mean, Herbert?'

'Have you heard of the artist Jackson Pollock, Marco?'

'No, Herbert.'

'When Pollock painted, he did not stop to think, he did not make preliminary sketches, he did not erase or revise a little here and there—he poured paint on canvas, straight from the tin, yet his works sell for millions. Tell me, Marco, who is the Pollock of literature?'

'I don't know, Herbert.'

'There is no Pollock of literature—which is my point. It is your destiny, Marco, to break the mold. You have the ability to write as Pollock painted—instinctively, pouring words onto the page without thought or revision. You look surprised, Marco.'

'Do some authors think when they write, Herbert?'

CHAPTER ONE

*In which Marco names his first character
in the manner of Jackson Pollock.*

As I started to type like Jackson Pollock, Doris Day sang *Que Sera Sera* in the pocket of my anorak.

"TV personality Marco Ocram speaking. How can I help you?"

"This is Lieutenant Como Galahad—Clarkesville County Police. You okay to talk?"

Como Galahad?

Cripes. Only three paragraphs in, and already I'd invented a character with a ludicrous name. That's the challenge of creating a masterpiece without thinking—you never know what's going to come out. Old Pollock must face it big time. Imagine he's got Beyoncé round to have her portrait done. *SPLAT*—down goes a tin of paint, and there's a stunning view of Mount Rushmore. Explain that to a disappointed diva. Well, no going back now...

"Certainly, Lieutenant. How can I help?"

"You know Herbert Quarry, the writer?"

"Certainly, Lieutenant. Not a crime, I hope. Ha, ha, ha, ha, ha."

There was a disturbing moment of silence in response to my hilarious quip.

"That depends. You been in touch with Mister Quarry in the last few days?"

"Not directly."

"Not directly. What's that supposed to mean?"

"We might have exchanged an email or two—nothing more."

THE AWFUL TRUTH ABOUT THE HERBERT QUARRY AFFAIR

BY

MARCO OCRAM

A Tiny Fox Press Book

Tiny Fox Press LLC
North Port, FL

To my lovely wife, Leona, hoping my repeated dedications do not make her blasé.

"Did they include an email from Quarry that read: 'Lola, I need to see you. Come now. Wear the lime green dress'?"

I pretended it did, wishing to nurture the flow of the dialogue.

"Yes, how did you know?"

"Why would Quarry send you an email like that?"

"I don't know."

"Don't try to be clever, Writer."

"I'm not being clever."

Which was true on several levels—one being that I'd probably forgotten some important detail of police procedure by allowing myself to be interrogated without a preamble about my rights and so on. Either that or I was dealing with a rogue cop. Yes, that was more like it—the Jackson Pollock technique was working after all. I typed another line of dialogue for my new character...

"What did you think when you saw the email from Quarry?"

"I thought Herbert had sent it by mistake. It was obviously for someone else."

"You know who Lola is?"

It was a stupid question—how was I supposed to know who she was when I'd only just made her up? However, Lieutenant Galahad wasn't to know, so I responded with gracious equanimity.

"I do not, Lieutenant. Perhaps you could say what this is all about," I added, teeing up an expositional reply to let us all know what was happening. I awaited his big exposé with huge excitement.

"This is a confidential police matter—I'll ask the questions." So much for the big exposé. "What did you do with the email?"

"I replied saying I thought he'd sent it by mistake. Then I deleted it."

"What did you type it on?"

"My iPad," I said, laying the foundation for a lucrative placement deal with Apple.

"What's your relationship with Mister Quarry?"

"He's my mentor."

"Mentor, huh. What does he 'ment' you in?"

"Writing. He's my literary mentor."

"He teaches you to spell and stuff?"

"Not exactly, Lieutenant. We go for walks on the beach, and I ask him questions about writing bestsellers."

"Okay, Writer, here's how it is. We're holding Quarry for questioning. There's been a crime, and the facts fit him as the perp. We just need to check you out since you're a known associate. This has been an unofficial chat, nice and easy. You get down here to Clarkesville with your iPad, and it stays unofficial. Or I come to New York, and everything gets official. Get me?"

There was something about the way he said *official* which implied rough treatment of various sorts, handcuffs pinching my delicate wrists, sleep deprivation, nights in a cell with ruffians, rectal searches performed with insufficient regard for my hemorrhoids, the harsh lights of news-hungry press crews, my Bronx mom tearful as her boy is led away, scandalous intrusions by the *National Enquirer*, and countless other tribulations I can't imagine quickly enough to type.

I told him I understood.

"Okay. Be at Clarkesville County Police HQ at three. Ask for me at the desk."

LESSON TWO

'So, Herbert, my novel should be like a Jackson Pollock painting?'

'Not quite, Marco. The chapter is the painting—a self-contained work which can be admired for its intrinsic beauty. The novel should be a collection of paintings—a gallery, if you like, in which the reader is carried, enthralled, from one object of beauty to the next.'

'So, Herbert, my novel should be like a gallery of Jackson Pollock paintings?'

'Yes, Marco. You look doubtful, Marco; what is it?'

'It seems such a daunting challenge, Herbert.'

'Nonsense, Marco. Have courage. If anyone can write a load of Pollocks, it is surely you.'

CHAPTER TWO

In which there is a fateful meeting.

I took the ramp onto an expressway to Clarkesville, imagining the route to be southbound and christening it the N66—the first designation that came into my head. No doubt I would be slammed for my lack of research into US highway nomenclature, such being the tragic state of literary criticism.

I was relieved to find that the car I had written for myself was not some knackered old Toyota but a top-of-the-range Range Rover in *Midnight Black* with *Llama Tooth* upholstery. As I familiarized myself with its minor controls, marveling at the smoothness of its tinted electric windows, I considered what sort of difficulty Herbert might be in. A violation of some traffic code, perhaps. A punch thrown at a love rival. A fracas with the paparazzi who dogged him and his celebrity consorts. Which of the many possibilities would my mind select when the time came to type it?

With a token hint of realism, I slowed to join a line of cars waiting to clear some hold-up. A police car drew up beside me, its driver coating her thighs with crumbs from the handfuls of corn chips she was munching. Contemplating the officer's nondescript appearance, I wondered whether Como Galahad should have some standout characteristics to allow the reader to form a vivid mental picture. Hmmmm. I would need to imagine something original but not too outlandish—perhaps a glass eye and rumpled beige coat. Or might he be the wheelchaired victim of a callous gangland shooting?

I was still composing variations on the theme of Lieutenant Galahad's appearance when an approaching sign announced the

Clarkesville exit. I eyed my dashboard to find the clock—I was two hours early for my appointment.

To kill time, I bypassed the homely town of Clarkesville and followed a quiet road through trees fringing the ocean shoreline. Just beyond a viewing point, I took the familiar track that led off between rocks and curved round to a lonely beach.

I killed the engine and sat in the car, suffused with a sense of shock. I'd stayed at Herbert's countless times, but to see it now—the house Herbert himself had designed, the house in which we had spent so many glorious days—to see it festooned with police tape...it brought home to me, in a gut-wrenching way, that festooned wasn't the right word, conveying, as it did, a sense of gaiety entirely inappropriate to the dramatic tension I was trying to build. Hoping my readers wouldn't spot the clumsy word choice, I wandered through the small patch of garden, noticing a grave-like excavation in one of the flower beds. Muddy footprints led from the grave to Herbert's porch, where a long-handled spade leant beside the door. Stepping through the crime scene tape, I felt behind the statue of James Joyce, where Herbert always left a key, and let myself into the house.

Walking into Herbert's study, I almost sensed his presence, as if the great man might appear and embrace me in welcome. There were the countless awards, the press cuttings, the photographs of Herbert with the actresses, models, artists, authors, poets, opera stars, pop singers, sportswomen, news anchors, heiresses and weather girls with whom he had been linked over the years. As my eye scanned the beautiful faces of Herbert's ex-girlfriends, it stopped at a picture I hadn't seen before. I lifted its frame from the wall. It showed a girl of about sixteen in a lime green dress. A dedication in a distinctive hand read:

To Herbert, with all my love, Lola.

I scrolled back to Chapter One—yes, there was the quote from the email Herbert had sent to me:

Lola, I need to see you. Come at once. Wear the lime green dress.

I wondered whether I should remind the readers about it. Deciding not to bother, I perused the papers littering Herbert's desk—the love letters, the draft novels, the uncashed checks for huge royalties—until I spotted a note in the same distinctive hand.

Herbert, my love, meet me tonight by the bandstand. PS don't forget the condoms, as I don't want to bear your lovechild, and your repeated rantings and threats to kill me won't make me change my mind. I would rather die. I love you, Lola.

I was pondering the implications of this remarkable memo when a giant black man stomped into the room, his gun covering my chest.

"Down on the floor! Down on the floor! Down on the floor!"

He bellowed the phrase as he stomped toward me, beating me to the ground with the impact of his words. His commands were redundant, however—I'd dropped to the floor at the sight of him, almost pooping my pants.

"Don't shoot! Don't shoot! I'm Marco Ocram, the writer."

A hand patted me down before lifting me to my feet by the collar of my anorak.

"What the fuck are you doing?" the man said. It was a good question—I had no idea. "Didn't you understand the '*do not cross*' on the tapes? I could've shot your dumb ass, and God knows what shit I'd've been in then."

I wasn't sure his '*I'd've*' was a sufficiently elegant expression for the literary tone I was struggling to set, but I decided not to push the point, partly because a nuanced discussion upon phrasing might spoil the pacey flow of the action, and partly because the speaker was about seven feet tall, about four hundred pounds, and about the meanest-looking person I'd ever seen—leaving aside my Bronx mom.

I straightened my anorak and tried to appear composed. "I'm a friend of Herbert Quarry's. He always lets me use his house."

"I know exactly who you are." He whipped out a badge. "Como Galahad, Clarkesville County Police."

LESSON THREE

'Herbert, how should I reveal my backstory?'

'How do you suggest, Marco?'

'I could have a flashback chapter in which I explain how I was adopted twice, how I was brilliant at many sports until I developed my middle-ear problem, how I postulated a new fundamental particle—the tau muon— how my popular science book—The Tau Muon—was an unexpected hit, topping the bestseller lists for over a year, how I was a regular guest on network chat shows, and all the other things the reader might need to know. Would that work?'

'No, Marco. You should tantalize the reader, revealing occasional glimpses of your background.

CHAPTER THREE

*In which Marco reveals untantalizing glimpses of his background
and is taken into Como Galahad's confidence.*

Without asking my permission, Como Galahad rifled through my satchel. Encountering the items within it, his face assumed three looks of varying expression: the first, prompted by a Barbara Cartland, quizzical and mildly censorious; the second, at discovering a max-pack of suppositories, somewhat more empathetic; the third derisive as he scanned my treasured photograph of Herbert—the one with the inscription *'To my ever faithful friend, Marco. Always write the first thing that comes into your head.'*

"*Always write the first thing that comes into your head.* Huh. That could explain those dumbass moves of yours, Writer."

I snatched the precious picture from his huge hand. He, in return, snatched my iPad. Having asked me to confirm it was the device I used for emails, he performed some technical tasks I didn't understand sufficiently to make up, then handed it back.

"I don't know what to make of you, Writer. You say you're best friends with Quarry, but you don't seem to know Lola Kellogg. Seems weird a best friend wouldn't know about his pal's love life."

"Not necessarily, Detective. Sometimes life's not so simple." I added the stock phrase to give myself time to think of a reason why I wouldn't know about Herbert's love life. Not enough time, as it happened.

"Where were you three days ago?"

I worked the dates in my head. "New York, why?"

"Anybody see you there?"

14

"Millions, probably."

"Huh?"

"I was on the Noosha Winfrey show. Talking about my book."

I meant my other book—the one about tau muons—not this one.

"Let me tell you why we're holding Quarry." Lieutenant Galahad scanned my face for reactions. "Three days ago, we get a call saying Herbert Quarry's up to no good at his house. We get here, and guess what."

I couldn't guess, so he told me.

"We find your best friend Herbert kneeling on the floor of his living room in a pool of blood. Lola Kellogg's body was in pieces around him. He didn't even register we were there. He was staring ahead and sliding his fingertips through the girls blood."

I was horrified by his revelation.

"Girl's, Lieutenant, girl's." What were they teaching in police college nowadays?

"You can spell it any way you like, Writer, but the fact is your best friend is facing the chair. He's killed a fifteen-year-old girl, and all the evidence says he was sleeping with her too."

I flopped back in Herbert's chair, swiveling it as an aid to thought, my eyes swiveling too as I tried to absorb what I'd just typed. Herbert, a murderer! There was no way I could believe it. There and then I formed an unshakeable conviction that Herbert had been framed.

The odd thing was, when I shared my conclusion with Lieutenant Galahad, he didn't laugh derisively, call me a dumbass, and generally pooh-pooh the suggestion. Instead, he looked straight at me, one eyebrow raised.

"What?" I said.

He paused a moment, giving me a chance to catch up with my typing.

"Let me level with you, Writer."

"Sure, Lieutenant."

"But this stays between you and me. Understand?" He prodded the air with a forefinger the size of a... of a huge forefinger.

I nodded.

"And if it doesn't stay between you and me, I'll have you slammed up with some real mean pieces of shit as Herbert Quarry's accomplice. Get me?"

It seemed an ungracious way to treat the writer who had gone to so much trouble to invent him, but I nodded, hoping he would get to the point.

"Everything points to Quarry having done this. And I mean everything," he said. "There's almost too much evidence."

"That can happen sometimes, can't it?" Especially when the writer makes it up as he goes along.

"Maybe." He looked around, checking we were alone. "But there are things I've seen at HQ."

"What sort of things?"

He shook his head. "Best if you don't know. But enough to make me wonder whether this whole thing's a set-up."

My chair-swiveling paid off as I thought of a question I should have asked earlier.

"What did Herbert say when you arrested him?"

"I wasn't there."

"But...I thought...but..." I redoubled my swiveling in the hope I might make sense of the Lieutenant's bewildering admission.

"Let me explain something," he said, much to my relief. "Clarkesville County has a small police department with a small budget. Three days ago, for the first time in more than five years, Chief McGee decided to send someone on a training course. It was me. I'm the lead homicide detective. On the day Quarry's arrested, I was out of town."

LESSON FOUR

'Herbert, does a writer need to experience love in order to write a truly great book?'

'No, Marco. A truly great writer can find inspiration in other emotions: greed, envy, pride, hatred, self-satisfaction, narcissism, rage, insecurity, overconfidence, a misplaced belief in one's ability, the desire to impress, repressed sexual perversions, resentment, fear of being outdone by contemporaries, escapist delusions, unconscious misogyny or misandry, nauseating complacency. You just need to let these emotions out, Marco.'

CHAPTER FOUR

In which Marco is put on the spot.

"Forensic taxidermy?"

I'd asked Lieutenant Galahad what the subject of the training had been, thinking he might have read too much into Chief McGee's decision to send him on a course—perhaps McGee considered the training essential for the performance of homicide duties.

"Does that sound essential to you, Writer? It was the only course with places free. In fact, all its places were free. I spent a day by myself with the taxidermy teacher while Clarkesville's biggest murder was going on."

Lieutenant Galahad kneaded his fist into his palm as if he needed to work off his frustration. I wondered if the readers would appreciate my wordplay on *kneaded* and *needed*, or whether I'd wasted the five seconds it had taken me to craft the sentence.

"I have a suggestion, Lieutenant."

"A good one, or a next-thing-that-comes-into-your-head one?"

"I think you will find it an excellent one. Why don't you confront the rascal McGee, forcing him to reveal the truth with rapier-like questioning?"

His fist kneading became more frenetic.

"That's an excellent suggestion? Writer, that's such a dumbass suggestion, I ain't gonna waste a breath explaining why."

I tipped back Herbert's chair to give myself something to write about other than swiveling it, while I waited for the next thing to come into my head. I could see Galahad's point. Confronting his Chief without evidence might not be a skyward career move. I, however, was not dependent on the goodwill of the police chief.

"What if I confront the rascal McGee?"

"What with? You gonna ask him why he sent me on a dumbass course the day the murder happens? I wonder how many milliseconds he's gonna take to figure out you got that from me."

I was beginning to wonder whether Herbert's advice about writing the first thing that comes into your head was more suited to literary fiction. In crime novels, you seemed to need a logic for everything. No wonder Como was kneading his fists—it was driving me nuts too.

I sprang from Herbert's chair. For the first time in four chapters I had an idea that made sense.

"Okay, then let's work together to find evidence. You can't go around making enquiries about whether this is all a setup, or you'll be shunned, spurned, snubbed, and ostracized by your police fraternity. But I can. I'm Herbert's protégé and friend. I've every right to ask the awkward questions no one else is prepared to ask."

A hot rush of moral righteousness inflamed my mind as I thought of Marco Ocram, the defender of Truth, single-handedly smiting her foes. Well, perhaps not single-handedly, as technically there would be four hands if I was working with Como Galahad—and since his were twice the usual size, I suppose an argument could be made for there being the equivalent of six standard hands, so I would be six-handedly smiting the foes of Truth. Anyway, don't get me bogged down in an irrelevant hand count. Where was I? Oh yes...

"That's nearly a good idea, Writer. But you got it the wrong way around. The moment Chief McGee finds you're investigating him, he's gonna have you banged up for something. Better if you seem to be writing a book to show what a great job McGee's doing. You said yourself, you were Quarry's big pal. Tell McGee you feel cheated by him. Say you wanna nail Quarry for being a sick bastard. You're gonna let the world know the truth about what he's done. McGee'll swallow a story like that."

The hot rush of moral righteousness abated a tad as I thought of how disloyal I would be to Herbert if I followed the Lieutenant's advice. How could I pretend Herbert was a sick bastard when he was my closest friend? How could I...

Thankfully Como's phone beeped, sparing the readers several boring sentences about my moral dilemma. He took the call with his back to me. I heard the usual meaningless interjections someone uses to move along a one-sided conversation, after which he said:

"I'm at Quarry's place. I need to call in at HQ, but I'll call round after that." He stuffed his phone in a pocket. "We're leaving. Come on."

"Great. Does that mean you need me to help?"

"No, it means there's no way I'm leaving you here to fuck up the evidence."

We took our own cars. I followed Como, my mind half on the job of keeping up with him—he drove like a maniac—and half contemplating the fact that I had started to think of him as Como rather than Lieutenant Galahad.

At Police HQ, Como stuck a beefy arm out of his window to point me at one of the bays marked *Police Vehicles Only*. I wasn't sure I should be parking there, but I did as he said, or, rather, pointed. He continued the pointing theme by tapping the dial of his watch as a gesture of impatience while I searched through the pockets of my clothes and my satchel for my key to lock the car.

"Sorry. Where are we going?" I jogged to keep up with his long strides as we crossed the car park.

"You'll see."

I followed him through an open office where people were performing the entire spectrum of activities shown in TV police procedurals: drinking coffee, making coffee, spilling coffee, making telephone calls with feet up on desk, making them with feet off desk, swiveling in chairs, shouting *Hey, Miko,* throwing pens and other items to denote a range of negative emotions, suffering the whoops and catcalls of a line of prostitutes awaiting interview, rewinding CCTV images, failing by one second to complete the trace of a telephone call, opening filing cabinets, punching a colleague, surrendering both badge and gun to begin a period of unjustly imposed suspension, comparing striations on closeup photographs of bullets, tampering with evidence, printing and photographing suspects, supervising lineups, revoking minor penalties in return for bribes, conducting case-conferences, sticking photographs to walls and drawing arrows between them, and countless other clichés I didn't have time to type.

We stopped at a pair of half-glazed doors, one of which bore the nameplate for *Chief McGee*.

"We need to give McGee the story," said Como. "That way, I've got a reason for letting you poke around in the case."

In a panic, I grabbed his arm.

"Christ, Como, you can't drop me in it like this—I don't know what to say."

"You need to have another look at your special picture of Herbert Quarry, Writer."

He knocked, pushed open the door, and pushed me into the room.

Como's hijack of the scene gave me no time to think. I did a natural Jackson Pollock and wrote the first thing that came into my head.

A heavyset man in a police chief uniform was standing near a window, a phone to his ear. He waved us toward his conference table and turned away to finish his call in confidential tones. After locking the phone in a drawer, he wandered over to join us.

"Who's your friend, Galahad?"

"This is Marco Ocram, Chief—the scientist guy off TV."

"Pleased to meet you, Mister Ocram."

He squeezed my hand so tightly I hopped on tiptoe with the pain.

"Likewise," I squeaked.

"Mister Ocram thinks it's time someone wrote a book about what a sick pedo Quarry's been, and what a great job the PD's done taking him off the street."

Como nudged my thigh with his knee to pass me the baton of the dialogue.

"Absolutely, er, Chief. This needs to be a lesson for all the other, er, sick pedos. Let them know Clarkesville PD is on their case."

"Great. About time we got a little credit instead of all the shit the papers say."

Chief McGee gave my shoulder a slap of appreciation, almost knocking me over.

"Mister Ocram's asked if I can show him around," said Como, "tell him about proper police procedure and stuff."

I didn't wait for another painful knee-nudge.

"Absolutely. Authenticity's my watchword. We can't have the readers thinking we're making things up as we go along, ha, ha, ha, ha, ha."

"He says he'll need some quotes and pictures of you for the publicity."

Chief McGee straightened his tie and put on his best police chief face.

"No problem, Mister Ocram. You let me know whatever you need. Galahad here will tell you, my door is always open."

"Thanks, Chief. Let's go."

Como ushered me out before I could say anything else off the top of my head. We went back to the car park.

"You did real good, Writer. I almost believed you myself. Notice anything about his office?"

"The new blinds?"

"That's the one."

"What about them?"

"He got'em three months ago—two days after he'd had a particular visitor in his office."

"Who?" I gulped the bait.

Como checked no one was close by.

"Lola Kellogg."

LESSON FIVE

'Are there techniques, Herbert, that writers use to keep readers in suspense?'

'Indeed, Marco, there are many. A sudden change in location, perhaps. Finishing a chapter prematurely to underline the significance of a revelation. But they are the cheap tricks of the hack. No serious writer would adopt them.'

CHAPTER FIVE

*In which Marco unexpectedly changes location and finishes a
chapter prematurely to underline the significance of a revelation.*

Astonished by his news, I followed Como in a trance all the way to 276
West 24th Street where a sign said *Clarkesville County Pathology
Center.*

Como led me into reception where we completed the tedious
formalities to record the start of our visit. I followed him through a
warren of corridors to a laboratory in which I, as a scientist, felt at
home after the alien surroundings of police HQ. My expert eye roved
over the room, clocking various types of scientific equipment far too
specialized for me to describe without holding us all up. We passed
between the benches to where someone was attacking a side of pork
with a harpoon. Hearing our steps, she turned to face us. Before I had
a chance to pad out a few lines by describing her appearance, bearing,
and manner of dress, Como introduced her.

"This is Doctor Flora Moran—Chief Forensic Scientist. She's a
specialist in knife crime." Como pronounced her name with an
emphasis on the last syllable as if to avoid it sounding like Flora
Moron. "This is Marco Ocram."

I held out a hand.

"*The* Marco Ocram?"

I gave a modest nod to show the beautiful pathologist I was
indeed *the* Marco Ocram, the scientist and TV personality renowned
for his bold theories about the tau muon. We exchanged various
pleasantries too humdrum to document, the gist of which being that

THE AWFUL TRUTH ABOUT THE HERBERT QUARRY AFFAIR

Flora Moran was thrilled and delighted to find me there. Como cut it short by asking Flora to summarize her provisional findings.

"The body is female, mid-teens. The blood group, DNA, appearance, hair color, eye color, dental configuration, and other distinguishing features match those of Lola Kellogg, who disappeared on the day the corpse was discovered. The rare Japanese cooking knife with which the corpse was dismembered matches a set of rare Japanese cooking knives in Herbert Quarry's kitchen. Herbert Quarry's DNA and fingerprints are all over the corpse. There are distinctive handprints on the sections of corpse showing where the body had been held steady as it was cut up, and the prints match those of Herbert Quarry."

I digested the implications of Flora's words—whoever framed Herbert knew what they were doing. I asked if I could inspect the corpse.

"Of course. The body is in the top drawer of the freezer," she said. "The head, arms, and legs are in the next drawer down."

I almost fainted at my first peek inside the drawer. I'd invented poor Lola's sensational death without a thought; now, confronted with its hideous reality, I was overcome by regret—not to mention squeamishness and the need to find a toilet. My blood seemed to have run off for a long weekend with my feet. Bucking the downward trend, my stomach was trying to climb out of my mouth. I cast desperate eyes around the lab for a chaise longue upon which I might swoon, and a brandy decanter to supply an antidote.

"You okay, Writer? You're looking a bit grey."

"I'm fine, thank you, Como, just a little tired after all the excitement."

I pulled myself almost together. If I was going to make a career of writing dramatic true-crime novels, I would need to master my weaknesses. Imagining myself a modern-day Sherlock Holmes, icily detached and objective, I removed the contents of the drawers and laid them upon a table.

I inspected the various parts with a scientist's eye and my rusty magnifying glass—sorry, my trusty magnifying glass—taking care not to contaminate the evidence with ash from my pipe. Nothing escaped my gaze. I deduced that Lola had received a pedicure and manicure shortly before she died—there had been little nail growth since the distinctive opalescent varnish had been applied. I also noticed she had no unusual birthmark on her right heel. Yes, that's right—I said no birthmark. I even checked it twice to be sure, just in case it became important later in the book.

Removing my heavy plaid Ulster, I donned surgical gloves to examine the poor victim's head. Dr. Moran was an expert in knife crime, so it was possible her professional bias might cause her to overlook other important signs. Yes, it was just as I expected: there was a slight softness to the right of the sigmoid talmata, a little-known area of the skull found only in the most advanced anatomical text-books.

Having found nothing else of note, I curtailed my examination before the readers had time to realize a frozen head would have no soft spots. I pulled off the gloves and dropped them in a bin, signifying that we had just disposed of several paragraphs of trashy prose.

"Thank you, Doctor Moran. I'm sure your observations have been entirely conclusive. May I?" I raised my iPad to show I meant to take photographs.

"Of course."

I took a number of closeups of the individual parts, then arranged them on a table for an overall shot.

"And if I could just get a couple with the two of you in the background to show to my mom...lovely...move together a bit...smile... perhaps if you could pretend to be examining that piece of left thigh... no the other piece...hold it...lovely..."

Curtailing the description of my photographic activities, I caught Como's eye and twitched my head to say I needed to speak with him outside.

"What?" he said, after we'd asked Flora to let us know when her final report was ready, said goodbye, left the forensic lab, wound our way back through the offices, got into our respective cars, driven to a remote layby where we wouldn't be overheard, got out of our respective cars and leaned against the immaculate paintwork of his offside front wing.

"Someone hit Lola on the back of her head before she died."

"You sure?"

"A thousand per cent. There was a distinctive softness behind the tabloid stigmata— just where you'd hit someone if you wanted to knock them out without doing obvious damage."

Como thought for a while. "Could still have been Quarry. He hits her, then cuts her up."

"What with? They found him with a knife. You don't knock someone out with a knife."

"Okay. I buy that. What d'you think she was hit with?"

I brought up the photos I'd taken and swiped through to the closeups, zooming in for maximum detail. "I'd say something with a bit of weight to it, but no sharp edges. Cylindrical maybe. Long enough to get a decent swing."

"You know what you've just described, Writer?"

I hadn't given it a thought.

"A baseball bat? A rolling pin? A frozen roll of puff pastry? A narwhal tusk?"

"Maybe. But what about this for an idea—what if you made it a police nightstick?"

LESSON SIX

'Herbert, what is a literary tradition?'

'A literary tradition, Marco, is a sustained collective view of what constitutes writing worthy of study, one passed down from generation to generation.'

'It's not a traditional way of writing, like sitting in a coffee shop with a Mac, Herbert?'

'No, Marco.'

'Herbert, from which literary traditions should the truly great writer draw inspiration?'

'The truly great writer finds inspiration in all literary traditions, Marco. She studies them avidly, appreciating what each has contributed. She would never disparage the literary tradition of any nation.'

CHAPTER SIX

*In which Marco makes the cheapest of jokes at the expense of the
French literary tradition and arranges a rendezvous with a minor
character.*

To betoken my emotion at Como's sensational suggestion, I smote the
wing of his car with my fist, immediately wishing I hadn't.

"Ow!"

"Easy, Writer, you could have damaged something." Como
watched with touching concern as I nursed my hand under an armpit.
"Why'd you punch the car?"

"It was meant to be a gesture—you know, to show excitement. I
was trying to build dramatic tension for the start of a new chapter."

"Well, punch your own friggin' car next time."

Perhaps I'd misread the touching concern. Flexing my fingers to
check they still worked, I thought about how to rebuild the dramatic
tension I'd just destroyed. Como, meanwhile, bent to examine his car.

"I only polished this yesterday. Now there's a smudge."

Not having much luck with my dramatic re-tensioning, I picked
up the thread of the dialogue where I'd dropped it at the end of Chapter
Five.

"Wow, what a great twist. Lola, killed by the police!"

"Trouble is, Writer, if she was, then McGee will have been in on
it. Which means we'll be at the bottom of the world's deepest shit-pit
if he thinks we suspect anything." He started pacing around as if he
were struggling to rationalize his thoughts. I knew how he felt—I was
struggling to rationalize my own thoughts, or, more accurately, the
absence of them. "Show me those photos again."

"Sure." I showed him one of the photos, a particularly fetching one of him and Flora.

"Not those, Dumbass—the ones of the mark on the head."

We studied the closeups together. The mark of the blow was faint but...

Como and I looked at each other as we absorbed the implications of the three dots I had typed. The mark of the blow was faint, but if dumbass Marco had spotted it why hadn't Flora?

"D'you think she could be in on it too?" I asked.

Como shook his head. "I just don't see it, Writer. Flora's straight, dead straight. Besides, she's clever, too. She wouldn't have let you take pictures if she was hiding something. I think she just didn't look closely—why would she go huntin' for other causes of death when the body's in pieces?"

"True." An idea mushroomed in my mind. "That's why they cut her up, Como! It all makes sense now. Herbert would never have killed her, and he never ever ever would have butchered the body. *They* did it, Como—*they* did it to throw Flora off the scent. Why would she bother with a full examination when the cause of death's so obvious? And the exsanguination of the body would have stopped a prominent bruise from forming where Lola was hit."

I started pacing in circles myself, wondering whether I'd invented a brilliant rationale for the dismemberment I'd typed at random in Chapter Three, or whether I'd just typed more random nonsense that anyone with the slightest understanding of pathology would see through in an instant. I crossed my fingers and hoped it was mold-breaking random nonsense.

"Maybe, Writer, but we're getting ahead of ourselves. For all we know, Flora might have seen it and might have logged it and just not mentioned it to us, so let's eliminate the obvious explanation before we go getting carried away with fancy theories." Como clocked his watch. "I'll go check it out, then I'm done for the night."

"Done for the night? It's only four-thirty. I thought we were working tirelessly in the pursuit of truth?"

"You can pursue truth all night if you like, but I've got a game to watch. Let's meet at HQ at nine tomorrow."

"But what am I gonna do?" *Stuck in this dump on my own*, were the words I almost added.

"Don't ask me. You're the writer, Writer—make something up." He gave the wing of his car one last pointed look, then climbed inside and drove off to HQ to check the logs for evidence of a bump on Lola's head.

I decided I needed caffeine to stimulate my exhausted brain. Conveniently forgetting I was parked in a remote layby, I crossed the street to my regular coffeeshop. The waitress recognized me immediately.

"Gosh, it's lovely to see you back in Clarkesville, Mister Ocram. I saw you on the Noosha Winfrey show. Would you..."

I signed Jacqueline's proffered copy of *The Tau Muon*, which she then hugged to her chest.

"Gosh, how rude of me. I haven't even shown you to your table. Mother, it's Marco Ocram."

Jacqueline's mother made a fuss of me, then shooed some other customers from the special table they always kept for me. "They've left such a mess." She wiped the table peevishly, in the exact manner of a character from a 1950's French novel I'd just read. I remembered the first time I'd called at the coffeeshop, all those years ago...

The waitress asked what I was doing in Clarkesville.

"I've come to see a friend, a great novelist who's bought a house on the beach just outside town."

"Oh, that must be Herbert Quarry. I saw his name in the paper. How exciting."

She pronounced Herbert the French way—Airbear.

"It's Herbert," corrected her mother, with an embarrassed laugh. "You'll be making this young man think we are very ignorant—if his friend's a great writer, he won't be French."

Jacqueline had become much more familiar with Herbert since, as he was the town's only celebrity inhabitant.

"We've heard rumors about Herbert and Lola Kellogg. Is it true he's killed her? We can't believe it, can we, Mother?"

Jacqueline and her mother shook shocked heads to indicate disbelief—I hoped it was prompted by the rumors and not my awful writing. I ordered a coffee to add an overdue touch of realism.

When Jacqueline returned with my drink, I asked her to sit with me, posing a question in lowered tones.

"I'm trying to get to the bottom of what happened with Herbert and Lola. Does Herbert have any enemies in town?"

"He's a famous novelist, rich and handsome, with many lovers, so all the men hate him, and some of the women."

"I can understand all the men hating him. But why do some of the women?"

"Have you heard the saying Hell hath no fury like a woman scorned?"

I pretended I hadn't so she could spell it out for the readers.

"It means if you scorn a woman, she will be more furious than anything in Hell."

"I see. And how does it apply in this case?"

"Some women in Clarkesville were scorned because Herbert chose not to make love with them, and some were scorned because Herbert did make love to them but spurned them afterwards."

"I see. Were some of these women more scorned than others? If, say, there was a scale of scorning from zero to ten, where zero meant entirely un-scorned, and ten meant utterly scorned, how would you characterize the distribution of the women of Clarkesville on such a scale?"

Jacqueline considered my remarkable question.

"I would imagine it to be a normal distribution, with most women around five somewhere and diminishing numbers approaching the extremes of zero and ten. A classic bell curve."

"Or belle curve!" I quipped.

We creased with laughter at my hilarious *bon mot*. After we had each wiped the torrents of tears from our respective cheeks, I returned to a more solemn line of conversation.

"Is there, then, a woman in Clarkesville who might score a perfect ten on the scale of scornedness?" I asked, typing an obscure abstract noun to impress the readers.

"Yes, there is; but she is my sister, Marcia Delgado, so I am not sure it would be right to betray a family secret to you."

"Come, come—you're being far too sensitive. The worst that could happen is I might reproduce her story in a bestselling novel, and where is the harm in that?"

"All right. I will tell you everything. But not here. Meet me at seven tonight at Kelly's bar and diner."

As Jaqueline slipped out of her chair, anxious to get back to work and to escape the horrendously corny dialogue I had typed, I noticed a beautifully made-up woman leave her seat at a nearby table. I was admiring the delicious ambiguity of the phrase 'beautifully made-up', which could refer to the clever way I'd invented her, when she slipped into the chair Jacqueline had just vacated.

"You must be Marco Ocram," she said.

I offered my hand courteously.

"Pleased to meet you, Miss..."

"It's Mrs. Tann but call me Quimara." She pulled her chair closer to mine and beamed at me. While I felt for my pen, expecting her to ask me to sign a copy of *The Tau Muon*, she said, "Did I just hear you're looking to dig up dirt on that sick pedo Herbert Quarry?"

Before I could decide how to answer, my attention-seeking iPad had a sulk about its battery and turned itself off.

LESSON SEVEN

'Tell me, Herbert, how do truly great authors describe their characters? Are there any golden rules?'

'Yes, Marco—since you ask, there is a golden rule. An author might describe a character's mannerisms, apparel, behavior, vices, opinions, emotions, actions, sexual preferences—indeed all of their attributes, bar one.'

'Which is that, Herbert?'

'The face, Marco. The truly great author never describes a character's face.'

'Why, Herbert? Is it to comply with postmodernist tenets about the primacy of indeterminist modal constructs of transformative plastic identity norms?'

'No, Marco—it is to make it easier to cast actors when the film rights are sold.'

CHAPTER SEVEN

In which Marco introduces Herbert Quarry in compliance with postmodernist tenets about the primacy of indeterminist modal constructs of transformative plastic identity norms.

By the time I'd pampered my iPad with enough juice to coax it back to life, I was already en route to the local prison to see Herbert. I couldn't type up Quimara Tann's amazing revelations while driving, so we'd have to leave them for later. Remind me to fill you in as soon as we reach a dull spot, otherwise I'll forget. Anyway, back to the plot...

The Clarkesville County Correctional Centre was a giant complex the size of five Olympic villages, perched upon a remote and forbidding moor sandwiched between two industrial parks. As I drove through its imposing gates, I wondered whether I'd made a huge gaffe in supposing Herbert would be held there. Might prisoners on remand be held in cells at police HQ? I'd have to ask Como. If necessary, I could always invent some story about the cells at police HQ being redecorated—perhaps increasing the plausibility of the explanation by embellishing it with authentic technical details, such as the need to find a wallpaper pattern that would hide blood stains.

I spotted a line of low-life scum waiting to visit the prison—the defense lawyers of Clarkesville trying to pick up business. I tagged on at the back and was eventually shown to a visiting room where I steeled myself for the tedious repetition of forenames which blights my dialogues with Herbert.

With a jangle of keys, a door opened. Herbert clanked in, his arms locked to his sides, his ankles shackled, his face a Hannibal Lector mask. He was overjoyed at my visit.

35

"Marco, I am locked up twenty-four-seven with illiterate murderers and rapists. I am so looking forward to a few minutes' conversation with an intellectual equal. But you will do for now."

"It's very kind of you to say so, Herbert. But why is your abdomen distended so?"

"The prisoners are brutal lifers, Marco. To pass time, they indulge in mindless games, one an egg-eating contest which I entered to prove myself as tough as they."

"Did you win, Herbert?"

"No, I was trounced, with endless coarse jests at my expense. However, I had the last laugh. I proposed a contest to write the most insightful critique of Barthes' theory of readerly positivism. I don't need to say that it was I making the coarse jests by the end of that bruising encounter."

"Herbert, I need you to tell me your side of the story. What was it between you and Lola? Who knew about it? Who could be trying to frame you?"

"We had better take those subjects in turn, Marco. Let me tell you about Lola. You might know that for almost eleven years I have been writing my bestselling books at the coffeeshop in Clarkesville, where the sympathetic proprietress reserves a special table for me."

"Yes, Herbert. She has done the same for me."

"That is typical of her, Marco. She is very accommodating to bestselling authors. Anyway, over the years, I dated many of the beautiful women who waited in the café."

"Herbert, do you mean the women who waited on customers, or women who just passed time there?"

"Both. I wasn't fussy. But with Lola it was different from the start. One afternoon I left my iPad at the coffeeshop, being deep in thought about the tagline for my latest novel. That evening, there was a knock on my door—it was Lola, bearing my iPad. I recall our conversation word for word...

"You left this," she said, proffering my iPad. "I spotted it contains a draft of a new bestselling novel. I hope you won't mind, but I read it all."

"All of it?"

"Yes."

"How could I mind when you are so beautiful and captivating?"

"Oh, Herbert, why must all the truly great writers be so sad? You, Brown, Grisham, Blyton—all giants of literature, and yet all such tragic figures."

"My darling Lola, writing is a disease, an all-consuming passion. For some of us, our writing is so important it leaves no room in our lives for anything else. The perfectly crafted sentence is the only thing our hearts desire."

"The only thing, Herbert?" she asked, looking deep into my eyes and touching me where she shouldn't.

"Well, no, now you come to mention it."

"Afterwards we smoked cigarettes and danced on the beach."

"Did you know she was fifteen?"

"So the police say, Marco. I took her to be twenty, or thereabouts. She was extremely sophisticated in her outlook and behavior."

I passed over the question of what sophisticated behavior Herbert had in mind, that kind of carry-on having no place in a mass-market humorous mystery.

"Who might have known you were having an affair with Lola?"

Herbert scratched a pensive armpit, which was ridiculous because I'd said his arms were chained to his sides. I typed his reply before the readers spotted my gaffe...

"It's a tough question, Marco. I honestly don't know. I did my best to keep our liaisons secret, as she'd told me her father was very religious and would be upset if he found she was having an affair outside of the holy bonds of matrimony. But we might have been spotted together, and there is always the possibility that our intimate communications could have been eavesdropped."

"How did you communicate?"

"The usual ways: postcards, tweets, Facebook."

"Don't you think it was rather careless, Herbert? Such messages could have been spotted by others."

"I hadn't thought of that."

Herbert was a bit of a dinosaur where social media were concerned. I prodded him to the third topic we needed to discuss.

"Who might have a motive to frame you for Lola's gruesome death, Herbert?"

"Frame me? I've no idea, Marco. What sort of person would want to frame me? What have I ever done to aggrieve anyone?"

I gave him some suggestions.

"A love rival? A rejected lover, perhaps? An author whose work you have criticized?"

"Ah, I see what you mean, Marco. It could be any of thousands of people."

That was a big help. I changed tack.

"Tell me then, Herbert—what happened on the day of the murder?"

"On the day of the murder, what happened was..."

But before Herbert could tell me what happened on the day of the murder, a bell drowned his words, a door opened, and a heavily armed warder entered.

"Time's up, Bud. Back to the guest suite."

Without giving Herbert a chance to thank me in broken words for rushing to his aid, the heavily armed warder dragged him out.

I wondered why prison warders were always heavily armed. Perhaps it was manhandling so many prisoners that built their muscles up.

LESSON EIGHT

'Herbert, what is Talking Heads Syndrome?'

'It is the tendency of the incompetent author to write passages of unrelieved dialogue, Marco.'

'What do you mean by unrelieved, Herbert?'

'I mean passages consisting only of spoken sentences, Marco, without descriptions of movements, gestures, settings or other factors that might illuminate the context.'

'Ha! A writer would have to be especially awful to do that, Herbert.'

'Indeed, Marco.'

CHAPTER EIGHT

In which Marco struggles with his Talking Heads Syndrome and imagines a character from a future book.

I parked my black Range Rover by Kelly's diner and edged my way through the crowd of revelers within. Within the diner, I mean, not the Range Rover. The atmosphere was tense and aggressive. Fights broke out sporadically between drunk men wielding pool cues, and drunker women chalking their tips. I found a dark and cozy nook where Jacqueline was waiting. She was dressed to kill. I asked her why.

"I have just finished a shift in the family abattoir. I came over without having time to change. I hope my attire does not make you uneasy."

"No, no," I reassured her, "not in the least."

But my reassurances satisfied her more than me—a woman who cut up carcasses was ideally qualified to dismember Lola Kellogg. Instantly I was on the alert. All of a clichéd sudden, the fighting crowd had withdrawn to the periphery of my mind—my absolute focus was now on the blood-spattered waitress.

"Tell me what you know about the affair between Herbert and your sister," I typed, preparing the reader for several huge dollops of unrelieved expositional dialogue.

"Herbert, as you know, was a bestselling novelist, so he commanded an instant overwhelming sexual attraction over all women. My sister was no stronger than the rest of us, and instantly succumbed to his charms. He took her to a province of northern India, where, he said, he wished to revisit a guru who was a master of the *Preveesh* yoga Herbert had practiced in his youth. According to Herbert, the guru had a needle passing all the way through his skull. He had achieved the extraordinary insertion through minutely small increments over tens of years, so the cells of his brain were able to accommodate it naturally."

"Unbelievable," I said, in what was probably the first accurate utterance in the book. "Did the guru not suffer any complications?"

"Only at the barbershop. When Marcia and Herbert arrived at the province, Herbert booked them into a luxurious hotel at the foot of the mountains; there they feasted on the exquisite cuisine, on the culture, and on each other's bodies. She told me she had never experienced such intense and profound sexual satisfaction before."

I nodded—Herbert was a bestselling author, after all.

"But even while they were there together, Herbert became infatuated with one of the village girls whose mother served at the hotel. Herbert made a pretext of wishing to be shown an ancient temple deep in the woods, to which, he claimed, the girl was one of few who knew the route. He was gone for three days, and upon his return all his libido was spent. It was clear to my sister that Herbert had seduced the young female. From then on Herbert found every excuse to be away from my sister, and eventually left the hotel altogether, leaving only a ticket for my sister's flight home and a hundred dollars for her incidental expenses."

"What happened when Marcia returned to Clarkesville?"

"When Marcia returned to Clarkesville, she was in a highly scorned state. I remember the night she got back. She drank a huge amount of whiskey and told me she would see Herbert Quarry rot in hell."

"What happened the next morning?"

"The next morning, people saw '*Herbert Quarry is a pedophile*' daubed in huge letters on the side of City Hall. It attracted the interest of the media locally and nationally, and Herbert was obliged to make various statements denying the accusation. After a supposed tipoff, which I imagine came from Herbert himself, the police arrested Marcia. They soon found she had no alibi; the paint daubed on City Hall matched a half-empty pot in her garage; discarded bristles in the dry paint matched those of a recently used brush in her garage; and her fingernails bore traces of the exact same paint. She was charged with defacing a public building; and it wasn't long before Herbert added a civil charge of libel. But before those charges came to trial, Herbert's lawyers made a motion to have my sister committed to an institution for nine years on grounds of insanity. Although the family fought it, we were outgunned by Herbert's expensive attorneys."

"What happened on the night they took her away?"

"I can never forget the night they took her away. Her anguished and full-throated screams echoed down the street. Again and again I heard her scream she would kill Herbert Quarry, until the threats were drowned by the sirens of the ambulance into which she had been constrained and taken away."

"When was this?"

"Exactly ten years before the day Herbert was found with the dismembered corpse."

Another coincidence—my investigation was becoming plagued with them. I glanced over our discussion thus far—almost two pages of pure dialogue. To avoid accusations of Talking Heads Syndrome, I made Jaqueline sigh, nudge her hair, sip a drink, wipe a tear from her eye at the recollection of her sister's suffering, wince at a *Village People* song being played for the third time running on the jukebox, smooth a napkin on her knee, and stick pins into a Herbert Quarry voodoo doll, before I asked my next question.

"Did your sister receive any psychiatric treatment when she was incarcerated in the lunatic asylum?"

"Yes. She developed a strange habit which attracted the interest of a researcher into the psychotic traits of the insane. He became virtually a daily visitor, such was his interest in the case."

"Interesting. Can you tell me his name?"

"Yes, if you are sure you want me to."

"Why shouldn't I?"

"Well, if I didn't remember his name, you would have an excuse for a couple of pages of padding in which you discover it through other means."

"Don't worry, there will be plenty of time for padding later. Tell me his name."

"It was Professor Sushing."

LESSON NINE

'How would a truly great author create names for their characters, Herbert?'

'They would not, Marco. Fiction is littered with the creations of profligate authors who imagine they are being clever by inventing new characters. Single-use characters are a wanton indulgence. The truly great author recycles characters.'

'But, Herbert, what if a character dies—how can you recycle them?'

'You are confusing fiction with reality, Marco. Realism in fiction is for the foolish and the reactionary. You must not allow your mind to be trammeled by a concept as petty as reality.'

CHAPTER NINE

In which Marco indulges in international travel.

"Professor Sushing!!!"

I'd once read that you should never, ever, ever end a sentence with more than one exclamation mark, so I wasn't sure why I'd typed three—perhaps some primal instinct was telling me that the name Sushing was to have a profound influence on my career as a writer. To cover the extreme nature of my punctuation, I invented a story about the Professor being the last person one might expect to take an interest in the case of a waitress's sister from Clarkesville...

"But Professor Sushing is a well-known billionaire with business interests all over the globe. He's the last person to take an interest in the case of a waitress's sister from Clarkesville."

"That's exactly what we thought too," said Jacqueline, helpfully going along with the nonsense I'd just typed. "We put it down to a philanthropic streak in the Professor's nature."

Unlikely. If you're a billionaire with a philanthropic streak, you try to cure cancer, or help the third world. However, who was I to argue? Jacqueline had been there, so she should know.

"Does the Professor live near Clarkesville?"

"No. He rented a property near Barton Hills while he was investigating my sister's psychosis, but he lives in Nassau."

Hmmmm—probably for some tax-dodge purposes. I thanked Jacqueline for her time and explanation, leaving her to socialize with her friends. She was cutting a dash on the dancefloor in her abattoir overalls by the time I'd visited the toilet on my way out.

I needed to hear what the Professor had to say about Marcia Delgado, the woman with a psychotic hatred of Herbert. Pausing, therefore, only to look up flight times, to text Como to say I would be busy for a spell, and to do something hilariously funny I can't quite remember, I headed to the Clarkesville County International Airport.

As I headed into Terminal Eight—the one reserved for TV personalities and the like—I wondered whether Herbert's arrest was still under wraps. I didn't have to wonder for long. On a giant TV in the first-class lounge, a presenter was spouting about *news just in from Clarkesville.*

I watched to see what spin they would put on it.

They started with footage of Herbert the playboy—clips showing him with a series of A-list beauties on his arm in the following situations:

The London premier of the film of Herbert's best seller, *The X and Y Coordinates of Evil.*

The post-awards party in Hollywood on the night he gained his best-screenplay Oscar.

A top nightclub in New York—the one that wouldn't let me in because of my anorak and corduroys.

A restaurant in St Moritz.

A water taxi in Venice.

They then struck a less glamorous note, with an image of Marcia's accusation daubed on the side of Clarkesville City Hall, old footage of Herbert—surrounded by reporters—denying it, and a photo of Lola, obviously chosen to exaggerate her youth and Herbert's culpability.

Finally, there was a clip of Chief McGee, sporting a straightened tie and his best police chief face, who said that thanks to the efficient law enforcement skills of his department, there was one less sick predator on the streets.

Ha! What happened to the presumption of innocence? Had Herbert already been condemned, without trial, in the unjust court of public opinion, or was it just the media turned against him? Surely the average person on the street would reserve judgment and...

My speculations about the fair-minded treatment Herbert might receive from the average person on the street were interrupted by the

46

strains of *Que Sera Sera*. I answered the call before I realized it was my Bronx mom.

"Markie, Markie, where are you?"

"I'm down in Clarkesville, Mom."

"Clarkesville!" She couldn't have sounded more shocked if I'd said downtown Sodom-upon-Gomorrah. "Clarkesville! You're not with that sick pedo Quarry? Tell me you're not with that sick pedo Quarry."

"Mom! He's not a sick pedo," I shouted, putting my hands over my mouth belatedly in response to the looks from those nearby.

"But he is, Markie, he is. It's on TV. He's killed that poor girl, Markie, and she only looks ten or eleven. And to think he sat in my house. The shame, Markie, the shame, the shame, the shame."

"Mom! It's not true. That's just what the TV people say. He's been framed."

"Framed! Who'd do a thing like that to frame someone?" It was a good question. "They caught him red-handed, Markie. How can he be framed? What am I going to say in the salon tomorrow, Markie? Mrs. Silverman is in at nine. She's seen him in my house. What's she going to be telling everyone—that your mom had a sick pedo murderer in her house. Oh, Markie, Markie, how's your poor mom going to find you a nice girl to give her grandkids if you're hanging out with a pedo?"

"Mom! Herbert's not a pedo, and he hasn't killed anyone. He's been framed by the local police."

"The local police!"

"They set him up, Mom, and now he's in jail."

"In jail! Is he eating right, Markie?"

I saw an opportunity to give my mom something to think about other than Herbert's alleged crimes.

"I don't think so, Mom. He was looking very thin. Really thin."

I remained silent, allowing the injected drug to suffuse through her neural system.

"Thin! Is no one cooking for him, Markie?"

"I don't think so, Mom. I think he's starving. I think he needs someone to send him some cookies and cakes." I could almost hear my

Bronx mom looking around her kitchen. "Shall I send you the address of the prison?"

"Later, Markie, later. Not now. Your mom needs to be baking. What are you holding your mommy up for, Markie? Keeping her on the phone when she needs to be baking."

"Sorry, Mom. Speak later."

I listened for the line to go dead, then killed my end of the call. Phew! To my Bronx mom, baking is an overpowering instinctive urge, rather as swimming is to a salmon.

I went quickly to the toilet, just in time to be called to board flight 1021 to Nassau. On the plane, I signed the cabin crew's copies of *The Tau Muon*, then settled into my luxurious seat. I put all thoughts of writing out of my mind—not that there'd been many there in the first place. I would use the time on the plane to prepare myself subconsciously for my looming encounter with Professor Sushing. I asked the steward to bring the drinks list. Things were looking up— they had both of my all-time favorite wines. Red and white.

LESSON TEN

'What attributes do publishers seek in an author, Herbert?'

'There is only one important attribute, Marco—productivity.'

'Why should that be, Herbert?'

'It is expensive to market a writer. If the writer subsequently produces only one or two works, the publisher gets little return on their investment.'

'I see.'

'If the writer can churn out book after book, they generate a highly lucrative revenue stream.'

'I see.'

'Do you have any other questions, Marco?'

'Not just now.'

CHAPTER TEN

In which Marco anticipates his next lesson.

On the flight to the Bahamas, I'd thought of a hilarious twist in which I would jump into a cab at Nassau airport, ask to be taken to the Professor's address, be told by the driver no such address existed, get into a big argument with him, Google the address to show him what a dumbass he was being, and find the Professor actually lived in Nassau in Delaware, so it was I who was the dumbass after all. But when it came to it, I wasn't sure the readers would find it believable, me being the dumbass. Besides, it wouldn't have been in keeping with my plan to break the mold of literature if I were to write about ideas I'd already had.

Instead, therefore, I jumped into a cab at Nassau airport, asked to be taken to the Professor's address, and found myself driven up the lanes of Nassau's most exclusive residential district, Thornton Heights. The Professor lived in a Frank Lloyd Wright house nestled in immature gardens with a spectacular view over the bay, all surrounded by a razor wire fence. I was patted down by rough-looking henchmen before presenting my card—the four of clubs—and being shown shown to his study.

"Doctor Ocram. This is an unexpected pleasure."

It was for me too—I hadn't expected to be a doctor. We shook hands, and he showed me to a seat with a spectacular view over the bay.

"What brings you to Nassau, Doctor Ocram?"

The Professor combined the most sinister characteristics of all eleven villains from the original James Bond novels. Wondering if that might include Rosa Klebb's curare-tipped brogues, I kept my eyes on his feet as I answered his question.

"I understand you were a daily visitor to Marcia Delgado when she was held in the insane asylum in Clarkesville. Can you tell me why?"

"From the day she entered the asylum until the day she left, she exhibited the most startling pattern of behavior I have ever experienced in more than thirty years' expert study of the insane."

I was intrigued by his words—I hadn't expected to type anything like them.

"You intrigue me," I admitted. "Can you describe her unusual behavior?"

"Having never in her life shown any aptitude for art, she unfailingly produced, each day, an exquisite painting or sketch. The graphic creations varied considerably in format, materials and style. Some were in charcoal, others in oil, gouache, acrylic, crayon, rudimentary herbal dyes or earthen pigments of her own manufacture. Some were on canvas, others on white cartridge paper of the finest quality, some on the walls of her cell. Regardless of the format, she produced exactly one artwork each day. The works represented an unparalleled collection of artistic primitives, as if every great artist of the last five millennia had been for a day her cellmate."

I wondered if that included Jackson Pollock.

"I have never heard anything so incredible. Is there a chance you might have preserved one of her works which you could show me?"

The Professor smiled before pressing a button on a pad set into the gleaming tropical hardwood of his expensive expansive desk. At the far end of his vast study, a door opened. The Professor motioned to me to follow him. After negotiating a labyrinth of corridors, we entered a cool, dark space in which our footsteps echoed. The Professor raised the lights to reveal we were in a huge gallery, the largest I had ever seen.

"Gosh," I said, "there must be hundreds of pictures."

"Three thousand, two hundred and eighty-five," he corrected.

"That's amazing. Which of them is by Marcia?"

"They all are."

LESSON ELEVEN

'Tell me, Herbert. Are there any other tricks hacks use in writing their trashy bestsellers?'

'There are many, Marco. The cliffhanger, the change in point of view, the flashback; these are all commonplace gimmicks.'

'Are some gimmicks gimmickier than others, Herbert?'

'Indeed, Marco. A gimmick much favored by the true hack is to end a chapter prematurely on an unexpected announcement, only to start the next chapter on the exact same announcement.'

CHAPTER ELEVEN

In which the Professor is revealed to be no friend of Herbert Quarry.

"They all are."

The Professor's dumbfounding statement echoed in my head. Here in the cavernous gallery was every one of the artworks produced by Marcia Delgado during her incarceration.

The Professor's august tones interrupted my stupefied thoughts.

"The works, although different in so many ways, share two common characteristics. Focus upon them."

I did. The first shared characteristic was obvious from a distant sweeping glance—every one of the works was a view through a window. The window in each picture was different from that in the next. Some of the artworks were views through modern panoramic windows; some were through ancient stone-framed windows of castles or temples; in others the windows were Tudor, or Victorian, or Jacobean, or of some western log cabin, or a Chang dynasty temple— there was no end to the variety of the windows. In some works, the view through the window was the dominant one; in others, the foreground was dominant, and the view through the window was secondary. Some were views looking out through the window; others were from the outside looking in. In some the window was central and prominent, in others small and peripheral. In some the window appeared full-on; in others the view was obliquely through the window to one side. What I am trying to say is that collectively the works of the mad woman depicted every conceivable type of window in every conceivable way, encompassing an incomprehensible spread of imagery.

It was only after I had taken in the first shared characteristic, and analysed it to some extent, that I began to see the second. At first, I saw it in a general way—it was a man; a man always appeared in the views through the windows, sometimes sitting, sometimes standing, sometimes alone, sometimes with others, sometimes clothed, sometimes naked, sometimes foregrounded, sometimes distant; the different representations of the man were almost as varied as the representations of the windows, except for one remarkable shared quality: they were all Herbert Quarry.

At first, I could not believe my eyes. Surely some of the paintings would not show Herbert through a window. But as I paced along the endless walls of the gigantic gallery—as I saw more and more of the infinitely varying artworks—so the truth became inescapable. Marcia had completely and utterly obsessed over the act of depicting Herbert through a window.

I barely managed to express the confused state of my overwhelmed mind: "What... what could it possibly mean?"

"Is it not obvious?" asked the Professor, almost as mystified by my lack of understanding as I was about the contents of his astonishing gallery.

"Certainly not. Please spare me and the readers the agony of my working it out for myself, which could spill over several chapters."

"Think, man. What does the window do to the figure seen within it?"

"It... it..." The enormity of what I was about to say almost prevented me from saying it... "It frames him."

"Exactly. It *frames* him. There you have the continually repeated unconscious story of Marcia's artistic endeavors: I don't care how long it takes, but one way or another I am going to frame Herbert Quarry."

My heart almost beat itself out of my anorak, such was the emotional impact of the Professor's words. Here, then, was the key to unlock Herbert's prison cell. I must get back to Clarkesville at once and alert the bumbling law and order officials. I thanked the Professor profusely and raced back to the airport just in time to catch a flight from Nassau to Clarkesville.

As the powerful airplane crossed mile after mile of the eastern seaboard, doubt ousted triumph from my mind. The Professor was world-renowned as a man of unmatched intellectual powers, yet he had willingly spared the time to see me and led me straight to a compelling conclusion. Was it possible he had manipulated me, just as, perhaps, he might have manipulated Marcia? Could the 3,285 artworks be an elaborate and painstakingly laid trail of diverting evidence, designed to lead investigators to the same conclusion I, with the Professor's help, had reached myself? Might the Professor have laid the trail for his own mysterious purposes? He had access to Marcia, and enormous powers of influence. Perhaps she had been his unwitting puppet. I realized there was one question I still needed the Professor to answer, so no sooner had the plane landed than I tore across the apron of Clarkesville County International Airport and boarded the companion shuttle just leaving for Nassau.

The Professor must have been surprised to see me so soon, but he clearly had enormous powers of self-possession, for he showed no emotion when I resumed my seat in his huge study.

"I forgot to ask," I said. "Exactly why were you in Clarkesville when Marcia was imprisoned? After all, you are a man with many international priorities. I cannot imagine you would have been in that quiet backwater without some special reason."

My question triggered the first signs of unease, and possibly anger, in the intellectual's granite countenance.

"Well, it is a matter of public record, so I suppose you would find out eventually. I was there to face trial."

"You?" The astonished ejaculation burst from my lips. "But for what possible charge?"

"Libel." Bitterness distorted his voice and face, as if the memory of the charges still evoked some powerful resentment.

"But who could possibly make such an accusation against Professor Sushing, the world-renowned beacon of objectivity?"

The Professor turned his penetrating gaze fully upon me before announcing his staggering answer.

"Herbert Quarry."

LESSON TWELVE

'Herbert, does it matter how I number my chapters? I heard an author achieved rave reviews for a book by numbering his chapters in reverse. Should I do that?'

'No, Marco, that was an unimaginative gimmick even in its day, and is now old hat. A great postmodernist author will realize that the identifiers traditionally given to chapters, namely the integers starting at one, are entirely redundant.'

'No, Herbert. I cannot agree with you. The chapter number tells the reader where the chapter fits in the book.'

'You are not thinking like a great postmodernist author, Marco.'

'How should I think, then, Herbert?'

'The number of the chapter is of no practical use. The book is bound, so the relative position of a chapter is fixed whether it is numbered or not. The great postmodernist author will abandon chapter numbers, and instead name his chapters in a manner signifying irony or a transcendent existential perspective of unparalleled breadth.'

'Can you say that last bit again more slowly, Herbert?'

CHAPTER HOLD THE MAYO

In which Marco's agent makes a figurative appearance, and the seed of a misunderstanding is sown.

With the Professor's astonishing admission ringing in my ears, I returned to the airport to catch the returning shuttle to Clarkesville. I slept throughout the flight, thereby sparing the readers the tedium of the thunderstorms, sick pilots, iced wings, engine fires, UFO encounters, loose tarantulas and countless other instances of melodramatic nonsense I might have written had I stayed awake.

After collecting my handsome leather-bound trunk from the first-class luggage carousel, I was queueing for customs checks when Doris Day began to belt-out the chorus of *Que Sera Sera*. She was just about to sing it for the fourth time, when the looks from the other passengers told me it was my phone and not theirs playing the cheery tune. I stopped whistling along with it and took the call. It was Barney, the literary agent I shared with Herbert.

"Hey, Kid, your mom says you're down in Clarkesville, digging around to find the truth about Quarry."

"Hi, Barney. Yes, I'm there now and I'm determined to expose the truth. I'm writing it all up as I go. The world needs to know what's been going on down here."

"That's brilliant, kiddo. Could be just the breakthrough we need for that first novel we want you to write. Amazing. New York's on fire to know what's really happened with Herbert. I can tell you this, Markie baby—if you can winkle out the truth, with all the juicy bits, mind, I'll get us the biggest book deal ever. The publishers will be gagging for it, Markie, gagging. And listen—I got Adaora Eze lined up to see you."

"Wow!" Adaora Eze was the society editor at the New York Times.

"Wow indeed, Kiddo. And guess what—she used to date Herbert, so she can't wait to get the lowdown. When do you think you can get back here?"

"Just a minute." I had to drop my phone while I unlocked my trunk for the customs officer to rummage through all the spare underwear my mom always makes me pack. "I'm not sure yet, Barney."

"Well don't make it too long—we've got a book to sell."

We said our goodbyes and killed the call. That was handy. If Barney could use his influence to sell the story, then maybe I could kill two birds with one clichéd stone, clearing Herbert in a book that broke the mold of literature. Speaking of which...

I nodded my thanks to the poor customs officer and found my way out of 'Arrivals' deep in thought. I needed to find more about the court case between Herbert and Professor Sushing. Perhaps some detail in the court's archives would give me a new insight into what to write next. Accordingly, I retrieved my black Range Rover from the VIP parking lot and drove straight to City Hall, leaving a message for Como, en route, asking him to meet me there.

The aforementioned building was the sole example of classical architecture in Clarkesville. Raised on an immense pediment of finest Portland cement, its massive portico was supported on slender columns topped with capitals of every classical order, including Doric, Ionic, Iconic and Ironic. The stone had been carried by specially hired dump-trucks from a quarry blasted into the side of Mount Clarke, almost eight miles away. Radiocarbon dating proved the building to be at least thirty-five years old. The bonds issued by the City Fathers to pay for the work were guaranteed to be redeemable at twice face value by 2146. The City Mothers had embroidered a memorial quilt, made with scraps of the stonemasons' overalls, which now hung proudly in the council chamber. The City Cousins had donated a tasteless plaque, which was kept in storage and leant against the wall of the building whenever they visited.

My phone buzzed to say Como was running ten minutes late. Not wishing to bore you to death by hanging about waiting for him, I followed the signs to the Court Archives. I pushed through an imposing set of ornate mahogany doors, along a filthy corridor in which the tenants of the public housing projects waited to argue about their rent arrears, up five sets of stairs, through the workshops in which the ceremonial regalia of the council members were maintained, down five flights of stairs, back through the imposing mahogany doors and over to a small hatch near the main entrance, above which was a sign reading 'Court Archives Department, Knock Here for Enquiries,' and below which was a sign reading 'Closed Indefinitely Owing to Industrial Action.'

As I had done to Como's car just seven chapters ago, I smote the hatch with my fist in a hackneyed gesture betokening impatience, anger, frustration and an inability to write anything more original. There was I, on the cusp, perhaps, of some dramatic revelation, and my breakneck narrative pace was being undermined by some petty dispute between the council and its court archivists. I'm not sure undermining is the right metaphor, if I'm honest, but let's not forget the point of all this—we're hardly going to break the mold of literature if we keep stopping to think of the right words. Anyway, back to breakneck narrative pace...

I turned to see Como run up the main steps two at a time, the tails of his ultra-cool overcoat flaring behind in the wind of his passage. I switched to slow-motion for our reunion. We floated toward each other across the busy foyer, stride by stride, while emotional background music underlined the significance of the moment. Here we were, the crime-fighting duo, reunited in an unbreakable bond of mutual respect and common purpose. My arms opened in greeting as Como spoke...

"What the fuck d'you think you're doing, Writer? Next time you decide to leave the country, you tell me first. I almost had a warrant out."

I aborted the man-hug I'd planned.

"A warrant! Christ, Como, what happened to working in partnership to get concrete evidence?"

"You fucking off to the Bahamas at zero notice—that's what."

"Como," I said, drawing myself up to my full height, at which my eyes were nearly level with his collar button, "the word partnership implies some degree of independence. It is not a synonym for any of the words bondage, subjugation, thrall, slavery, vassalage, serfdom and so on. If we are to be partners, we must operate in a framework of unquestioned mutual trust."

"It's easy for you to say, Writer, but it's me who'll have Chief McGee's boot up my ass if you turn out to be Quarry's accomplice."

"Then the sooner we disprove the possibility, the better. Speaking of which, what did you find at police HQ about the impact wound on Lola's head?" I asked in an attempt to regain the initiative—not a very successful attempt, as it turned out.

"Nothing. You sure you didn't make up all that shit about a blow to the skull? Anyway, what were you up to in the Bahamas?"

I told Como about Sushing's court case, the amazing collection of paintings and the theory about Marcia Delgado framing Herbert, hoping he wouldn't find them even less believable than the blow to Lola's skull.

"That's why I came to City Hall—to look at the court records."

"You should have told me, Writer: I could have saved you the wasted trip."

"You mean you knew about the Court Archives Department being closed indefinitely on account of a petty industrial relations dispute?"

"No, I mean I knew about the trial. I was there."

LESSON THIRTEEN

'Tell me, Herbert, aside from extreme productivity, is there any other attribute a publisher might hope to see in a prospective bestselling author?'

'Why yes, Marco, there is one: versatility.'

'What do you mean by versatility, Herbert?'

'Bestsellers must fall into established categories of subject matter, known as genres, otherwise the staff at the bookshops cannot work out where to place them on the shelves. A versatile writer can produce content for any genre. That is important to the publishers, Marco, for if one genre becomes unpopular, their stellar writers can shift their output to another.'

'I see. What is an example of the more commercial genres, Herbert?'

'A good example, perhaps, is the courtroom drama, as popularized by authors John Turow and Scott Grisham, whose many works, such as Grisham's 'The Formula,' all share similar plots, characters, socioeconomic settings, and so on. You are more likely to be picked up by a publisher if you demonstrate an ability to churn out thousands of words in a variety of genres.'

'I see.'

CHAPTER LOSING THE WILL TO LIVE

In which Marco proves his versatility.

"No, there doesn't seem to be anything here either."

We were back at Herbert's house, looking for old newspaper articles or diary entries about the court case, after Como confessed he could hardly remember anything about it. *It was nearly ten years ago* was his excuse.

"Let's admit defeat, Writer, and go for some lunch—I'm wasting away."

I was about to make some sarcastic comment about how Como did indeed seem to be wasting all the way from four hundred pounds to three hundred and ninety-nine pounds fifteen ounces, when I had a brilliant idea.

"Gorging yourself with food can wait, Como. I have just remembered I have an international reputation as a hypnotist. With your permission, I will simply put you into a deep trance from which you will be able to recall the events of the trial in vivid and compelling detail."

Como rested on a divan in Herbert's study and watched a watch I was dangling until he fell into a deep hypnotic coma.

"Tell me about the court case," I prompted.

Under my powerful hypnotic influence, Como recounted his memories in the manner of Scott Grisham...

Portly, middle-aged Harry Rex Horgan—a fearless litigator with a brutal work schedule, a brutal drink problem, and three brutal ex-wives —is conducting a brutal cross-examination of the defendant—

the renowned Professor Sushing, a dignified elderly personage accused of libeling famous author Herbert Quarry. The case is being heard by Judge Miriam Oldenshaw in the ceremonial court in Clarkesville, a town many miles away from Kindle County.

Harry Rex inclined his head doubtfully at the defendant. 'So, Professor, if I understand you correctly, you are asking us to believe that in dismissing my client's books as...' Harry read from a paper in his hand...'formulaic, over-padded, cliché ridden junk that no self-respecting person should be seen dead reading,' you are expressing a genuinely held belief.'

'Correct,' answered the Professor from the witness box.

'And we can take it, therefore, you are not a fan of my client's work?'

'Correct.'

Harry Rex raised a manila envelope from which he extracted a glossy nine-by-seven print of what seemed to be a luxuriously appointed bathroom. The area around the toilet was strewn with books. He held the photograph in front of him and addressed the defendant.

'Professor, do you recognize the subject of this photograph?'

The Professor shifted uneasily in the witness box. 'I do.'

'Would you please tell us what it shows?'

The Professor cleared his throat. 'It shows one of the bathrooms in my Central Park apartment.'

'One of the bathrooms?' Harry's eyebrows were raised, as was the incredulous tone of his voice. 'Is it just one of the bathrooms in the apartment?'

The Professor ignored the question and stared across the crowded courtroom with a look of regal defiance.

Harry Rex appeared to change tack. 'Who is Eva Hauptmann?'

The Professor sighed. No, make that the Professor sighed wearily. 'You must be more precise. Eva Hauptmann is a common name. There must be thousands of Eva Hauptmanns.'

'More precisely, then, who is the Eva Hauptmann who, according to the United States Revenue Service, is employed by your charitable research foundation at a Central Park address that also happens to be your New York residence?'

'A cleaner, a char.'

'I see. And how long has this 'char' been working for the Sushing family?'

'Some time.'

'Some time.' Harry Rex echoed. 'If it please the court, Eva Hauptmann has been a cleaner for the Sushing family since 1946.'

'Objection!' The leader of the Professor's team of hotshot lawyers—twenty-thousand-dollar-a-day boys from Manhattan—had leapt to his feet.

'Overruled,' barked Judge Oldenshaw. 'However, counsel had better get to his point.'

Harry Rex bowed his thanks to the Judge, then turned to the defendant. 'I have here a deposition from Eva Hauptmann, an Argentinian member of the domestic staff at your Central Park apartment. In it, she states the bathroom appearing in this photograph is your own personal bathroom, and I quote: reserved exclusively for the Herr Professor's private use. Is that correct, or has a woman who has been a servant of your family for more than seventy years not yet had an opportunity to assess your habits?'

Harry Rex bowed again, this time to acknowledge the chuckles from the packed courtroom.

'It is correct,' admitted the witness.

'Thank you. So, if the bathroom in question is reserved for the Herr Professor's own private use, then presumably the well-thumbed paperbacks strewn all around the toilet are the Herr Professor's own private reading matter. Correct?'

'Objection. Prosecution is leading the witness'. The Professor's lawyer made the point wearily. Going through the motions for the sake of form. He could guess what was coming.

'Overruled,' barked the Judge, 'but counsel will refrain from leading the witness.'

'Apologies your Honor, it was the slip of a humble country lawyer who is out of his depth against these city experts.' Harry Rex raised another chuckle from the jury. He returned to the cross.

'Professor Sushing, do you know what chained pixel interpolation means?'

'I should—I invented it.'

'Then perhaps you could summarize it for the benefit of the court.'

'It is an algorithmic technique for extracting detail from images through a scalar interpolation of tri-spectrum color depths, reliant upon parallel tensor processing.'

'Or, in other words, a way of revealing hidden details in digital photographs.'

'Crudely, yes.'

'Is the technique reliable?'

'Absolutely. Correctly programmed, a six-nines success rate is practically guaranteed.'

'And by six-nines you mean a ninety-nine point nine nine nine nine percent success rate.'

'Yes.'

'In other words, the chances of the extracted detail being incorrect are roughly one in a million?'

'Yes. Provided, as I said, the technique was correctly programmed.'

'Indeed. And am I right in thinking, Professor, that Nassau Image Services, a commercial offshoot of your charitable research foundation, is a world leader in the application of the technique?'

'It certainly is.' A trace of uppish pride was clear in the Professor's quick reply.

'And the CIA, NASA, DEA, NATO, and a dozen other organizations rely upon Nassau Image Services to perform chained pixel interpolation to extract details from images?'

'Yes.'

'Thank you, Professor; that is most helpful. You have confirmed there is less than a million to one chance that details extracted from images by Nassau Image Services could be incorrect.'

Harry Rex extracted a sheaf of glossy nine-by-seven prints from the manila envelope and walked to stand directly in front of the jury. He held the sheaf at arm's length so the jury could plainly see the top print in the bundle.

'This is an image of one of the many books surrounding the Professor's private toilet, an image magnified by Nassau Image

Services using the technique of chained pixel interpolation, an image that stands a one in a million chance of being wrong—an image, ladies and gentlemen, that shows the well-thumbed book to be Fool's Epiphany by Herbert Quarry.' Harry Rex let the glossy print fall to the floor, revealing the next in the pack.

'This image, also extracted by Nassau Image Services, also with a million to one chance of being wrong, shows another item of the Professor's personal reading matter, this time Of Love and Larceny, also by Herbert Quarry.'

Again, Harry Rex dropped the print to show the next.

'This is The Love Seed, another Herbert Quarry.'

One by one, Harry Rex showed the magnified images of the books scattered around the defendant's toilet, each a Herbert Quarry, until the floor in front of the jury was carpeted with the discarded prints. He spun to face the witness.

'By the technique you developed, through the company you own, we see the reading materials you choose are precisely the works which you said no self-respecting person would be seen... dead...reading.' The masterly repeated emphasis on 'you,' and the pauses between the final words, gave Harry Rex's delivery the effect of huge drama, electrifying the court. Turning to Judge Oldenshaw, his face flushed with indignation, his outflung hand pointing accusingly at the defendant and his hotshot lawyers, Harry Rex...

"And you're back in the room."

LESSON FOURTEEN

'I heard someone say on a podcast, Herbert, that appalachians should be capitalized. Does that mean I should spell appalachians with a big a?'

'I think you mean appellations, Marco.'

'Do I?'

'The Appalachians are mountains, Marco. Appellations, loosely, are names, and should take an upper-case initial letter.'

'Writing is very confusing, Herbert. What if I sometimes forget to spell appellations with big letters at the start?'

'You will annoy certain readers. Your proofreader, particularly, will think you a careless idiot.'

'Does that matter, Herbert?'

YET ANOTHER CHAPTER

In which we hear the tale of como Galahad, fries go missing, and a two-chapter gag is set up.

Having brought Como out of his hypnotic trance, I shifted the scene to a burger bar for some much-needed sustenance. Como seemed to be eating more than his fair share of the fries—and the burgers too, now I think about it—presumably to restore his emaciating physique. I decided to divert him from his frantic ingestions by asking about his backstory.

"How about you?" I asked. "How did Como Galahad get to become a police lieutenant?"

"Oh, the usual way. My mother was a gifted woman with high expectations for her children. Although we lived on the wrong side of the tracks, she worked all hours to ensure we had what she thought we needed. She took us to church school and arranged for us to have extra tuition given voluntarily by rich and cultured white folk who were impressed by her dignity and noble bearing."

Como's face assumed a faraway look as he recalled his mother and childhood. I took the opportunity to move the bowl of fries from his encircling arms while his concentration was elsewhere.

"My father was a drunken brute who beat my mother savagely. He beat us kids too, until I grew bigger than he. One night he came in drunk and surly and told my mother to shut her filthy mouth or he would shut it for her. As he raised his hand to strike her, I stood from the dining table, folded my napkin and grabbed his wrist. 'You've struck that woman too many times already—you are not going to do it again.' 'Why you insolent young pup, I'll fix your hash,' he said, and went to hit me, but I was stronger than he, and my body hadn't been ruined with drink and drugs, and so I dragged him into the street and beat him to a bloody pulp. All the neighbors were out on their porches watching the commotion. When my hot wrath subsided, I waited for the police to arrive; I waited to face justice. But the local sheriff turned up, a wise old man who went to the same church as my mother and who respected her noble dignity. He knew my father had bad blood— he had arrested him too many times to count. When the neighbors explained the background to the thrashing I had meted out to my father, the sheriff took me under his wing. He could tell I was a good boy, but he knew it would be easy for my life to go off the rails if I was sent to prison, so he persuaded my mother to enroll me for police college. It was tough there, as I was the only black student in a faculty staffed by white officers, and their prejudice against me was extreme, but I remembered the advice the sheriff had given me: 'Don't let the bastards grind you down' and his unique words of wisdom kept my soul afloat in even the darkest hours. And from there…. Hey, Writer, are you asleep?"

"No, no, just closed my eyes to concentrate."

"Where have all the fries gone?"

"I didn't see. Maybe the waitress thought we'd finished and took the bowl. Listen, why don't we get back to the plot—do you think we should check Delgado's whereabouts on the day of the murder? If Sushing's theory is right, maybe she was at Herbert's place."

Como reluctantly agreed, and even more reluctantly paid half the tab. He was still crabbing about the 'missing fries' when we got back to his desk at police HQ to look up Marcia Delgado's address. His police computer was fitted with the latest security software—he was presented with a five-by-ten array of randomly generated photographs of houses, and asked to select, in order of preference, the five houses in which he would most like to live. An algorithm compared his choice with a prediction based on a personality profile and let him login after finding a match. Como told me the system was 99.999% reliable and funded by a local realtor. It seemed utter nonsense, but I typed it anyway, Pollock-style.

THE AWFUL TRUTH ABOUT THE HERBERT QUARRY AFFAIR

We made a note of the address—Apartment 1007, Block D, Hacienda Apartments, Clarkesville—and headed out to find it, Como first having to close about thirty popup windows advertising real estate. I asked Como if we should ring ahead to check that Marcia was at home. He laughed.

"You sure you wanna be a crime writer? You know frig-all about police work, that's for sure. You wanna ring and tip her off we're coming? Give her a chance to hide stuff, rehearse a story?" They were rhetorical questions, obviously—he answered them himself with three head-wags of contemptuous disbelief at my dumbass suggestion. "When we get there, you leave all the talking to me, right?"

"Right."

The Hacienda Apartments were nothing like I'd imagined, which was a bit of a mystery given that I was responsible for inventing them. They were five identical buildings constructed without regard for taste, architectural merit, the dignity of their inhabitants, or any of the ten tenets of Feng Shui. We trudged through the communal areas, ignoring the special offers touted by the prostitutes and drug pushers, and found Apartment 1007. I was dithering about whether to say its poorly maintained door was no different from any of the others in the block, or to make it stand out in some way, when it was opened in response to Como's knock by Jacqueline, the waitress from the coffee shop.

"Marco Ocram! Gosh, what a surprise!" she said, ignoring Como—much to his annoyance—and looking round to see if we were being filmed for some sort of candid camera show. "Why..." she paused, utterly lost for words, as was I. "What...I mean, why are you here?"

I would have thought it obvious, given our recent conversation at Kelly's, but I explained it anyway, not wishing all of us to be held up by the doziness of a minor character.

"We were hoping to speak with your sister."

"But she's not here, Mister Ocram, she's working a shift at the family abattoir."

Hmmm. I gave Como a rhetorical look, one conveying the question *Who's the dumbass now, Galahad, for not phoning ahead?*

71

but he was too thick-skinned to notice. He asked Jacqueline for the address of the abattoir, before nudging me in the ribs to say we should get a move on.

LESSON FIFTEEN

'How would you define style, Herbert?'

'As anyone else would, Marco—an arrangement of steps designed to allow people, but not animals, to cross a field boundary.'

'No. I mean style with a y.'

'Ah. Style is a distinctive way of writing. All good writers possess style.'

'Should I strive to develop my own style, Herbert?'

'No, you must never consciously create a style; you must let style enter you and suffuse your being, like a huge snort of coke or the touch of a... Sorry, what am I saying—please forget that, Marco.'

'Can you name an author with a very distinctive style, Herbert?'

'You should read Damon Runyon, for example, who wrote a series of humorous short stories written entirely in the present tense.'

'OK. Dame Anne Runnion. I will look her up.'

CHAPTER MOBIUS STRIP

In which police time is wasted.

"I thought we agreed you'd leave all the talking to me."

I'd been expecting Como's criticism all through the walk to the car. He fired the engine and turned us round in the street.

"But she blurted my name, Como. I could hardly stand there and ignore it. I'd have looked a dumbass."

Como said nothing, but his face expressed the view that since I was so obviously the world's biggest dumbass, my concerns about being made to look a dumbass were somewhat misplaced. I gave as good as I'd got, my face expressing the view that it was easy for him to sit there, spouting visual criticisms, but I had the added burden of trying not to appear a dumbass while making everything up on the spot, and he ought to try it himself if he thought it was easy.

We drove through the dreary Clarkesville suburbs in silence, each projecting our facial opinions, until Como changed the subject with an anticipatory frown which said we were just about to make a right-hand turn into the visitors' car park at our destination.

The abattoir was a state-of-the-art installation, conforming with all local, federal and international animal welfare regulations. A stream of trucks brought the animals intended for dispatch, reversing against ramps carpeted with the finest AstroTurf, up which the animals were tempted with potpourris of the sweetest herbs. Giant TV screens either side of the holding stalls projected stunning pictures of the lushest pastureland, while the animals were hand fed by dungareed cowherds at the peak of their profession. After slaughter, the animals were butchered with the most expensive Japanese knives, whose blades were made from recycled bullet-train rails, the metal being refolded sixty-four times to form a laminar structure with layers only three atoms thick. The prime cuts were automatically wrapped in vacuum sealed packaging, while the offals and other viscera were piped to a fast-food outlet on the opposite side of the car park.

"Now don't forget, leave the talking to me."

Como flipped his badge at the receptionist and asked to see Miss Delgado. We browsed the display cases housing the abattoir's impressive collection of memorabilia—a golden stun-gun, a 'Best Eviscerator' certificate, a framed photo of the foundation stone being laid by the mayoress of Clarkesville—until a figure in blood-spattered overalls and boots came out to meet us. She removed her faceguard and shook out her hair. It was Jacqueline—the waitress from the coffee bar.

"Marco Ocram! Gosh, what a surprise!" she said, ignoring Como—much to his annoyance—and looking round to see if we were being filmed for some sort of candid camera show. "Why..." she paused, utterly lost for words, as was I. "What...I mean, why are you here?"

The three of us stood in silence by the display cabinets. I was trying to figure out which of us was the most confused, when Como said:

"OK. You wanna tell me what the frig's goin' on, Writer?"

I wished I could.

"But you've just told us to come here to see Marcia," I said.

"Who?" said Jacqueline.

"You did."

"I did?"

"Yes. At Marcia's place. Ten minutes ago."

I was starting to think they'd been right to bang-up Marcia in the loony bin, if she was half as nutty as her sister appeared to be.

"But I've been here all morning...wait, have you just been to Marcia's?"

"Yes."

"And you think I was there and told you to come here?"

"Yes."

She put a hand to her nose to stifle a snort.

"That was Marcia, Mister Ocram. She's my twin. I'm sorry—I shouldn't be laughing, but..."

But I'll laugh anyway at what a dumbass you are, was what she thankfully didn't say.

"You're saying we've come all this way for no reason?" said Como. "Don't you know there's a law against wasting police time? I could get you locked up for this."

I sprang to Jacqueline's defense.

"Come, Como, she was hardly to blame."

"It wasn't her I was talking about."

LESSON SIXTEEN

'Herbert, how can I be sure I will become a rich and famous novelist?'

'You can never be certain, Marco, but you can feel the conviction within you.'

'What signs can give me confidence I am going in the right direction?'

'If your writing can be more than just the words you write, then you are heading in the right direction.'

'When you say more than the words what do you mean?'

'You should aim to be associated with a special word, so readers will always think of you when they hear it. For example, if you use the word 'seagull' in the right way, readers will associate it with you forever, so when they see seagulls they will say 'Seagulls. I wonder what Marco Ocram would make of them'.'

'Can the special word be any word at all? An adjective such as incompetent, for example?'

'Yes, Marco. With your natural gifts, I am sure you can make people think of you whenever they hear the word incompetent.'

CHAPTER CAN WE PLEASE GET BACK TO USING NUMBERS?

In which a lie is swallowed, and Marco spots a possible clue.

We drove back to the Hacienda Apartments and re-knocked on the door to 1007. I left the talking to Como. When Marcia answered the door, he flashed his badge and asked if we could go in.

She led us inside, where my eye played like a powerful searchlight over the contents of her shabby apartment. Immediately apparent were recently purchased dresses from Faratali, Carpaluci, Tagliateli and half a dozen other top fashion houses—exclusive couture, entirely out of place in the home of a poor member of the Clarkesville working class. I nudged Como and twitched my head to draw his attention to them. He nudged me back to acknowledge receipt of my nudge and began to question Marcia as I nursed my ribs.

"Miss Delgado, I know about your past involvement with Herbert Quarry." At the mention of the name, Marcia's eyes became like those of a cobra. "You know he's been arrested in connection with the death of Lola Kellogg?"

"Yes, and I hope he fries in hell for it."

"Well, we're gonna make sure he gets the justice he deserves. But can I ask if you know anything about what happened? Anything that can help us?"

"What more do you need to know? He was a sick pedophile, and he was caught red-handed. The sooner you get him in the chair, the better."

"You watch TV, don't you? You've seen what happens when the fancy lawyers get involved. They could get Quarry off the hook unless we cover all the bases. We need to eliminate any reasonable doubt, so we're just trying to see if anyone was around who might know anything that could add to the case. You weren't around Quarry's house that day, by any chance?"

"No. I wasn't even in Clarkesville."

Como waited for her to go on.

"I...I was out of state at a game. The Clarkesville Giants were playing away. I was in the crowd watching. I can prove it—look. My friend saw me and sent me a clip."

She picked up a tablet and showed us a video. It was from the local TV coverage of the game. The sexist cameramen had been zooming in on various beautiful women in the crowd, one of their victims being Marcia. Her friend had spotted her on the replay and forwarded the clip.

Como made a few notes.

"OK. Thanks for your help, Miss Delgado. You're very like your sister."

"We're practically identical. The only way to tell us apart is she's got a scar on her left hand by her thumb knuckle."

I wished she'd told us before—it would have saved us a trip to the abattoir.

"No need to see us out," said Como. He gave her a card. "Just make sure you call me if you remember anything."

We tipped our hats, or would have done had we been wearing any, and left her studying Como's card in her living room. On our way out, I took the chance to flick a finger through a pile of open letters on a table near the front door.

LESSON SEVENTEEN

'Herbert.'

'Yes, Marco?'

'How important is the cover of a book?'

'That depends, Marco.'

'Upon what, Herbert?'

'Upon whether the author is already famous. If so, the cover is of little importance. The millions the publisher has pumped into promoting the author will have conditioned the minds of purchasers to buy the product regardless of its intrinsic merits. For a new writer, however, the cover must appeal to the reader.'

'But, Herbert, in these days when it is possible to read sample pages of a book before ordering it, surely the quality of the author's writing will overcome any shortcomings of the cover.'

'True, Marco. If the writing is superb, the cover need not be. I hope, Marco, you have engaged a superb cover designer.'

CHAPTER SEVENTEEN

In which Marco is threatened, meets a billionaire, remembers not to think, and encounters a spectacular clue.

"There was a compliments slip in her post, Como. It said *Please find our check attached.* Don't you think that was suspicious, especially given all the expensive new things in her apartment?"

"There could be a million and one reasons why someone like Delgado gets a check."

"Well can't we at least check the check, and trace who paid it?"

"Not without a whole load of paperwork and justification. This is a free country, Writer. The police can't just pry into people's financial affairs."

I stared out of the un-tinted window of Como's police car. Yet again his pedantic preoccupation with proper police procedure was preventing me from developing my narrative in a freeform, mold-breaking, Jackson Pollock manner.

"If you feel, Como, that observing petty police rules is more important than fanning the flame of Truth, then I will just have to investigate that particular lead myself."

"That lead's not strong enough for a nano-poodle, Writer. But maybe it won't hurt for you to be off chasing rainbows—I've got some admin to do back at HQ, so it'll keep you out of trouble until I'm finished."

Como kindly dropped me back at Herbert's place, or wherever it was I said I'd left my black Range Rover. As I went to unlock the car, I saw a folded card tucked under one of the wipers. I untucked and unfolded the card. It was a handwritten note...

We don't like snoopers in this town.

I called Como.

"Galahad."

"Como, it's me."

"For fuck's sake, Writer, I only just dropped you off."

"I know, but someone's left a threatening note on my car."

Even through the tinny quality of the phone's speaker, I could hear the tone of Como's voice change to one of concern.

"What's it say?"

I told him what it said.

"OK. It's probably someone harmless havin' fun. But keep the note safe. Don't touch it more than you need to. We can get it dusted for prints, just to check it's not linked to anyone serious."

"OK."

"And Writer..."

"Yeah?"

"Keep yourself safe too."

Having finished the call and blipped down a tinted window or two to let out some heat, I sat inside my black Range Rover to Google the business whose letterhead appeared atop the suspicious compliments slip I had spotted in Marcia's hallway. According to the official Clarkesville County business register, the company was privately owned by Elijah Bow, a secretive and reclusive billionaire industrialist with a huge ranch-style property, otherwise known as a ranch, about ten miles from Clarkesville on the N66. The business was a holding company, performing no trading in its own right; it had one director—Bow—and no other declared staff.

I entered the coordinates of Bow's ranch in my satnav and drove in accordance with her instructions.

En route, I called Como.

"Christ, Writer, am I ever gonna get ten minutes' peace?"

"Do you know Elijah Bow?"

"The reclusive billionaire industrialist?"

"Yes."

"Yes."

"He owns the company that sent the check to Marcia Delgado. I have reason to believe he may be implicated in framing Herbert. I'm on my way to see him right now and will be relentless in my examination of his affairs."

"You're crazy, Writer, but that's what I love about you."

"Love you too."

I hung up, as I was getting close, and needed to muster all my powers to write a short scene of unsurpassed corniness.

"Turn left towards the billionaire's ranch," said the satnav.

Bow's grand front door was opened by a maid who motioned me into a vast circular hall tastelessly adorned with garish works of art. In the center of the hall a large bronze of a naked young girl surmounted a pool, water spouting from the figure's pouting lips. Having taken my card, the maid beckoned me to follow him and lumbered along a corridor before showing me into Elijah Bow's study where the billionaire was at work. Bow dismissed the maid and read my card.

"We don't like snoopers in this town?" he said.

Ooops, wrong card. I swapped it for the right one, which he scanned before asking the purpose of my visit.

"I am investigating the gruesome murder of Lola Kellogg."

I observed him closely through narrowed eyelids as I made my announcement. I could see at once my words had unsettled him. His eyelids narrowed too, as if in answer to my steely gaze.

"I would have thought," he said, in measured tones (he was speaking into a frequency analyzer), "such an investigation was entirely unnecessary, since the police have caught the perpetrator knife-in-hand."

"So the media would have it," I replied with an unwavering gaze. "However, I know Herbert Quarry to be incapable of such a heinous crime. He must therefore have been framed. Moreover, he must have been framed by someone with significant resources and infinite cunning, the sort of person who might have founded an industrial empire centered in Clarkesville."

"And you are stupid enough to imagine Elijah Bow tied up in all this?

"I do not imagine so. I know so."

"This interview is at an end." Bow's hand reached to a richly bejeweled Turkish bell-pull, prompting the entrance of another maid. "Mister Ocram is leaving. Please see him out."

"Don't think you've seen the last of me," was my parting cliché.

I bowed at Bow, clicked my heels, turned on them, and followed the maid out of the room.

My mind raced feverishly as we walked back through the maze of corridors to the front door. Other than uncovering Bow's defensiveness, I had not acquired any tangible proof from my visit. I knew Como could not act on my suspicions alone, however well-founded he believed them to be. I had to find concrete proof. But how? Think, Marco, think.

As we neared the entrance hall, I had an inspiration. Then an expiration. In fact, I was breathing quite deeply, when I remembered Herbert's advice: Don't think, Marco, don't think.

Like an automaton in a trance, I let my subconscious take over, and stared at the huge bronze statue spouting a fountain from its lips. At once I recognized the face from the picture in Herbert's study—could it be? There was a plaque on the low wall surrounding the fountain. I pretended to tie a loose shoelace, hoping I hadn't mentioned I was wearing sandals, and bent down where I could read the inscription on the plaque.

Lola, I will love you always, Elijah Bow.

LESSON EIGHTEEN

'Herbert, how should a writer develop the plot of a bestseller?'

'Without trying, Marco.'

'What do you mean?'

'You must not deliberate, Marco—you must let the plot come out of you organically. The human mind, Marco, is the most complex structure in the known universe. The plot is already in your mind, like a seed in the soil. The seed does not consciously develop the idea of a plant; it becomes one through a preordained process. You must let the plot grow out of your mind like a vegetable from the soil.'

'Like a vegetable...'

CHAPTER EIGHTEEN

In which four opportunities for padding are lost through bad luck.

I drove back to Herbert's, hoping the readers would forget it was meant to be a sealed-off crime scene, and flopped on a settee. I called Como.

"Galahad."

From the background noise I could tell he was driving.

"Como, it's me. You okay to talk?"

"Sure. What happened at Bow's—he have you thrown out on your ear?"

I heard Como chuckle.

"No. I found some evidence. Bow has a giant statue of Lola in his hall."

I heard a long screech of tires and the noise of Como's engine stop.

"You *what*?"

I told him about the fountain and the inscription on the plaque.

"Does he know you recognized it?"

"I don't think so—he wasn't there, by the statue, I mean. What shall we do? Shall we go and arrest Bow? Shall we tell Herbert's defense team? Should we call a press conference? Shall we confront McGee? Do we need to..."

"Writer, just shut the fuck up—I need to think."

I shut the fuck up in compliance with Como's suggestion and waited for the fruits of his thinking.

"I'm out of town. McGee's got me on some crap case that isn't going anywhere, just to keep me busy. Don't say anything about this to anyone else until I get back."

"How long will you be?"

"Fuck knows. I'll text you."

After fond farewells I killed the call, wondering how I was meant to sustain a breakneck narrative pace while my main character was out of action. Deciding to indulge in formulaic padding, I walked along the beach reflecting upon the lot of the writer, I cooked an imaginative and healthy snack from the few ingredients in Herbert's fridge that had yet to go off, I performed an hour of meditation, I showered, I sat on the toilet reading Herbert's copy of *Autotrader*, and I trimmed my toenails. Thus refreshed, I sat at Herbert's desk and drew-up a list of suspects who might have a sufficient grudge against my mentor to want to frame him for the grisly murder. It read as follows:

Professor Sushing—lost a court case brought by Herbert.
Marcia Delgado—extremely scorned by Herbert.
Elijah Bow—possible rival for the affections of Lola.

It wasn't much of a list—perhaps an interview with Lola's father might identify some other names I could add to it. From news reports I forgot to mention earlier, I knew the Kelloggs lived within walking distance of Herbert's place. I picked up the Clarkesville City Gazetteer and flicked through it, wondering whether to write that there was only a single entry for the surname Kellogg in Herbert's area, or whether I'd be better off with several, thus giving me the opportunity to visit various spurious addresses before finding the right one. I was just trying to decide whether thirty would be too many spurious addresses to visit, when my finger finished tracing down through the Kellermans, the Kellerways, the Kelletts, the Kellet-Clarkes, the Kellibers, the Kellighers, the Kelliwells, and the Kellochs, to find five entries under Kellogg near Herbert's zip code. Hmmm, not as many as I'd hoped, but I supposed five opportunities for padding were better than none.

I got into my black Range Rover, forgetting to mention its tinted windows for once, and punched one of the Kellogg addresses into the satnav. As I rounded a corner to reach my destination, I saw a house submerged in commemorative bouquets. Cursing my luck, I yanked on the parking brake, locked the car with an embittered blip of its remote control, and trudged over. The bouquets were of every size and shape, with cards bearing the sentiments of well-wishers, sentiments which left no room for doubt: this was Lola's father's place. So much for my opportunities for padding. I straightened my cravat and tapped respectfully on the door. No answer. I tapped respectfully a second time. No answer. I respectfully hammered on the door, respectfully rattled the handle, and respectfully shouted through the mail slot. No answer.

I looked around. The Kellogg place was in the woods near a lake. There was only one other house nearby, so I sauntered over to it, hoping the neighbors might have some interesting beans to spill. As I approached the house, I heard Wagner being played at full blast inside. When I got closer, I heard above the music a heated argument between two of the occupants. Without wishing to reveal my presence, I edged to the jamb of the door. These were the very words I overheard:

Woman's voice, full of rage: "You sick perverted bastard. If it hadn't been for you, Lola would never have run to that creep."

Man's voice, indignant: "How *dare* you accuse me of being a sick perverted bastard? If you and those witches you call your friends hadn't dabbled in satanic rituals with those bloody Kelloggs, we wouldn't have been in this shit-hole in the first place."

I backed away. It obviously wasn't a good time to call.

LESSON NINETEEN

'Herbert, what do you think of the sample I showed you?'

'It is crap, Marco. As I have told you until I am blue in the face, you have greatness within you, but you have still to let it out.'

'I don't understand, Herbert. Please give an example of what I need to do better.'

'You must choose your words with greater care, Marco. You write 'I looked at my watch and discovered it was teatime'. Discovery implies endeavor, or the revelation of a thing hidden. You discover cures for cancer; you discover the existence of tectonic plates; you discover lost temples in the jungle. You don't 'discover' it is teatime.'

'What should I have written, Herbert?'

'You might have said that you 'saw' it was teatime, Marco. It would be more concise and more appropriate.'

'Need I take such care with every word, Herbert?'

'If you are to be a great writer, yes.'

'But Herbert, there must be literally hundreds of words—finishing a book could take weeks!'

CHAPTER NINETEEN

In which Marco's recollection of Herbert inspires a truly Pollock-like development.

I went for a walk around the lake, hoping to give the Kelloggs' neighbors a chance to finish their heated argument. As I picked my way over the rocks, I thought back to when Herbert and I first met. I was a sophomore at an elite university at which Herbert was a visiting professor in English literature. I did not fit in with the other students: they had money, privilege and social status; whereas I was an orphaned boy living with impoverished foster parents in a poor part of the Bronx. I had gained a place at the university through sheer brilliance and the encouragement of my Bronx mom.

"Markie," she encouraged, "you can get to the elite university with all that sheer brilliance of yours. Now eat your cake like a good boy."

Herbert coached boxing in his spare time, a sport I had taken up to discourage older bullies from bullying me. And younger ones, now I think about it. I developed a special technique that guaranteed I would never lose a bout—the technique of never taking part in them. Herbert was often around when I was sparring. One day he approached me as I removed my gloves.

"Not bad. Not bad," he said. "You have quite some technique there."

"Thank you."

"And yet you never take part in competitive bouts?"

I wasn't sure how to reply without giving my secret away, so I merely shrugged.

"Anyone can spar," he said. "Perhaps you're not man enough for the real thing."

As usual, Herbert had a clutch of beautiful girls in tow, the sort of girls who would ignore me if I walked by. They giggled at Herbert's taunt. Something snapped within me.

"*Au contraire*, Quarry. I will fight any opponent of your choosing, at any venue of your choosing, at any time of your choosing."

"Oh? By coincidence, the heavyweight boxing champion of the United States is due to meet me for some advice at the gym next door. Come along now and we can see what you are made of."

I was trepidatious, and worried about ending a sentence with 'of', but I knew it was my destiny to impress Herbert Quarry or die trying, so I went along. Within minutes I was in the ring with my giant opponent—six inches taller than I, and a hundredweight heavier. We eyed each other from our respective corners as we warmed up. My trainer rubbed my shoulders, wiped the beads of sweat from my forehead, and murmured advice. *Keep low. Watch his left. No biting. Get in close. He cuts real easy if you can hit his face. Tie that shoelace.*

Ding. The bell rang and we were off. I can now barely recall the fight itself. Round after round of grueling effort, pain, and weariness. But eventually came the final bell. My legs could hardly support my weight, but we stood there, my opponent and I, on either side of the referee. I shall never forget the disappointment I felt when victory was awarded on a split points decision to my jubilant foe. All I could do was to shuffle wearily to my corner, picking up my teeth as I went. However, my depression was short lived, for as I climbed down from the ring in my robe, Herbert Quarry clapped me on the shoulder.

"Ow!" He'd clapped me right on one of my many huge bruises.

"Man, you must have balls like space-hoppers" he said. "I will now be your firmest friend for life. Let us go and share a beer overlooking the sea."

It seemed a strange suggestion to share a beer, but perhaps he was low on cash, I thought.

Stumbling over a rock brought me back to the present. My circumambulation of the lake was almost complete. I headed once more to the Kelloggs' neighbors' house.

As I approached, I heard Wagner still played at full blast. Wondering whether the heated argument had now given way to love and kisses, I edged to the jamb of the door. These were the very words I overheard:

Woman's voice, full of rage: "You sick perverted bastard. If it hadn't been for you, Lola would never have run to that creep."

Man's voice, indignant: "How *dare* you accuse me of being a sick perverted bastard? If you and those witches you call your friends hadn't dabbled in satanic rituals with those bloody Kelloggs, we wouldn't have been in this shit-hole in the first place."

The blood froze in my veins and my hair stood on end as I realized those were the exact words I had overheard the last time I eavesdropped at the house, freshly copied and pasted. I pushed open the screen door. It was too dark to see inside, so I decided I would just have to risk it: I burst into the living area.

The sight that met my eyes was at once both normal and horrifying. In seats either side of a coffee table were a man and a woman, their mouths open as if in speech. Their eyes stared vacantly across the room. I continued to hear their noisy argument, but the words came from hi-fi speakers behind me. The two people were motionless and silent. A thrill of horror came over me as I realized they were dead!

In disbelief, I approached them. Their fingernails were unnaturally long. Their glassy stares were glassy for a reason—their eyes were glass. What I was seeing were two stuffed human bodies, possibly long dead. An endlessly looping recording was playing on the hi-fi to project sounds of life outside the house, but life was long gone within. Who could have done this? How could they have done it? When could they have done it? Why could they have done it? How come nobody had spotted this before I did?

With those and other questions racing through my startled mind, I called Como. I remembered his forensic taxidermy course, and I reflected on how handy that would now become, as I waited impatiently for him to answer.

"Detective Galahad. How may I help you?"

"It's me, Como. If you're driving, pull over."

"It's OK, Writer—police officials are allowed to use their phones while driving."

"No, I didn't mean that. I meant what I'm about to say will startle you so much you'll be unable to steer safely. I'm at the house of Lola's father's neighbors. They're both long dead. Someone has expertly stuffed their bodies to make it look to a casual observer that they are sitting in their lounge, and a tape recording has been playing on a loop to give the impression they are talking inside the house."

I heard another long screech of tires and a thud.

LESSON TWENTY

'Herbert, you are often telling me that writing a book is like a sport. What sport is it most like?'

'It depends on the book, Marco. Sometimes when I write I feel I am taking part in a boxing match; other times I feel I am weightlifting or competing in the pole vault.'

'What will my experience of writing a book be like, Herbert?'

'It will be like the Cresta Run, Marco'.

'You mean... thrills and excitement at every turn?'

'No, I meant you would get off to a slow start then go downhill fast.'

CHAPTER TWENTY

In which there are thrills and excitement at every turn. Well, nearly every turn.

So startled had he been by my report, Como crashed his police car. I went to pick him up. We watched his mangled motor being winched onto a transporter.

"Maybe you'll get a new one," I said, hoping to cheer.

"Yeah, and maybe I'll shit gold ingots next time I get five minutes in the men's room. And I don't see me getting five minutes any time soon with all the forms I'm gonna have to fill. McGee'll go nuts."

I made a note to remind myself to work on my cheering technique, then drove us to the Kelloggs' neighbors' place to let Como investigate the incredible scenario I'd invented there. I was impressed by the expert way in which he examined the stuffed bodies.

"This is taxidermy of the highest quality, Writer. See how the facial expressions are so lifelike. The curl of the fingers in repose is most exquisite. I would estimate there are not a hundred taxidermists in the world with the skill to make such realistic forms from dead humans."

"And to think, Como, we have Chief McGee to thank for your remarkable knowledge of taxidermy." I smiled at the irony of it. "What should we do next?"

"Let's take a look round."

The house had a dusty, neglected look. None of the rooms showed signs of recent habitation, bar one. It was upstairs, the room with the best view of the Kelloggs' place. At its scrupulously clean window, a pair of gyroscopically-stabilized, military-grade binoculars with the finest triple-coated optics was mounted on a five-way adjustable tripod. Someone with a predilection for hyphens had been monitoring the Kellogg family.

Any question about the subject of the mysterious surveillance was more than adequately answered by dozens of photographs loosely stacked on the window ledge. Each portrayed Lola Kellogg. In some she was alone; in some she was with a man dressed as a priest— presumably her father; in some she was with Herbert; in the remainder, she was with another man—a man in a distinctive uniform: Chief McGee.

Como leafed through picture after picture, a look of utter bewilderment on his face. I knew how he felt—I'd expected to see Lola with Herbert, but McGee?

"Writer, look at me." I looked at him. "Don't say a word about these pictures to anyone—get me?"

"Christ, Como, they're evidence—we can't just sit on evidence that might have a bearing on the case."

"We can sit on what the fuck we like, Writer, especially where my ass is concerned. Right now, McGee thinks we're going along with his bullshit story. What's he gonna do if we say we've found two stuffed bodies in the house next to Lola's, and guess what—the house is full of pictures of him with Lola?"

I'd no idea what to write for the best. Unable to concentrate on the dilemma, my thoughts strayed to the fancy binoculars.

I leaned to the eyepieces. The superb instrument furnished the clearest possible view of the Kellogg house—as if I had been standing within arm's reach of the place. I was panning from one window of the Kellogg house to the next, wondering who had been at these eyepieces before me, when...

"Como, I think there's something you need to see."

I stood away from the binoculars to let him take a look. He had to pull over a chair as he was too tall to bend down to them. He looked for maybe a second and a half.

"Let's go."

I followed as Como ran down the stairs, outside and across to the Kellogg place. Smashing a pane of glass in the front door, he put his hand through to unlock it from inside.

"Don't touch anything."

We walked warily upstairs to find the room we had previously seen through binoculars. Como eased open the door. Flies buzzed. A man's body was hanging on a rope from a hook in the ceiling.

"Do we sit on this too?"

I asked the question as Como examined the hanging body.

"Looks like Lola's pa. He was a priest. The set-up's classic for suicide."

By 'set-up' I assumed he meant the way a chair was tipped over near the hanging body. His next words confirmed my guess.

"Kellogg stands on the chair; he gets on his tippy toes to put his head in the noose; then he kicks the chair away."

It was very plausible—except I didn't think Como would speak in semicolons.

I tried not to wonder whether it was a real suicide or a staged one—I needed to let the story grow on its own, without interference, like a vegetable.

"Zucchini," said Como. He was inspecting the shoes on the dangling legs of the body. "That's weird."

He could say that again.

"Why's it weird?" I asked, ignoring the obvious reason.

"There's zucchini squashed in the grooves on the sole of the right shoe. Where would that be from?"

"The grocery store? Don't ask me, Como—you're the detective."

Como used his hanky to pick up the chair.

"No sign of zucchini on the seat." He let the chair down. "Let's look around."

"OK."

"Don't touch anything."

"OK."

"Tell me if you see any zucchinis."

"OK."

We failed to find zucchinis in the bedrooms, the bathrooms, the conservatory, the dining room, the lounge, the kitchen, the study, the hall, the billiard room, the ballroom, the library or the cellar.

"Let's take a look outside."

"OK."

Outside we found a huge raised bed upon which grew zucchinis of every variety, including exotic and heritage strains of exceptional rarity. No expense had been spared in preparing the ground to promote the growth of the magnificent fruits. Fertilizers and feeds of every kind filled the shelves of Father Kellogg's gardening shed. A huge heap of recently delivered manure steamed in the sunshine.

"Como, look at this."

I called him into the shed. On the table was the schedule for the Clarkesville County Annual Horticultural Show—a booklet setting out all of the classes for which competitors could submit entries. The schedule was held open at a certain page by a terracotta pot performing the role of a paperweight. Certain zucchini classes were marked with a penciled asterisk, presumably indicating those for which Father Kellogg had fancied his chances. The rear wall of the shed was entirely covered with rosettes from Father Kellogg's previous outings to the show.

"So?" Como seemed entirely unimpressed by my discovery.

"I take it, Como, you are not a keen gardener?"

"Writer, if I want vegetables, I get them from the store. I hardly have time to eat them, let alone grow them."

"But imagine you had grown them, Como. Imagine they were your pride and joy. Imagine you had spent your every spare moment lavishing every care upon them. The flower show is this weekend, the show at which you expect to sweep the board, bringing home rosettes by the armful. Would you abandon your glorious fruits, walk upstairs, and top yourself?"

"Maybe not."

"What are we going to do?"

"We'll call it in, but we won't say it's us who found it. You can make the call."

"Me?"

"Yeah, they'll know my voice if I do it."

"What shall I say?"

"Don't tell them about the body—just say there's been a break-in. And don't give them your real name."

"What if they trace the call to my mobile?"

"We'll use Kellogg's landline."

We went downstairs and found Kellogg's landline. Como told me what number to call. As I was starting to dial, I thought '*What if they record the call and play it back just after hearing me on one of my many TV appearances and realize it's me?*' I asked Como if I ought to put on a stupid voice.

"No, it's already stupid enough."

Smarting at Como's hurtful comment, I dialed the PD and fought my way through a horrendously overcomplicated system of menus, pressing an eight, a four, three threes, a one, two sixes, another eight and a five, to signify I wanted to report signs of a break-in. After a computer voice asked me to hold the line, I finally spoke with a human, to whom I enunciated the Kelloggs' address and zip code before being asked for my name, address and phone number. Wondering if I was committing perjury, I gave Herbert's name and contact details, and killed the call.

"Shit, Writer—why'd you give them Quarry's name?"

"Why d'you think? It was the first thing that came into my head. It can't do any harm, can it?"

"Let's hope not. Ok, let's go wait and see what happens."

We went back to keep watch in my black Range Rover. I drove it into the shade of the Kelloggs' neighbors' carport, which would keep us hidden behind our heavily tinted windows.

We didn't wait long before a car arrived. A man stepped out in a decidedly alert and business-like manner. It was McGee. He strode directly to the Kelloggs' door, inspected the damaged pane, reached inside to let himself in, disappeared for two minutes, came out, went to his car, got a cloth from the trunk, went to the house, wiped the door handle, went to his car and drove off.

I must admit it was an impressive performance—McGee's I mean, not my writing, which was even more drearily pedestrian than usual.

"Well, Como, credit where credit's due. You have to hand it to Chief McGee." I looked at my watch. "Less than ten minutes since I called the PD, and he's been here—in person mind, no sending a junior—examined the damage, and even polished the Kelloggs' door handle. Now that's what I call service."

"Writer, you're a bigger dumbass than I thought you were—and I thought you were a fuck of a big dumbass. You think McGee's responded to your call like a proper concerned police chief doin' his job the proper police way? Jeez—you're such a dumb fuck."

LESSON TWENTY-ONE

'Herbert.'

'Yes, Marco?'

'Is my writing getting better?'

'No, Marco. You are still making far too many rudimentary mistakes.'

'Such as, Herbert?'

'Here, where you say 'She collapsed down to the ground' the words 'down to the ground' are superfluous—she could hardly collapse up to the ceiling. And here, where you say 'It was a warm summer day in June', the word summer is redundant—it could not be a warm winter day in June. Expunge the unessential.'

CHAPTER TWENTY-ONE

In which the boys get a proper car for the job.

I tactfully started a new chapter, drawing the veil, as it were, over Como's regrettable outburst. Como, meanwhile, had turned up the volume of his police walkie-talkie, clicked a few of its buttons, and placed the device on the armrest between us.

"Listen," he said.

I listened.

There were all sorts of chatter, none of which I understood, but I feigned interest lest Como think me rude. After a few minutes, I heard the dispatcher telling someone to check a reported *ten sixty two* at an address that sounded like the Kelloggs', following which someone else said *ten four* then *ten seventeen* then *ten twenty-six* then *fourteen thirty,* or maybe some other numbers altogether, but it was that kind of thing.

"See?" said Como.

I had no idea what any of them were talking about. Thankfully, he spelled it out.

"They've dispatched Fuego and Taft to investigate. They'll be here in fifteen minutes. Chief McGee was here on his own account—strictly unofficial."

I was learning that *unofficial* had a wide range of meanings where Como was concerned. I wondered if the readers would appreciate the nuanced echo of the very first page, where Como's use of the word had led me to imagine he was a rogue cop. Quite how big a rogue I was still finding out.

"What are we going to do about it?"

"Nothing, yet. We'll find out who's been spying on the Kelloggs. Maybe they'll have seen something suspicious."

"How do we do that, Como?"

"We'll make a list of all the taxidermists within fifty miles. One of them will have stuffed those bodies. Now let's go before Fuego and Taft find us."

Taking care to avoid the use of unnecessary superfluous redundant words, we returned to police HQ. I paced up and down not chain-smoking while Como methodically combed through periodicals such as *The Clarkesville Taxidermist, Taxidermy Today, and North American Taxidermy News*. At last, Como snatched a list from the printer.

"These are the suspects."

I took the list from Como and scanned the names and addresses of the taxidermists he had identified.

"There are twenty-six people on this list, scattered over ten thousand square miles. How do we know where to focus?"

"We don't. We'll just have to start from the top and work down. The list's in alphabetical order, so it's as easy as ABC."

"No way, Como, we're not falling into that old trap."

"What old trap?"

"The trap of working a list from A to Z. We all know the guilty one ends up being the last suspect on the list, and I don't want my mold-breaking book to be marred by that horrendous cliché. We'll work the list from Z to A, so we find the guilty one straight off."

"Have it your way, Writer."

We went out into the lot and picked up the replacement vehicle Como had been temporarily allocated—a red '74 Ford Gran Torino with white 'vector' side darts, 5-slot mag wheels, un-tinted windows, and a 'Huggy Bear' doll hanging from the rear-view mirror. There was something familiar about the car, but I couldn't place it. I raised the collar of my thick woolen cardigan against the cold of the evening and got into the passenger seat. Como fired the engine and radioed our call sign 'Zebra three' to let the dispatcher know we were on our way. I marveled at how my subconscious had picked a Zebra call sign that mirrored our Z-to-A search method, and wondered if my readers would be smart enough to appreciate the cleverness of it without me pointing it out.

The first taxidermist on the list, or, rather, the last, was Zaquette Zorab, whose small ad in the classified section of the Clarkesville County Gazette suggested she specialized in stuffing trophy fish for anglers—two for a thousand dollars, display cases extra. Como carped at this.

"I don't mind working the list in reverse order, but someone who stuffs fish? That's work for beginners—I stuffed three in the introductory practical class on my course. No way someone like that would be up to the job."

"Ha! Exactly. That's my point, Como—in books and films it's always the person the cops least expect. If we follow your logic, we'll fall right into that clichéd trap. We'll end up investigating all the others only to find it's her. I just know it. Do we want the readers tutting at the weary predictability of it all, or do we want them marveling at our originality?"

"What we want, Writer, is results."

"Yes, well, the sooner you stop complaining and get us to Zorab's the sooner we'll get them."

"What's the address again?"

I read it off the sheet.

"Mason's Ridge? That's fifty miles away!"

With some relief on my part, Como engaged a reluctant gear and we set off, he continuing to cavil while I typed a paragraph of blatant padding about our journey. After clearing the sleepy suburbs, we pootled along the scenic two-laner that circled the southern flank of Mount Clarke before rising to the arid plateau to the south west. The contrast between the cacti and tumbleweed of our new surroundings, and the lush coastal vegetation we had left behind, was a salutary reminder of both the looming threat of global warming and my tendency to write unrealistic nonsense during the quieter moments in the narrative.

The fortunes of Mason's Ridge had been in constant decline since the closure of the aluminium smelting plant that had once been the town's largest employer and foremost example of inappropriate

British English. The sidewalks of its run-down Main Street were strewn with garbage and peopled here and there by knots of idling ex-smelters.

Zorab's place was a trailer in a rubbish-filled lot next to a wrecker's yard, its frayed chain-link fence showing no sign of ever being polished. My Bronx mom would have stern words to say about Zaquette's standards of housekeeping. A mean pit bull prowled the lot—it bounded over and leapt at the gate, growling and snapping to get at us.

"What now, Writer?"

"You mean the dog?"

"What else would I mean?"

"Don't you have one of those things like a noose on a pole?"

"If I did, I would have used it by now—and I don't mean on the dog."

I ignored his hurtful quip.

"I must say, Como, you seem lamentably ill-prepared. What if there had been an emergency—how would we get past the dog then?"

I regretted the question the moment I typed it. Como would probably say something about shooting the dog, and I'd have all the world's animal welfare societies on my back. I held up a silencing hand to preempt any reply.

"Never mind. Do you watch *The Dog Whisperer*, Como?"

"Never heard of it."

"*It* is a him. The Dog Whisperer has an innate understanding of the psychology of the canine class—he demonstrates in countless astounding episodes his power to quell the most vicious and unruly behavior. You need simply emulate his techniques to pacify the beast, and we can go about our business."

"I ain't emulating nothing, Writer. If you want to emulate yourself into trouble, that's up to you, but I vote we call the local cops and get them out with the right kit."

I pondered Como's suggestion—very level-headed and pragmatic but hardly a plan to enliven the dozing reader. They'd be nodding off in hordes if we did things Como's way and waited for the Mason Ridge police to turn up. Besides, would Jackson Pollock wait for his local art-shop to deliver a special brush, when he's all for thrashing his canvas in a frenzy of artistic expression? I think not.

"Very well, Como, if you do not feel up to the task, I will take it upon myself. The key is to personify calm assertion. I will back into the compound, thus allowing the dog to realize I am not about to attack. There is a rope by the door of the trailer—I will ease my way over there and form a leash with it. In the meantime, please remember the Dog Whisperer's mantra—no touch, no talk and no eye contact. With the dog, obviously."

I backed up to the gate and waited for the ensuing paroxysm of aggressive barking to die away.

About twenty minutes later, the paroxysm still showed no sign of abating—the dog was snapping at the gate like a crocodile. Concluding that we needed a Plan B, I rewound my memories of the *Dog Whisperer* episodes.

"Clearly the dog is nervous, Como. I remember now that in such cases it is important to reassure the animal by respecting dog etiquette. You will doubtless have seen how dogs stand and allow themselves to be sniffed. I will do the same. Here."

Handing a skeptical Como my writer's satchel, I got down on all fours and slowly moved my rear near to the fence that separated me from the enraged canine. To my surprise the aggressive barking morphed into a whimper more of excitement than of fear.

"See, Como, it is just a matter of psychology. Open the gate and I'll back in."

Como eased the mesh gate aside just enough for me to squeeze in backwards. I could hear the dog's snuffles and feel its nose prodding inquisitively at my nether regions.

"What's your plan now?"

It was a good question. For a moment I dithered about whether to ask myself *what would the Dog Whisperer do?* or *what would Jackson Pollock do?* The dog was more decisive—it mounted me and proceeded to hump with remarkable passion and energy. It felt like a jackhammer on my back.

"Don't laugh—get it off me!"

Como was bent double.

"Writer, you sure got your dog psychology mixed up. Keep him busy while I get the rope. Don't put him off his strokes."

I clenched my jaw—and buttocks—and wished I'd had the forethought to raise the collar of my cardigan as some kind of prophylactic against the dog's germ-laden breath and slobber, both of which were warming the back of my neck. I encouraged Como to be quick about his task.

"Christ, Como, are you making that rope?"

I heard his returning footfalls above the noise of the dog's frenzied panting.

"I'll say one thing—you sure have some balls."

His words induced a glow of pride. I might be humiliated by an oversexed pit bull, but at least my resourcefulness and courage had gained Como's respect.

"Thank you, Como, but if you could please hurry."

"I was talking to the dog."

Como hauled off the beast and tied it to a sturdy bench. I thanked him as he proffered my satchel.

"My pleasure, Writer. It ain't every day you get to see dog psychology practiced by a master. You should do your own dog whisperer show. C'mon, let's knock up Zorab."

I dusted myself off in an attempt to patch up my threadbare dignity as Como rapped, knocked and rattled the door of the filthy trailer. Eventually his efforts yielded a result in the form of a coarsely voiced question, thus:

"Alright, alright. We're coming. What's the big fuss about?"

The door opened to a person between thirty and seventy holding a tumbler and blinking at both the harsh light and the contrasting forms of her unexpected visitors—one giant, dapper and authoritative, the other slender, disheveled and authorlike. Como flipped his badge.

"Zaquette Zorab?"

"Sure."

"Can we ask you a few questions about taxidermy?"

"Sure, though I don't do much of it these days."

"Can we ask you inside?"

"Sure."

We followed Zaquette into the gloom of her trailer, Como stooping in the limited headroom.

"Want one?" She gesticulated with the tumbler.

"No thank you, Ma'am, we're on duty."

"Suit yourself. Take a seat."

We made space between old magazines, discarded wrappers and other detritus and perched on the edge of a filthy couch.

"We understand, Ma'am, that you practice taxidermy. Can you tell me whether you have taken on any unusual commissions recently?"

"Did. Did practice it. Don't no more. Don't see too good. Besides, I got nerve trouble."

She held out a hand Saint Vitus himself might have envied, her fingers waving like the tentacles of a hungry polyp.

"I can see that might be a handicap," acknowledged Como.

"Yes, but you'd be a demon on air piano," I added, to show there was a bright side.

Ignoring the bright side, Como asked if we could see an example of her most recent work.

"Sure. Help yourself. It's in there."

We followed the direction vaguely indicated by her wobbling arm, and entered a room that was part office, part workshop, part study, and part bottle-storage depot. We had to burrow through several years' junk before we found any evidence of actual taxidermy, namely a medium-sized mirror carp that looked like it had been stuffed as a communal exercise in a kindergarten class. I stared at its mournful eyes, at least one of which had been sewn in the wrong place.

"We're wasting our time here," Como announced, overlooking the twelve hundred words I'd invented with very little help from him. "Let's go."

We thanked Zaquette for her cooperation and made our excuses. Como released the pit bull after I'd sought sanctuary beyond the fence. It stared at me with eyes that seemed to ask *Don't you love me anymore?* as I got into the car.

"OK, Writer. What was all that about? You said we'd do the list from Z to A because the last person on it would be our man."

"Or woman, Como—we might be writing things off the top of our head, but we must still take care with our gender balance."

"Man, woman, what difference does it make? Half the day's gone and we're nowhere."

I pondered Como's prosaic complaint. It seemed to me that the challenge of breaking the mold of literature was horribly compounded by the innate conservatism of characters, who seemed to need a reason for everything. It was alright for Jackson Pollock—he didn't have to explain his paintings as he went along. I thought of an excuse.

"Hardly nowhere, Como—we have eliminated at least one red herring. Besides, when I said the last person on the list would be our man, or person, I was speaking figuratively. I didn't mean the actual last person—that would be as ridiculous as making it the very first person—I just meant it would be someone near the end of the list."

"You better be right, Writer. I've got a shit load of other work back at HQ."

"Time will tell, Como, so let's not waste any more of it moaning about our lot." I retrieved the list from the glove compartment. "Yuri Yousef's next."

"Where does he live?"

"Barton Hills."

"Barton Hills? That's fifty miles the other side of Clarkesville!"

"Christ, Como, don't blame me."

"Don't blame you? You're the writer, Writer. You're the one making up this shit."

"Yes, well, but which of us compiled the list? Huh?"

I didn't quite catch Como's response, as it was muttered through lips preoccupied with the production of a petulant pout. He slammed the car into gear, and with a screech of tortured rubber we were off.

With another screech of tortured rubber, we lurched to a stop two hours later next to a sign welcoming us to the Barton Hills Craft Village, Motel and Diner, a hideously tacky development on the site of an abandoned self-storage facility. The old lockups had been converted into units in which the artistic members of the Barton Hills community made and purveyed a variety of quaint goods to sell to tourists with time and money on their hands. We looked up the location of Yousef's unit—*Pets N Stuff*—on a board showing the layout of the site, then found the unit itself sandwiched between one selling cookies shaped and decorated to resemble famous religious figures, and another selling patio ornaments made from old beer cans. Yousef's window display displayed a narrow range of unconvincingly stuffed creatures of the pet class. There was a cat with a flattened face and kinked tail, a spherical gerbil with no visible limbs, a hamster whose cheeks were stuffed more realistically than its trunk; the only exhibit with a remotely convincing body-shape was a tortoise. The glass door was locked. A yellowing hand-written note taped inside said *Closed Until Further Notice.*

Como looked at me. Although he voiced no words, I knew exactly what was in his mind and answered accordingly.

"Okay, okay—stay cool. I'm sure there's a simple explanation."

We got the simple explanation from the neighboring stallholder, who furnished it while decorating a cookie of Pope Pious the Tenth ...

"He's in the can. Got twelve months. Tax fraud. Can you believe it? A nice regular guy. You work all day in this place, and you can barely pay the rent and some asshole from the IRS starts poking his big nose in. Jeez."

"Thank you, Sister—you've been most helpful." We put ten dollars in the nun's mite box and wandered outside where I tried to forestall the tsunami of criticism soon to be swamping me from Como's direction.

"Before you say it, Como, I know, I know."

"You know? Saying you know doesn't change things, Writer."

"Yes, but—you can't blame me for him being in prison, Como. I admit I'm the writer, but I'm not the police. I am quite happy to accept full responsibility for matters within my area of expertise—punctuation, word choice, syntax and so on—but I fail to see how I can be responsible for the imprisonment of a minor character."

I said all that to Como's back as I followed him to the car. We buckled in in a tense silence which Como maintained while I retrieved and unfolded the list. I read out the third name from the bottom.

"Ximena Ximenez."

"Where does she live?"

"Harmony Pines."

"Shit, that's right by Mason's Ridge."

Two days later we had visited the addresses of all but one of the taxidermists and crossed out twenty-five of the twenty-six names on the list. Two of those we had visited had been in prison, one had died, one had been declared insane—a condition Como claimed he was close to sharing—and one had emigrated to Guatemala over a year ago; the work of the rest had been far too crude, according to Como, to have matched the exquisite perfection of the taxidermy in the Kelloggs' neighbors' house. Only one name remained on the list: Aaron Aaronovitch.

Exhausted and stubble faced, we sat in the Gran Torino on a curve of a mountain road, munching burgers and fries while contemplating the towns and villages spread below us, at least twenty-five of which we had recently visited. The car was littered with the discarded containers of the armsful of fast food Como had bought to fuel our epic search. I had asked him if there was an organic vegan option, but he told me it would spoil the mood of the scene. As we nourished our bodies, we nourished our minds also, talking philosophically of this, that and the other. Mainly the other.

"You don't have a girlfriend, Writer?"

"No."

"How come?"

I picked out a particularly long fry as I thought about the question.

"I dunno, Como. I never seemed to meet anyone before I was famous. After my book topped the charts, I met lots of women, but they only wanted the celebrity Marco, not the real one."

"They didn't lust after you because of your irresistible sexual charisma?" Como smirked.

"No." I tried to make light of my complete lack of irresistible sexual charisma. "Hard to believe, isn't it?"

"Yeah. Just like the rest of the crap you write." Como rubbed a reassuring hand on my shoulder to compensate for his hurtful quip. "Speaking of which, why don't you just write yourself a girlfriend?"

It was a good question. I wagged the fry to conduct the orchestra of my thoughts. "It's not that easy, Como. I'm meant to be breaking the mold of literature, so I'm not supposed to actually write anything on purpose—I just have to type whatever comes out. If I did type a girlfriend..."

My words petered out as my mind was enveloped in a struggle of competing visions. In the blue corner, my ideal soulmate, beautifully conceived and wrought for a lifetime of perfect compatibility. In the red corner, a hastily drawn Jackson Pollock character, overly influenced by subconscious thoughts of my Bronx mom. I put the fry back in the box and closed the lid, suddenly off my food. Thankfully Como changed the subject.

"Tell me, Writer, how did you cope with all that fame you got?"

I fondled the burger box reflectively as my mind went back. "It was strange. At first, I thought it was brilliant. The lonely spotty gangling kid everyone ignored had become someone everybody wanted to meet. I had money and success. I bought a loft apartment in Greenwich Village and had a really mean time there."

I paused again, this time to wonder whether my readers would appreciate the Greenwich Mean Time reference without me having to labor it. "I found myself invited to parties with rock stars and actors— people I'd idolized. It was incredible. But still I felt lonely, and the fame became intrusive. I couldn't jog around town without hordes of kids running after me wanting to know about my predictions for the magnetic moment of the tau muon."

Como nodded, either in sympathy or boredom.

"How about you, Como—is there anyone special in your life? Ever think about settling down?"

"I came close once or twice, but settling down doesn't really fit with police work—know what I mean?"

Of course I knew what he meant. The trope of the lonely cop was one of the most overworked themes in fiction—I was appalled that he'd contaminated my narrative with such a cliché. I hurried us to another subject.

"Speaking of police work..."

Como took the hint and started the car. "What's the address?"

I found the list among all the food wrappers and looked at the only entry I hadn't crossed out.

"Five Marlow Court, Clarkesville."

"Marlow Court? Christ, Writer, that's right next door to police HQ. If we'd done the list from A to Z, we'd have nailed Aaronovitch two days ago without even having to get in the frigging car. You're such a fucking asshole, you know that?"

Thinking it best to treat the question as rhetorical, I maintained a philosophical silence as Como drove us moodily back to Clarkesville.

LESSON TWENTY-TWO

'Herbert, when I last checked, I was managing to write five thousand words per hour. Is that a sufficient rate of productivity to attract the attention of a publisher?'

'More than sufficient, Marco, assuming, of course, that what you have written is not total garbage.'

CHAPTER TWENTY-TWO

In which the reader is astonished by two revelations.

We parked the '74 Gran Torino outside the Aaronovitch house. Como switched off the sirens and I slid over the hood to get to the sidewalk in a more dramatic way—instantly regretting it, as I bruised myself horribly.

Como rang the bell while I rubbed my coccyx. A refined elderly gentleman opened the door, walking with a stick. Como flashed his badge. "Detective Como Galahad of Clarkesville County Police. This dumbass is Marco Ocram off TV. We'd like to ask a few questions. Can we come in?"

"Of course."

Aaronovitch led us along a musty hall crammed with the most spectacular and exotic taxidermy I had ever seen. Peacocks, a snow leopard, the rare Carisco monkey, two giant turtles, male and female, a huge anaconda entwined around the newel post of the stairs, an eight-foot polar bear towering over us with paws outstretched ready to strike, a tiny humming bird, its delicate tongue questing for pollen, three iguanas, a chameleon cunningly colored to match the flock wallpaper behind it, a brace of partridge that...

Como nudged me heavily in the ribs to bring my attention back to the case. We walked into an old-fashioned parlor where a little old lady rocked back and forth in a chair. Como removed his hat gallahadly, sorry, gallantly.

"Evening, Ma'am. We are sorry to intrude."

Old Aaronovitch laughed.

"She won't mind, Detective. It's a long time since anyone disturbed my wife."

Como and I looked at the old lady, then at each other. She was stuffed. In an instant Como had his Colt Sauer PPK service pistol in his hand. He pinned Aaronovitch to the wall by his throat, kicked his feet apart and frisked him expertly. Finding no weapons, he released the old man, who sat in an armchair in a paroxysm of coughing. I went to get a glass of water—and one for the old man too. When he recovered, we began an impromptu interrogation.

"How do you explain this?" Como pointed with his gun at the figure still rocking in the chair.

"I can explain everything," said the elderly taxidermist.

"Make it snappy," said Como, with a touch of impatience that did no credit to the police force he represented, although it did allow me another two lines of padding.

On the far wall of the room was a large mirror through which I caught the surreal tableau: the stuffed old lady, serene in her rocking chair, the huge figure of Como staring at the frail taxidermist, and I scratching my left buttock as I waited for my mental pot to fill with word-paint I could splat onto the page.

Eventually Aaronovitch spoke...

"As you can see, I am a master taxidermist, one of the best. My work is sought by the rich and famous the world over. My beautiful wife and I retired to Clarkesville to enjoy the last of our days together. But within a month of settling here she was killed in a tragic road accident, her beautiful body totally disfigured. I could not bear the sight of it, nor the thought of being without her, so I asked if I could stuff her, as I knew I had the skills to make her beautiful once more. It was a request that had never been made before, and the local authorities were very conservative in their outlook, so I had to fight a long legal battle, going all the way to the Supreme Court to get permission to stuff my wife, whose mangled body was in cold storage. But I won out, and the body was released to me. Never in all the thousands of commissions I undertook for the rich and famous did I exercise as much skill and care, and now you can see for yourself that my wife looks alive and radiant in her favorite rocking chair, to which

I added a small electric motor with an offset spigot and crank to rock it just as she loved to do herself.

"Eventually, however, my money ran out. I had an idea born of desperation. Why should I be the only person to be consoled by the stuffing of a loved one? Why not offer the service to others? Surely there would be huge demand. I secured a loan and advertised my new taxidermy service for the recently bereaved. But, alas, I underestimated the conservatism of small-town Americans. No one took up my offer."

"No one?" Como asked doubtfully.

"No one."

"So how can you account for this?" Como took out an iPad and confronted the master taxidermist with a video of the two stuffed neighbors of the Kelloggs.

Aaronovitch was as engrossed as he was astonished. "Such incredible work. Such mastery. I have never seen the like outside my own studio." He replayed parts of the video again and again, marveling at the exquisite examples of the taxidermist's art.

"Only one hand could have performed such delicate work," he went on.

"Whose?" asked Como and I in unison.

"I didn't know his name at the time, his real name that is. He told me to call him Mister Vmith. He came to me one day having seen my advertisement for stuffed bodies and asked if I could teach him the art. Money would be no obvtacle, he told me. He was a huge strong brute, horribly disfigured, and unable to pronounce his esses, all of which came out as vees, but he was the perfect pupil. Not only did he readily assimilate my skills; in some ways he surpassed them. Many of the stupendous pieces you were admiring in my hall were stuffed by his hand. It was only later I found the true identity of the disfigured brute. He was..."

In the mirror, Como and I stood with our respective mouths agape in matching Os of suspense.

"...Bluther Cale, the manservant of the billionaire industrialist Elijah Bow."

There was a pause of some minutes while we waited for our astonished mouth-gapes to relax to the point at which we could speak, after which Como said:

"I'm sorry to reawaken your grief-laden memories, Mister Aaronovitch, but did they find the driver responsible for your wife's fatal accident?"

"Did they? Oh yes, they found that son of a bitch alright, but he had something over the police chief and they never touched him. Too little evidence they said, when half my wife's face was squashed into his radiator grille."

"Who was he?"

"That bastard pedophile writer, Herbert Quarry."

LESSON TWENTY-THREE

'Tell me, Herbert, how did you become a bestselling novelist?'

'It was a long time ago, Marco. I knew it was my destiny to write, as writing is a disease, an inherited disease, in one's genes as surely as cancer, or red hair, or any other inherent characteristic. For me writing was everything. It was food, it was drink, it was sun and rain, it was wakefulness and sleep, it was sex and abstinence, it was like boxing. It was everything. Do you understand, Marco? Everything.'

'I understand, Herbert.'

CHAPTER TWENTY-THREE

In which police brutality prompts the spilling of beans, Marco has second thoughts about Herbert's innocence, and Como starts a trend for subsequent books.

Como and I looked at each other in amazement, as we seemed to be doing in virtually every chapter recently.

"Wait a minute," I said, "are you saying Herbert Quarry killed your wife but had something over Chief McGee that allowed him to evade charges?"

"That is exactly what I'm saying, and if you had any gumption you would already have left to confront Quarry and check the truth of my words."

Stung by the old man's bitter admonishment, Como and I stormed out of the house and leaped into the Gran Turismo. Or was it a Gran Torino? It's all very well Herbert saying that chapters are like paintings in a gallery, but in a gallery you don't expect consistency between one painting and the next. In a book it's different. I can just imagine the readers going nuts if I get the name of the car wrong—and how are you meant to break the mold of literature when you're forever worrying about trivia? Nodding an exasperated head at the tedium of it all, I returned to the plot.

"Where to now?" I asked.

"You know where, Writer." Como rammed the selector into 'Drive' and we left rubber half-way down the street as we raced off to the county jail.

Slam! Como drove Herbert's head into the wall of the visiting room while I looked-on with concern for my mentor.

THE AWFUL TRUTH ABOUT THE HERBERT QUARRY AFFAIR

"I'll give you one last chance to level with us Quarry, and then it's no more mister nice guy."

Herbert felt his way into a chair, blinded by the blood from a cut on his forehead. "Ok, ok, I'll tell you all I know."

I set up the reel-to-reel recorder I carry with me everywhere, nodding to Herbert to begin his story as I adjusted the gain.

"It was some years ago. My last novel wasn't selling, and the publisher was breathing down my neck for the next. Millions were riding on it, as an advance was about to be negotiated, and there was a bidding war for the film rights. I couldn't cope with the pressure, so I got drunk, blind drunk, in a bar in town. A young woman walked in, an ex. I tried to talk with her, but she blanked me and stormed off. I suppose she was disgusted by my drunken appearance and lack of self-esteem. It was as if a mirror had been held to my face. I realized I was a pathetic loser. I had everything to live for—a lifestyle most people could only fantasize about—yet I was letting a little pressure get to me, pressure that was nothing compared with the day-to-day agonies of existence endured by nobodies everywhere. In a mood of utter self-disgust, I staggered to my car to drive home, determined never to touch a drink again. But as I was getting close to my house on the beach overlooking the ocean, an old lady lurched from nowhere into the path of my car. I can never forget the look on her face, a face blinded by my headlights before a sickening thump as I mowed her down. I skidded off the road and hit a tree. McGee was first on the scene. He found me slumped over the wheel, but I was sufficiently awake to recognize him. When his eyes met mine, he knew I knew his guilty secret, and he put me in the back of his car. Squad cars and an ambulance arrived. He left another officer in command, drove me to police HQ and locked me in a cell. The next morning, after I had sobered up, he made me give a urine sample, which showed little sign of alcohol in my body. Later he said the sample had been provided immediately after the accident, so I could not be prosecuted for drunk driving. The fact that the old lady was in the middle of an unlit road on a bend made it look like an understandable accident, and no attempt was made to prosecute me. But the old lady's husband received a tip-off, and ever since then he has vowed to bring me down, even if it takes him until his last breath."

"What was McGee's guilty secret?" asked either Como or I—it doesn't matter which, so take your pick.

"Two days earlier, I had been walking in the woods near my house on the beach over-looking the ocean. It was a beautiful morning, warm and sunny. Shafts of golden light filtered down between the pristine foliage. Damsel flies hovered in the pure air. The world had a newly created quality, Eden-like, the scent of the air enchanting the mind with its infinite promise of..."

"Get on with it, Quarry." That was definitely Como.

"And don't use a hyphen in overlooking." That was me.

"Sorry, sorry. I saw a police car had been driven between the trees, about a hundred yards off the road. Thinking there might have been an accident, I went to see if I could help. I saw a couple lying on a blanket. One was a girl of perhaps fifteen or sixteen—the other was a man in police uniform. He jumped up sharply at the sound of my approach. It was Chief McGee."

Wow. I rewound the tape while Como paced around the room like a caged tiger wondering what to do next.

Como punched the wall. "We've been idiots. We've missed some obvious clues." Herbert and I waited for him to go on. "McGee says he caught you red handed through a tip-off. Somebody called the emergency line. How would that somebody know, unless they were looking through the window of your house? And who looks through a window to see someone cutting up a body, and then calls the emergency line without giving their name?"

It was a good question—two good questions, actually—and I was surprised I hadn't raised it, or them, earlier.

"Someone's got some answering to do. Come on, Writer." He gestured for me to follow, leaving Herbert to be led back to his cell by a guard.

As we cruised back to police HQ in the Gran Torino, Como seemed in a more philosophical frame of mind. "So, Writer, explain this. Here we are, thirty thousand words in, and yet a fundamental plot device has only just been deployed. How could that be?"

For a moment I had no answer. I had to think. Then I realized it was the result of Herbert's advice. Write the first thing that comes into your head. Don't overthink it. Don't plan out a plot. Spontaneity is the writer's friend. Plans are poison. Again and again in different words Herbert had convinced me it was wrong to think ahead. And here we were looking foolish amateurs through a lack of planning. A thought lurking in my subconscious mushroomed into my mind like a...like a giant mushroom. What if Herbert too had been trying to mislead me? What if all this talk of writing like Jackson Pollock was designed to distract me from thinking through to the obvious truth, that my mentor Herbert really was guilty after all? I wasn't ready to share my doubts with Como, so I parried his question with a suitable sporting analogy...

"Investigating a death is like a boxing match, Como. You can't plan punches far in advance. You have to react to the motions of your opponent. When the bell dings for the first round, you don't know you'll need a left hook two minutes into the fifth. With hindsight it's obvious we should have asked what triggered Herbert's arrest, but we shouldn't be too hard on ourselves for missing it at the time."

"True." Como appeared consoled by my words, and we drove a few more miles in companionable silence.

"Know what I think?" he asked at last.

"No."

"I think we need a case conference in a room with a glass wall where we can stick photographs and draw arrows between people with connections to the case. They have them in all the TV cop shows, so I don't see why we shouldn't have one too."

LESSON TWENTY-FOUR

'Herbert, for a book to be a bestseller, must it be well written?'

'No, Marco. Some bestsellers are well written, but the two qualities are not related.'

'Then what makes a bestselling book?'

'Money and contacts, Marco. Sales are in proportion to the number of palms that are greased. The critics will say anything if they are paid enough.'

'But surely there must be more to it. Surely the book must have some merit.'

'Well, there are some basics, admittedly. The book must have at least a certain number of pages. The text should constitute recognizable sentences. Clearly, Marco, the words cannot be a random jumble.'

'But can truly mediocre writing become a bestseller purely through the perverse machinations of publishers and their marketing advisors?'

'For your sake, Marco, let us hope so.'

CHAPTER TWENTY-FOUR

In which a malodorous episode precedes a passage of proper police procedure.

Como dropped me at Herbert's place where I had set up camp in one of the many guest bedrooms. Or maybe I dropped Como at police HQ and drove to Herbert's myself, depending on whose car we were in last. Como's suggestion, that we should insert a dollop of realistic police procedure by holding a case conference, seemed to have two major drawbacks, viz:

Drawback #1—Realistic police procedure might not have a place in a mold-breaker a la Jackson Pollock.

Drawback #2—I had no idea how to write it.

However, with my usual gritty determination I decided to give it a go. After all, if we always downed the pen every time we found something we didn't know how to write, we'd never get past Chapter One. Accordingly, I spent my free time performing the most diligent preparations for the forthcoming case conference—charging my iPad and having a nap.

In good time I roused myself, packed the necessaries in my satchel and went out to blip open my black Range Rover, admiring the view of the ocean reflected in its tinted windows. Ordinarily my car flashes its lights when blipped, greeting the owner who feeds it gas and other nourishing fluids. There was no such greeting today—I must have left it unlocked. Never mind. Herbert's house was very isolated—it was unlikely there'd be car thieves about. I opened the driver's door.

On the squab of my seat, contrasting with the immaculate cream leather, were several moist blobs of dog doo doo. Stuck into the doo doo was an envelope addressed to *'Snooper.'*

Recoiling from the dreadful whiff, I pulled the envelope from the blobs and gingerly opened it, hoping not to get any of the poo on my fingers. Inside was a card showing a view of Clarkesville harbor, the rear bearing the words:

'We don't like snoopers, especially when they stick up for pedophiles. If you know what's good for you, you better leave. We'll give you forty-eight hours to pack your bags.'

The words were in 16-point Incredula, a font normally found in books on the occult. What could it mean? Who could have done this? Who knew I was helping Herbert? Engrossed in my thoughts, I flopped onto the driver's seat, having forgotten the doo doo.

An unpleasant change of trousers later, I went into Herbert's garage to search for cleaning aids to deal with the excreta my buttocks had pressed into the grained leather. Among the paraphernalia cluttering the place, I found a mannequin of the sort department stores have in window displays. It was about the size of a fifteen-year-old girl. Lines had been drawn across its limbs, with the instruction 'cut here'. What could it mean? Perhaps it meant writing the first thing that came into your head was a daft idea after all.

Having cleaned the seat, I drove into town to join Como at police HQ. He was just about to brief his team—a mix of young, eager detectives and seasoned cynics who had joined Clarkesville PD before I was born.

"Ah, Writer, good of you to come," said Como.

We made introductions; I shook a dozen hands; the team complemented me on my stylish use of semicolons; then the briefing began in earnest.

"Gentlemen. Ladies. Let us go through what we know about this case," said Como. "At 2:47 p.m. on the ninth a call came through to the Clarkesville PD emergency line." Como nodded at one of the technical specialists to play a recording.

"This is Clarkesville County Police Emergency Line. Please state your emergency, Caller."

"There's a famous novelist with a house over-looking the ocean who's been having a secret affair with an underage girl, and now I think he has killed her and is cutting her body into pieces at his house."

"Thank you, Caller. I'll dispatch a patrol car right away. Is there anything else I can help you with today?"

"No, thank you."

"Thank you for calling Clarkesville County Police. Have a nice day."

"Any questions?" asked Como.

I put up my non-typing hand.

"Yes, Writer."

"Have we been able to trace the call?"

"Not yet. The caller withheld their number. It's technically possible for the telephone company to trace the call, but we need a warrant to give them permission to do it, as it would otherwise be a breach of the caller's rights."

"And how long will it take us to get a warrant, Lieutenant?"

"Usually two working days, but there's a case going through the state court challenging the right of law enforcement authorities to apply for warrants in such circumstances, so we have no idea how long it might take in this case."

"That's literally unbelievable. How is a small-town police department expected to clear a writer framed for a grisly murder with one arm tied behind their backs?"

I scowled at my coffee cup with ill-concealed disgust for my inept mingling of the singular and the plural, and for the do-gooders responsible for hampering our investigation. I was also very annoyed about the anonymous caller's hyphenation of overlooking, which was making me look a rank amateur in the spelling department. Looking on the bright side, however, the court case did set up the possibility of a *deus ex machina* ending in which Herbert would be saved from frying in the chair thanks to a last-minute issue of a warrant to trace the call.

"Let's move on," said Como. "At 3:06pm Chief McGee arrives at the scene of the reported crime with heavy back-up. Upon entering the premises, the police find the suspect Herbert Quarry kneeling in a pool of blood within which are scattered large pieces of a dismembered corpse."

Como affixed to the glass wall a large color print showing Herbert kneeling among the blood and cuts of meat. Three of the younger members of the team threw-up and two fainted. I almost threw-up myself at having to write such rubbish. The older members of the team, however, were hardened cops, inured to the clichés of crime fiction—they crushed their cans of soft drink to denote their anger at the brutal murder.

Como ignored the commotion.

"Forensic examination has shown the dismembered body was of a girl aged fifteen or sixteen. Her blood group, DNA, appearance, hair color, eye color, dental configuration and other distinguishing features match those of Lola Kellogg, a young girl who disappeared on the day the corpse was discovered. The rare Japanese cooking knife with which the corpse was dismembered appears to be one of a set of rare Japanese cooking knives in Herbert Quarry's kitchen. Herbert Quarry's DNA and fingerprints are all over the corpse. There are distinctive handprints on the sections of the corpse showing where the body had been held steady as it was cut up, and the prints match those of Herbert Quarry. We also know from many independent sources, including a confession from Quarry himself, that he had a long illicit love affair with the poor child."

At this, Como affixed a photo of Herbert to the glass wall and drew thick arrows between the photo and one of the dismembered Lola, thus signifying the strong evidential links between the two.

One of the more seasoned detectives raised her hand, shedding salt and pepper over the conference table. "Does Quarry have an alibi?"

An alibi. I knew there was something else I had forgotten. I decided a brief flashback was necessary to correct my omission...

Six days earlier...

THE AWFUL TRUTH ABOUT THE HERBERT QUARRY AFFAIR

After my first visit to see Herbert had been ended prematurely by the heavily armed warder, I realized I hadn't asked Herbert all I needed to know. At the next available opportunity, I returned to the prison and once again went through all the formalities to find myself alone with Herbert in an interview room. I asked him to tell me about the day on which he had found Lola's dismembered body...

"It no longer seems real to me, Marco," he said. "It seems like an impressionist painting viewed from afar through smudged spectacles. However, the day before was the happiest of my life, and the happiest of Lola's too. We had settled into a routine, she and I, one we had to hide from the world. Every morning she would arrive at my house, having convinced her parents with some story that she would be visiting friends for the day. She would cook breakfast while I sketched ideas for the next few pages of my book. After breakfast we would tell each other how much we loved each other, and dance on the beach. She took to looking after me and liked nothing better than to darn my socks while we discussed literature. She said she wanted to be my wife and look after me forever. Never again would my socks be un-darned. We would have children and move to Canada where we could live in peace. She would be my muse, my editor, my wife, my lover, my best friend, and my agent, all rolled into one. She left messages for me around the house, penciled on paper, or written in lipstick on the mirror, or cut into the lawn with a lawnmower, or arranged with trails of toilet paper in the bathroom, or let into the surface of my desk in exquisite marquetry. All expressed her undying love for me. Then one day she came to my house with angry livid bruises all over her body. I asked her what had happened, and she told me her father beat her, that she was a wicked, wicked girl and she deserved all of the beatings. I had never heard anything so outrageous, and I went to look up the telephone number of the appropriate authorities to whom the beating should be reported; but Lola was wiser than I, and pointed out that our relationship was just as illegal as the beatings, and if we were to report the latter then surely we would end up exposing the former, and our love would be torn asunder."

I gave a small nod of sleepiness which thankfully Herbert misinterpreted as one of understanding. He went on...

"It became clear to me that the only way to save Lola from her abusive parent was to elope. We agreed on a time and a date. I started rumors about a promotional trip to Europe, hoping to throw people off the scent once we had left for Canada. On the fateful day, I had arranged to meet Lola at my house at 1pm, but that very morning she called to say she wanted to meet me at the beach instead, to dance there one last time. She also said she might be running up to two hours late, so I should wait for her from 1pm to 3pm and only return to the house if she had not arrived by the aforementioned time. (Yawn, yawn.) I went to the beach at exactly 1pm in a state of supreme relaxation. The worries and tensions that had been such a constant part of our secret life had vanished. We were on our way to our new life. Soon all of our troubles would be behind us. Reflecting on my good fortune and golden future, I fell asleep, awaking at exactly 3pm. At once I was worried that Lola had not arrived, and in accordance with our agreement I returned to the house. What did I find but my beautiful darling Lola in pieces on the floor. I sank to my knees in shock, incapable of thought or movement, as if in a trance, and I touched my fingers to the bloody pool to see if it was real or the continuation of my dream on the beach. After all, it was easier for me to believe I was still sleeping than to accept the horror surrounding me. It was then the police arrived, Marco, and the rest you know."

Back in the present...

"No," I heard myself saying. "He has no proper alibi. He said he spent the two preceding hours sleeping alone on the beach waiting for Lola, then returned to the house only after she failed to turn-up."

Elevated eyebrows indicated the cynicism with which my words were received by the more-experienced members of the team.

"So, Herbert Quarry does indeed appear to be the most likely suspect," asserted Como.

"I disagree," I contested. "I know Herbert to be incapable of committing such a crime, especially against his one true love; but putting that aside, his story is consistent with the known facts, and there are others with both the motive and the opportunity to have committed the crime."

"True," acknowledged Como, with what seemed to me to be remarkable fairness. "Let us get on to what else we have established about the case. Firstly, we have Marcia Delgado." At this, Como affixed to the wall a photograph of the waitress's scorned sister, one taken at the mental asylum, showing her in some sort of fit, the very image of a psychopathic lunatic. He went on:

"Delgado had a strong motive for ruining Quarry. She had been deeply scorned by him, had accused him of being a sick pedophile, had publicly vowed to see him rot in hell, and had, according to one of the world's most renowned psychologists, subconsciously betrayed an implacable desire to frame the bestselling author."

Como told of the 3,285 extraordinary artworks Marcia had produced in the lunatic asylum, each showing Herbert framed in some way. Como drew an arrow from the photo of Marcia to the photo of Herbert, writing the word 'FRAMED' next to it, and a reverse arrow from Herbert to Marcia, which he labelled 'SCORNED'.

"Our honorary colleague here," Como nodded at me, "has pointed out that Professor Sushing has taken a remarkable interest in the Delgado case, and that his powers of subconscious influence could have been directed at Marcia then, and at us now, to lead us to the conclusion that Marcia was likely to be framing Herbert. The Professor could be framing the framer." Como fixed up a photo of the stern and austere countenance of Sushing—one that highlighted his villainous mien—and drew another arrow to show the potential relationship to Delgado.

"We also know bad blood existed between the Professor and Quarry, who had taken him to court for libelous reviews of his books." Como drew another pair of arrows, marking one 'JEALOUSY' and the other 'COURT CASE.'

"Next we have Aaron Aaronovitch," Como added a photo to the wall, "an expert taxidermist who professes to have no direct link to the killing, but whose wife was killed by Quarry in a tragic accident." Como added more photos and arrows showing the links between Aaronovitch and Herbert, writing 'KILLED WIFE' next to them.

"Then we have Elijah Bow, the billionaire industrialist who was found to have a huge bronze statue of the naked victim. Could he be a love rival to Quarry, anxious to suppress evidence of his own illegal love for Lola?" Another photo hit the wall, with six more arrows.

"Finally, we have Bluther Cale, two people we believe he stuffed, and a chameleon who may be unrelated but whom we have yet to rule out." Como added four more photos and a whole quiver of arrows to the glass wall.

"Okay, now what have we got..."

Como stepped back to assess the overall picture. It was an indecipherable mess of scribbles with everyone connected to everyone else.

I took a nice picture of it with my iPad.

LESSON TWENTY-FIVE

'Marco, what were you trying to convey with this sentence 'I felt like a volcano preparing to erupt'?'

'I was trying to say I was suddenly excited and energized, Herbert. Is there something wrong?'

'Volcanic eruptions are never sudden, Marco—they are always preceded by months of seismic activity.'

'Oh.'

'In any case, it is nonsense to say volcanoes prepare to erupt. Volcanoes do not make preparations, Marco.'

'Oh.'

'You must understand, Marco: writing spontaneously is not the same as writing tripe.'

CHAPTER TWENTY-FIVE

In which Marco continues to confuse tripe and spontaneity.

I returned to Herbert's house on the beach overlooking the ocean and sat in a recliner on his deck. I was beginning to have doubts about the whole business: about my ability to solve the case, about my ability to write a bestseller, about the plot I had developed, or, rather, not developed. I tried to clear my mind and live in the moment for a moment. The sun was setting, and the surface of the ocean was iridescent. I felt a pang of loneliness. In spite of all my fame, wealth and success, and in spite of my growing camaraderie with Como, and in spite of the *esprit de corps* I shared as an honorary member of his crack squad, I still felt I was missing someone to share my life. The hot actresses who pestered me to father their babies were one thing, but I missed something more fundamental. I wanted a special companion. I wanted someone to dance on the beach with, someone who would share my taste in books and music, someone who would talk with me on long, romantic walks, someone I could surprise with romantic gifts, someone who could argue with me about which of us was doing our fair share of the housework, someone who could criticize my Bronx mom for interfering in our life, someone who could daub accusations about me on the side of civic buildings, someone who...

Que Sera Sera put a stop to my romantic reflections. It was Como. He said he had some startling news for me for a change, and he was on his way and I'd better be ready to leave as soon as he got here.

I heard Como's siren long before I saw his Gran Torino hurl round the bend toward me. I was waiting for him by the roadside. He executed a perfect handbrake turn to stop alongside me after a spectacular tailskid, so all I had to do was open the door and get in.

"Belt up good and tight, Writer," he advised, flooring the pedal to jerk me back in my seat with the force of our acceleration.

"Where are we going?"

"You'll see when we get there, but there's a dead Bluther Cale waiting for us."

"Bluther Cale! Dead?!"

"You bet. A patrolman saw a black Lancia Monte Carlo down in the surf where the road runs near the cliffs. He climbed down and there's a body in the car. The description of the deceased suits Cale to a tee."

"Do we know how long he's been dead?"

Como paused to concentrate on skidding the Gran Torino through a hairpin. "Two weeks."

Two weeks? That was almost exactly the time since Lola was found in pieces in Herbert's study. Connections started to form in my mind, but before I could reach any conscious conclusion Como skidded the Gran Torino to a halt just yards from a cordoned-off section of the road in which a wrecking truck, surrounded by prowlers with flashing lights, was winching something up from over the edge of the cliff.

We wandered over, Como acknowledging the greetings from the uniformed officers, while I wondered why cops on TV always skidded their cars everywhere. I leaned on the fence and peered over the edge. About twenty feet down, a black car was being inched up the cliff, water seeping from its doors. The front of the car had been concertinaed by its impact with the rocks. I could see a vague shape hunched over the steering wheel. As the car was winched closer, I could smell the vague shape too—it was a foul stench of hell's vilest corruption. I vomited all over Como's left police shoe.

"I'm sorry," I gasped, wiping my mouth with the back of my hand.

"Here." Como offered me his handkerchief.

"Thanks," I said. I was about to use the handkerchief to wipe my mouth, but Como lifted his foot and made me wipe his shoe instead.

The black Lancia had been hauled to the road; it sat on flat tires, dripping water. Como donned plastic gloves and used his giant strength to yank open the deformed driver's door. I reflected that while I had meant the deformed door, what I had written could also mean the door of the deformed driver, which would turn out to be a pretty witty pun, albeit an unintentional one, if the driver was indeed the horribly disfigured Bluther Cale.

Braving the dreadful pong, Como glanced over the body inside. It was badly decomposed after two weeks in the surf, but Como's expert eye missed no detail.

He strode back to me, stripping off the gloves.

"It's Cale alright. No doubt about it. But there's also no doubt he was dead before the car went over the cliff."

"How can you tell?"

"His kneecaps were smashed, his face was pulped, and he was finished off with several blows to the back of the head."

"Someone beat him to death?"

"Yeah. And not just any someone—someone with a police nightstick."

LESSON TWENTY-SIX

'What is plagiarism, Herbert?'

'Plagiarism is the act of presenting the ideas of others as if they were one's own. You seem very quiet, Marco.'

'I was thinking, Herbert.'

'Yes, Marco?'

'Does that mean you have to have ideas of your own if you want to write a book?'

CHAPTER TWENTY-SIX

In which Marco strictly observes the tenets of good security.

I started a new chapter to allow this latest revelation to sink in, and shifted the scene to the Clarkesville coffeeshop, where Como and I had gone after we had seen the decomposing body of Bluther Cale bundled into an ambulance. We were sitting at my specially reserved table. I put the obvious question to Como as he stirred sugar into his coffee.

"How many police officers are there in Clarkesville County who are equipped with the type of nightstick that finished off Bluther Cale?"

Como said a number which I decided not to type in case it proved to be a ludicrously implausible overstatement of the capacity of a typical small-town police department.

"Could we get them all to submit their sticks for inspection?"

"What, and start a riot?"

"How else can we develop the lead? We can't just ignore it!"

"That's easy for you to say, Writer." Como tore fifty paper napkins into shreds as he considered our predicament.

"Wait a minute," I said. "I've had an idea. Could we invent some other reason for getting the crew to hand in their nightsticks? An equipment audit, for example, or a product safety recall."

Como looked at me. "I suppose that's an occupational hazard for you writers."

"What is?"

"Making up shit."

"Well I don't hear any better ideas coming from you," I said, a touch piqued.

"OK. How about this? The guys are all based at HQ. When they go off shift, they keep their kit in lockers in the basement. We slip into the basement at night and check each of the lockers."

"But won't they be locked?"

"Yeah, but there's a master key for emergencies."

I wasn't convinced.

"I'm not convinced," I said.

"Why not?"

"It doesn't seem a promising plot line. Apart from the difficulties of getting hold of the master key, what would we be looking for? It's hardly likely anyone would be dumb enough to be carrying around a nightstick caked with bits of Cale's skull and kneecaps. Even if there were microscopic quantities of DNA on one of the sticks, we wouldn't be able to tell which. We'd have to swab every stick in secret, keep track of which of the swabs was associated with which of the sticks, and get all the swabs analysed in secret."

"Not necessarily," countered Como. "You could arrange it so the first locker we opened just happened to contain something suspicious, like another photo of Lola, and we swab that stick and lo and behold it's covered in Bluther Cale's DNA."

"True. But wouldn't that identify the perpetrator, and risk the whole story ending prematurely?"

"Not necessarily," Como countered again. "You could invent a processing hold-up at the lab. Then you could have one of those X-machine endings you were talking about, where Herbert's saved from the chair by last-minute DNA results."

I was starting to warm to Como's thinking. "Ok, let's give it a go."

Having driven us back to Police HQ, Como led me down to the basement where the janitor had a small workshop full of tools and spares and the like. Como kindly indulged in a few paragraphs of unimaginative cop banter with the janitor to spare me the trouble of inventing some dialogue.

"Hey Marty, how's it going?"

"Hey Como, how's it going with you? Long time no see."

"I got me a big case, that Lola Kellogg thing."

"You mean the poor kid who was raped, murdered, and cut to pieces by that bastard pedo Herbert Quarry. Him and his kind need to have their cocks sliced off and fed to them with mustard."

"My sentiments entirely. By the way, this is Herbert Quarry's best friend." Como waved his giant hand at me.

"Hi," I said.

The janitor peered into the gloom of the basement. "Don't I recognize you? Aren't you that Marco Ocram off the tee vee? I was talking to my wife only last night about the magnetic moment of the tau muon, and she was saying that..."

"Listen, Marty," Como interrupted, "I've only gone and left my locker key back at home. Any chance of borrowing the master?"

"Well... you know I ain't supposed to, Como."

"But if you lend it to me you can tell Mister Ocram here all about that magnetic moment you had with your wife, while I go get my stuff."

"Okay... but don't go getting me into trouble." Marty unhooked a key from a ring on his belt, and Como left us talking about tau muons. He was back in a couple of minutes.

"Here's your key, safe and sound, Marty. I owe you one."

We left the basement and went back to the car. Como said nothing the whole way, but I could tell he was bubbling with suppressed excitement.

"OK, whatcha got?" I said when we'd slammed the doors.

"Only this!"

"Wow!"

Como handed me a golden locket on a chain. Inside was a picture of a police officer and a strip of paper bearing the words '*I love you, and I feel so safe now you've said you would kill anyone who tried to hurt me. Signed, Lola Kellogg.*'

"It was in the first locker I opened," said Como. "Scoobie McGee's. I swabbed his stick. We just need to take the swab to Flora, and we should know within 24 hours whether there's any DNA matching Bluther Cale's."

We drove in a state of elation from Police HQ to the pathology labs at 276 West 24th Street. The car park barrier was down.

"Shit!" Como thumped the dashboard of the Gran Torino with his meaty fist.

There was a keypad next to the barrier, so I said, "Why don't you call Flora and ask her for the entry codes?"

"Good thinking, Writer."

He got Flora on the hands free.

"Hello, Big Boy. Need me to examine that nightstick of yours?"

You could have made toast on Como's blush. "I'm in the car with Ocram."

"Oh, right."

"We're just outside but it's all locked up. What's the code for the barrier?"

"Just a minute. You got a pen?"

Como looked at me. I nodded.

"Go ahead."

"The code for the barrier is XCJ425b39J4"&&}{nnnPQw99. The code for the door is 6^%BfffC812<<<F8."

"Okay. See you in a minute."

Como killed the call.

"You get that all written down?"

"Don't be ridiculous, Como. One doesn't write down access codes—it's against every principle of good security."

"So how are we meant to get in, dumbass?"

"I have committed them to memory, Como. Unless I am tortured by evil scientists who inject me with truth serum, they will remain a secret."

With a look too nuanced for me to describe, Como powered down the window of the Gran Torino, and leant out his arm ready to punch the code into the keyboard that controlled the barrier.

"Go ahead," he said.

"Six."

"Okay."

"Up arrow."

"Okay."

"Percentage sign."

"Okay."

"Upper-case B."

"Okay."

"Lower-case f"

"Okay."

"Lower-case f"

"Okay."

"Lower-case f."

"Another one? You sure?"

"Of course I'm sure."

"Okay."

"Upper-case C."

"Okay."

"Eight."

"Okay."

"One."

"Okay."

"Two."

"Okay."

"Less-than sign."

"Okay."

"Less-than sign."

"Okay."

"Less-than sign."

"Okay."

"Upper-case F.... no, hang on a minute, maybe that's the code to the door..."

I couldn't remember which code was which.

"Ok, ok, start again, try this.... Upper-case X, upper-case C, upper-case J, four, two, five, lower-case b..."

It took about six goes and two more calls to Flora before we got into the car park. Luckily Como knew a back way into the building, so we didn't have to go through the ordeal all over again to remember the code for the front door.

Entering the morgue, we found Flora Moran examining Bluther Cale, or, should your beliefs incline you that way, the body of Bluther

Cale. Sensing our presence, she turned, removing a glove to shake my hand.

"Mister Ocram, how nice to see you again. And you too, Lieutenant Galahad," she added with feigned formality.

"Should we don special plastics suits, masks and gloves to inspect the body?" I asked.

"No, smart casual is fine on Fridays."

"What do we know about the victim?" asked Como.

"He's Bluther Cale, the deformed manservant of...oh, sorry," I interrupted myself when I realized Como's question was aimed at Flora Moran. She smiled at my gaffe, and took over...

"He does indeed seem to be Bluther Cale. There was ID in a wallet that was still on the body. What's more, the gross disfigurements and cleft palate match the medical records we have been able to trace at the Clarkesville County Hospital."

"What do we know about how and when he died?" asked Como, staring into the beautifully shaped eyes of the beautifully shaped pathologist.

"The when is easy," said Flora. "Here." She handed Como a stainless-steel tray on which rested a wristwatch inside a transparent evidence bag. She went on: "The watch glass was cracked, presumably by the blow that broke Cale's left forearm. The impact of the blow has stopped the watch at exactly 1pm on the 3rd of this month."

"But that's..." I was lost for words at the corny improbability of Flora's announcement.

"Exactly the time when Herbert Quarry said he went down to the beach to wait for Lola," finished Como. "So, we've established the when. What about the how? Was it the blows to the back of the head?"

"As far as I can tell, yes," Flora confirmed, ignoring Como's clumsy syntax. "Apart from his deformities, Cale appears to have been in excellent health when he was attacked. And before you ask, yes, the blows were from a police nightstick. Lord knows I've seen enough nightstick injuries in my time."

Phew, that was a relief. My plot could have been in all kinds of trouble if Flora had introduced conflicting theories about the nature of the cylindrical object that had caused the damage. My eyes pivoted to the top left as I had another moment of distracting introspection about pool cues, tire irons, stale baguettes, and so on.

"What about his other injuries? What else can you say about the manner of his death and the tragic events preceding it?" asked Como.

"To judge by the nightstick blows, by the small scratches on his face and arms, and by the traces of pollens, leaf molds, mushroom spoors, and other microscopic matter on his hair, clothes, and shoes, I should say he had been running through the woods and had stopped, as if confronted by one assailant, when a second assailant hit his left knee with a wide swinging blow from a nightstick."

"What? The officer who did this had an accomplice?" I asked, hardly able to believe my own words.

"Yes," said Flora. "And the accomplice was also a police officer. While one confronted him, the other broke his kneecap. Police nightsticks lead a hard life. From the time they are allocated to a patrolman (or woman, let's not forget) they begin to gather all kinds of nicks and scratches. Since each leads a different existence, each nightstick collects its own unique combination of small marks, like a signature or fingerprint that can be uniquely attributed to the officer who owns the stick. I have examined Cale's wounds and there can be no doubt that two separate nightsticks contributed to his demise."

Wow. I hadn't expected this development at all, and nor had Como. We took some moments to get our heads round the implications of Flora Moran's startling revelation. The implication foremost in my mind was the possibility that Flora's statement, having been made up on the spot by an author utterly ignorant of police matters, might be entirely incorrect—perhaps nightsticks weren't permanently allocated to individual officers, but shared in a pool. I could just imagine the slagging-off I'd get from reviewers for my inadequate research. Como had other concerns:

"So, this DNA swab I've taken was a complete waste of time. We can identify the offending stick by a direct visual comparison of its microscopic marks with those found on the body."

"Yes," confirmed Flora Moran.

"We've been stupid, Writer," said Como. "Instead of swabbing the nightstick we should have just taken it and left mine behind in its place so no one would have suspected anything."

"*We've* been stupid? It was your idea, remember, not mine."

"OK. Let's not argue about it now," said Como. "We need to get that nightstick." He turned to Flora Moran. "Have you anything planned for tonight?"

"No, I'm going to be in bed all on my own, Big Boy."

Como's blush reignited. "No, I meant can you wait here to examine the nightstick if we get it now?"

"I suppose so," she answered, somewhat sulkily.

"Come on, Writer."

LESSON TWENTY-SEVEN

'Tell me, Herbert, are there any similarities between credulity and, say, an elastic band?'

'Yes, Marco—it's funny you should ask. Credulity is like an elastic band. You can stretch it so far, then it breaks.'

'Are there any other parallels, Herbert?'

'What did you have in mind, Marco?'

'Well, you can ping an elastic band across the room into a waste basket if you practice for long enough. Can you ping credulity into a waste basket?'

'I honestly cannot say, Marco, but if anyone can do it, I am sure it will be you.'

CHAPTER TWENTY-SEVEN

In which we meet Barney—not for long, thankfully—and Marco explains himself.

Como drove us to police HQ in the red '74 Gran Torino with the white side darts. As I followed him to the basement, I wondered how he was going to handle Marty.

"Hey Marty, how's it goin'?"

"Hey Como. You get a big case and I see you twice in a day. What's all that about?"

"Marty, I've only gone and left my stupid locker key at home again. Can I borrow that master if I take real good care of it?"

"Hell sure. Take what you like." Marty threw the entire bunch of keys at Como. "As long as I can talk to Mister Ocram here about tau muons, I'm happy."

Marty and I chatted contentedly about tau muons for several minutes. I was just explaining how a tau muon was a hypothetical cross between a tau and a muon, first proposed by me to account for unexpected transients in neutrino scattering coefficients, when Como came back. He tossed over the keys.

"Cheers Marty. I guess I owe you another one."

"No, I owe you, Como. It's not every day a humble janitor gets to talk tau muons with the great Marco Ocram."

We made our apologies and left, I promising to email Marty some papers on neutrino scattering.

As Como drove us fast towards the complex where Flora Moran was waiting, I wondered about this latest twist. While I was talking with Marty, Como had substituted his own nightstick for Scoobie

McGee's, which was now on the back seat of the Gran Torino. Within minutes we would be back at Flora's lab, and she would confirm whether Scoobie's nightstick was one of the weapons that killed Bluther Cale—the whole mystery could unravel like a house of cards, a hundred pages short of the target. If only we had stuck to relying on DNA. I gnawed on the problem as Como drove through the heavy Clarkesville traffic.

"What's on your mind?" he asked at last.

"This business with the nightsticks. It seems too clean a way of wrapping up the mystery. We've worked so hard to tease out a mass of complex evidence, and now it seems that five minutes with a microscope could sort the whole lot out."

"That's not my problem, Writer," said Como. "But haven't you overlooked the silver lining?"

"What silver lining?"

"The name of the patrolman. What was it?"

"Scoobie McGee?"

"Yes. And who does that remind you of?"

"Scoobie Doo?"

"No, stupid, the McGee part."

"You mean...you mean Chief McGee?"

"Exactly. Scoobie McGee is Chief McGee's nephew. We haven't simplified the plot, Writer, we've added a whole new twist."

I was still puzzling over the significance of the whole new twist, when we got to the pathology center. Como left the Gran Torino on the street, so we didn't have to go through the farce with the key codes, and eventually we found ourselves in Flora Moran's lab. Of Flora Moran, however, there was no sign. We looked around and found a hand-written message on a piece of paper on one of the stainless-steel dissection tables.

"What's it say?" asked Como.

"The darned microscope has gone on the blink," I read, "so I won't be able to do any more forensics until I can get a technician to look at it on Monday. In the meantime, why don't you come around to my place with that big nightstick of yours and we can..."

Como snatched the message out of my hands, finished reading it, then fed it to a shredder.

"Come on," he said. "I'll drop you at Herbert's on the way."

I woke the next morning before dawn and went for a brisk run into Clarkesville and back. There's something special about an early morning run, the quiet, the freshness in the air, the expectancy of a new day, the fact that yours is the only car on the road. In the shower afterwards, I decided I needed a break from the case. It was the weekend, and there would be little chance of progress until Monday, so I decided to drive back to New York, as I had some catching up to do with my Bronx mom and with Barney. It was a while since I'd seen that tough face, and listened to that tough voice, a voice that had hammered out deal after deal, a voice that took no nonsense from anyone. It was even longer since I'd spoken with Barney, so I headed for his place first.

"Marco!" He gave me a great bear hug and slapped me on the shoulder. "Am I glad to see you. Champagne?"

Barney gestured towards a bottle of vintage Krug in a cooler on his huge desk.

"No thanks, Barney. You know I never drink between 12:13 and 12:22."

"Your funeral, Markie. So, what's happening with that crazy pedophile bastard Quarry?"

"I wish you wouldn't talk about him like that, Barney."

"Why not? That's what everyone else calls him."

"Christ, Barney, what happened to loyalty? You're his agent— aren't you supposed to be looking after his interests?"

"Not anymore, kiddo." Barney nodded at an overturned picture frame in a wastebasket next to his desk. I fished it out and wiped the dust from the glass. It was a photo of Herbert with an arm around Barney's shoulder. "I can't be associated with a child-killer—it's bad for business."

"A child-killer?" I thought back to the many times Herbert and I had discussed his Buddhist faith, the many times he had lectured me about the sanctity of life, the many times he had stayed my hand as I'd been about to crush some bug or other. *All creatures have a right to life,* he would say. "Jesus, Barney, Herbert's no killer. How can you think it for even a second?"

"It's not a question of thinking it—the cops caught him red handed. Every paper's got the story."

"Yes, but they're wrong, and I intend to prove it."

"Wrong? Whaddaya mean wrong? I've got a five-million-dollar advance for your book because everyone thinks you're gonna expose that pedo bastard and prove he sliced up a fifteen-year-old kid. Don't tell me *wrong* for Chrissakes."

"But Barney..."

"Don't you but Barney me. Quarry deserves all that's coming to him. And we deserve all that's coming to us, all five mil' of it, and you can't go ruining all that now."

I threw my hands in the air in a gesture of defeat. Barney continued:

"Now where are those sample pages you promised me? I need to hand them over to Templeman and Newie by noon on Monday."

I dug into my satchel and handed over the sample pages for Barney to show to the publishers. Barney put them in a drawer in his desk.

"Aren't you going to read them?" I asked.

"Not now, Markie, not now. Listen, I've set you up with that interview, with Adaora Eze at the New York Times." He checked his watch. "You need to get those skates on, Kid, or you'll be late." He put an arm over my shoulder. "Keep her focused on Quarry, and what he's been up to—don't go wasting the interview talking about that mold-breaking crap. What the world wants is a good story, not your crazy theories about literature. Eze used to date Quarry but he two-timed her, so she'll lap up all the scandal. Button your cardigan right and get your tie straight for any photos. That's better. Here's the address. Now you run along like a good kid. I got AJ and Paulie coming over." The doorbell rang. "That'll be them."

AJ and Paulie were two of Barney's many godsons who were always popping in to give him money. I often wondered about that, especially since some of the godsons were way older than their godfather. Barney said it's a tradition in the part of Italy he comes from. I high fived them on the way out.

LESSON TWENTY-EIGHT

'Herbert, what can a writer do to appear more intelectual?'

'Learning to spell intellectual would be a start, Marco.'

'I'm sorry, Herbert. Aside from learning the correct spelling of intellectual, is there anything else a writer can do?'

'The most intellectual literary tradition is that of France, Marco. Camus, Sartre, Gide, Duras, Sarraute, Perec—the list of great French authors is as long as that of the iconic characters they created.'

'Should I try to copy some of the truly great characters of French literature, Herbert, like Maigret, Asterix, and Tintin?'

'Tintin was Belgian, Marco. No, you do not want to appear merely derivative. You should refer to the French literary tradition in a subtle way, without being obvious about it.'

CHAPTER TWENTY-EIGHT

In which Marco makes unsubtle references to the French literary tradition.

After Barney shooed me out of his office, I drove over to the New York Times building at 225b Fleet Street, rehearsing answers to the questions I might be asked at my imminent interview. There was a free parking slot right alongside the main entrance—yet another brilliant demonstration of the power of the Pollock technique. Imagine if I'd been one of those realist writers instead. Right now we'd be circling the same blocks over and over looking for a space, then spending five minutes rooting under the seats of the car for change, then squeezing along a congested sidewalk stuck behind a couple of hedge-fund managers boring us all to death with their boasts about the deals they'd struck before breakfast, then finding I'd left my iPad in the car and having to walk all the way back to get it, and having to stop every few yards to sign copies of *The Tau Muon*, and getting distracted by the window displays in the shops, and...I mean, who wants to read rubbish like that?

I blipped the car shut and pushed my way through the revolving doors into the offices of the famous newspaper, where the air was thick with the smell of cheap cigars, the clack of typewriters, the clamor of reporters yelling for the front page to be held, and the noun that means the noise of hundreds of pencils being sharpened. At reception, I learned the disappointing news that glamorous society editor Adaora Eze had been called away, and I was to be interviewed instead by Denis Shaughnessy, the literary sub-editor known in publishing circles as Mister Panoramic because he had views on everything. So much for all my wasted tie straightening. But as I was led to Shaughnessy's basement office, I reflected that every *nuage* has a silver lining, as the French say—at least Shaughnessy might be more interested in my literary aims than in scandalous accusations hurled at Herbert.

Office turned out to be rather a grand word to describe the cubicle in which the unpopular literary critic turned out his opinionated reviews, its door being so narrow that Shaughnessy's nameplate was affixed to it vertically. I edged inside and was invited to perch on his half-width desk.

"Sorry, we're a bit cramped. Perhaps if I move these."

Shaughnessy shunted a couple of stacks of books to give me an inch or two of extra space—they were French paperbacks. I picked up one of them—*Les Gommes,* by some hopeful called Robbe-Grillet.

"I suppose it must be one of the hazards of the job, being sent books in foreign languages." A blank look was the response to my Dale Carnegie attempt to create empathy. "Some authors are such dummies."

"I can imagine. Thank you." He took the book off me, no doubt to return it to the sender with some polite note of explanation: Dear Author, I am afraid the New York Times is able to review only those books published in English. We wish you every success in seeking reviews elsewhere. Yours etc.

"Mind you, you can't blame them for trying. Everyone likes a nice review." I would have underlined the hint with a subtle nudge to his ribs, but there wasn't enough room to move my arms.

"Your agent tells me you're Quarry's protégé—I wouldn't have guessed."

"You know Herbert?"

"We were at the Sorbonne together."

"Never been there, I'm afraid. Good meal?"

"It's not a restaurant, Mister Ocram—it's a French university."

"Oh. Right."

Talk about pedantic! Mind you, to be fair, I suppose nitpicking goes with the job when you're a literary critic. I spotted an opportunity to atone for my blunder with a witticism.

"Herbert said he'd taught at a university in Paris, but I wasn't sure if he meant Paris Texas. Ha ha."

Shaughnessy's eyes swiveled up and to the right somewhere.

"There isn't a university in Paris Texas—the nearest is in the neighboring city of Commerce, forty minutes to the southeast."

"Oh. Right."

I was beginning to see why he wasn't invited to many parties. I decided to ditch the attempts at ice breaking and get down to business.

"Herbert wants me to break the mold of literature."

That got a response. He frowned, put his palms together, crossed one leg over the other, and slid his hands between his thighs.

"Fascinating. Tell me more."

"Herbert says all books ever written have the same basic ingredient: thought. He says someone should break the mold by writing a book without thinking. He's coached me to do it because he says I'm naturally gifted in that direction. I'm on Chapter Twenty-Nine already, and I only started a few days ago." I hoped he didn't think me boastful.

"Yes, yes, I see. That makes sense." His eyes swiveled even further to the right, or at least one of them did, as he withdrew into his memories. "Herbert used to rage about the conservative nature of literature, about the need to abandon the *idée reçue*, to go so much further than the authors of *nouveaux romans* had ever dared. The ideal book, he used to joke, would be written by an articulate imbecile."

My eyes swiveled too at the phrase he had just used. *Nouveaux romans*. Surely there was a pun to be made about Romans.

Shaughnessy droned on about subjects he and Herbert had debated when they were teaching in the French version of Paris. It was *scriptable* this and *lisible* that, and *logocentrism* versus *phonocentrism*, and a whole pile of other words that freaked-out the spellchecker. I let him get on with it and made a huge effort to work out a pun on *nouveaux romans*. I went through all the well-known phrases: *Go tell it to the nouveaux Romans*, or was that the Spartans? *When in Rome do as the nouveaux Romans. Friends, nouveaux Romans, Countrymen*. None of them worked.

Ten minutes later I was still puzzling over potential nouveaux Romans puns when I realized Shaughnessy had stopped droning and had extended his hand towards me. I took it and shook it.

"Thanks for a fascinating discussion," he said. "If I have any other questions, I'll follow them up through your agent."

Other questions? He hadn't asked any! I never had a chance to answer the ones I'd rehearsed—*When was my favorite time to write? What books did I like best? What was my favorite letter?* I thanked him anyway, and said I'd send him a review copy of my book. He led me back upstairs.

"Don't you want to know why Herbert's in prison?" I shouted over the clack of the typewriters.

He shook his head. "I'm strictly fiction. True crime's not my department. Ha ha."

"Ha ha ha ha ha."

LESSON TWENTY-NINE

'Why do authors write prequels, Herbert?'

'Authors write prequels opportunistically, Marco, to exploit the popularity of a series when they have run out of ideas for sequels.'

'Might an author write a prequel for some other reason— perhaps to provide an explanatory backstory for certain aspects of a book that mystified its readers?'

'Perhaps, Marco, but a book would have to be exceptionally confusing and poorly conceived to require a prequel to be written for that purpose.'

'Are there golden rules for the writing of such a prequel, Herbert?'

'Only one, Marco. If you are writing a prequel to clarify the meaning of existing books in a series, then you must ensure it does not increase the sense of confusion already inflicted upon the unfortunate reader.'

CHAPTER TWENTY-NINE

In which Marco continues to break the golden rule of prequel writing and makes the world's least credible excuse to escape his caricature Bronx mom.

Imagine, if you will, a face bearing an expression of utter perplexity, a face framed with the unruly locks of an Afro escaping the hood of an unfashionable anorak, a face with eyes that stare at nothing, possibly two separate nothings, through the windscreen of a Midnight Black Range Rover. Yes, dear reader, the face was mine, as I tried, and failed, to think of a quip about nouveaux Romans until a kindly policeman tapped on my tinted window and asked if I was going to be there all day. Emerging from my creative reverie, I headed across town, or downtown or uptown, to wherever the Bronx is, having promised my mom I'd call in to see her.

En route, I reflected upon the unfairness of Shaughnessy making a crass crack about true crime when the charges brought against Herbert were anything but true. Perhaps I could forge a new literary genre—untrue crime—populated exclusively by my mold-breaking untrue memoirs, each ironically entitled *The Awful Truth* about this that or the other.

As I neared my Bronx mom's place with all my mental distractions still in play, my Pollock technique let me down: I found no free parking space. Instead I circled the same blocks over and over looking for a spot, then spent five minutes rooting under the seats of the car for change, then squeezed along a congested sidewalk stuck behind a couple of hedge-fund managers boring everyone to death with their boasts about the deals they'd struck before breakfast, then found I'd left my iPad in the car and had to walk all the way back to get it, having to stop every few yards to sign copies of *The Tau Muon*. With all that and getting distracted by the window displays in the shops, it was almost an hour before I reached the building in the Bronx in which I'd spent so many unhappy days in my teens. I climbed the familiar stairs to the familiar landing and rang the familiar bell of our familial apartment. My Bronx mom opened the door.

"Oh my God it's Markie. You're safe. Let me see you."

She withdrew a handkerchief from somewhere up her sleeve, spat on it, then started to wipe my face.

"Mom!"

I fended off her unsanitary grooming maneuvers.

"Aren't you going to come inside? Imagine, keeping your poor mom out in the cold. All the heat, Markie—it's pouring out of the house. My cakes, my cakes!"

My mom ran off to do something she'd forgotten to do with her cakes. I checked through the post to see if there was anything for me, then followed her to the kitchen.

"Where's Dad?"

"Where he always is, in the park playing chess. I told him he was a lazy bum and he was getting in the way, so he says he's going to the park, and I say what about Markie, what's Markie going to say when he gets in and finds his mom's here but not his bum of a dad? And he says Markie's not coming home, so don't kid yourself, and yet here you are, you came to your mommy, Markie, you came to your poor old mommy like a nice boy. Here..." She gave me a big slobbery kiss that tasted of nutmeg. "Have you had any lunch? You're looking very thin, Markie. Have you been eating?"

I assured my mom I'd been eating.

"What's the news about Herbert? I need something to say at the salon, Markie. On the TV they keep saying he's a sick pedo who's murdered that poor girl. I've told everybody at the salon it's wrong, that my Markie is going to prove it all wrong. Have you proved it all wrong, Markie?"

"Not yet, Mom, but I'm working on it with Como."

"Como, who's Como?"

"Como Galahad. He's a police lieutenant."

"Como Galahad? That doesn't sound like a nice Jewish name, Markie."

"It probably isn't, Mom."

"Does his mom look after him? Does he get enough to eat?"

"I don't think he needs looking after." I thought of Como's colossal frame and burger intake. "I'm pretty sure he gets enough to eat."

"Here." My mom passed me a huge sandwich, a glass of milk and four different types of baked confectionary the names of which I refuse, on principle, to research, this scene being tedious enough without us all getting bogged down in extraneous detail. "I met Phyllis Bugolyakov's middle daughter, Alexandra. Such a sweet girl. She's Russian, but she's very nice."

"Mom! You can't say she's Russian but she's very nice."

"Why not? She is very nice."

I flourished my sandwich in the manner of Socrates holding aloft a scroll. "Because you're implying Russians aren't usually nice."

"Who says they are? You should see her house, Markie. Her kitchen's to die for. Four ovens, Markie, and she doesn't know how to use any of them. Mister Bugolyakov's one of those oilygarks, all money but no taste. I do her hair Thursdays. She doesn't come to the salon much since she married him, so I go to her. She shows me around the place. Markie, you never saw so much money spent on a house."

She lifted my plate to wipe away a crumb I'd dropped, while I chomped my snack and wondered why a Russian oligarch would have a house in the Bronx and marry one of my mom's salon customers. Maybe I'd have to write a prequel to explain that.

"While I'm drying her hair, I say to her, Phyllis, what's that meant to be, over the fireplace? You never saw anything like it, Markie. It looked like a mess the decorators had made. I don't know, she tells me, but Van paid forty million for it. Forty million, Markie, for some splashes of paint. Van's her husband. Very nice man. And he's Russian—who'd think it? That's when Alexandra comes back from her mom's, her real mom's, with some flowers for Phyllis. Isn't that nice, Markie, flowers for her stepmom? I know someone round here who never buys flowers for his stepmom." Lest I be in any doubt about the identity of the someone, she hit me on the back of the head with a wooden spoon.

"Ow!"

"She's such a nice girl, says Phyllis, not like those other two stuck-up fairies, meaning Van's other girls, Markie. I can't say they are stuck-up—I never met them. She says they never say thank-you for anything. Imagine that. No breeding. That's Russians for you. If I was their stepmom, I'd sort out that nonsense in three minutes flat, and they'd thank me for it, mark my words."

Luckily my phone rang before my mom could further alienate my Russian readers. It was Jenna Duplessis, PA to a famous British rockstar who lives in Mustique and asks me to any parties he's holding. I shushed my mom and answered the phone.

"Marco Ocram speaking. How may I help you today?"

"Oh, Marco, great. It's Jenn. How are you?"

"Hi Jenn. Fine thank you, fine. I'm writing a book about Herbert Quarry, but I'm fine thanks."

"Well good for you. It's about time someone shamed that sick pedophile bastard. Listen, Mick's having a party tonight in Mustique and wants to know if you can make it. I've checked the flights and there's one leaving Kennedy in an hour and a half. I've booked a first-class ticket and sent a stretch limo to your mom's in case you're able to come. It should be with you any minute now."

"Sounds good. Alright then. Tell Mick I'll see him later."

"Great. He'll be really pleased. He wants to finish that conversation you were having about the tau muon. He's got a crazy idea it might be possible to create an entangled quantum state of a tau and a muon, and that could account for the neutrino scattering transients. Simple when you think about it. See you later."

"Mom, I've got to go. A car will be calling for me any minute now." The doorbell rang. "That will be it." I grabbed my satchel, but before I could scoot, my mom had me pinned against the sink, brandishing a cake-slice laden with menace.

"But, Markie, you can't go now. You only just got here. What about these cakes? When can I get you to see Phyllis Bugolyakov's beautiful daughter if you keep going off in cars like this, Markie?"

"I'm sorry, Mom, I've got to go. I'll miss my flight." I inched along the drainer, planning my escape to the door.

"Flight? Flight?" She thew up her hands, giving me a chance to edge past a pile of recently greased baking trays. "Where are you going?"

"Mustique." I had reached the corner unit, heading for the oven.

"Musteek? Don't talk to your mom in riddles, Markie. Where's Musteek?"

"Don't ask me, Mom. It's where all the popstars live," I explained, sidling across the front of the oven—next objective, the ironing board.

"But look, Markie, you've got mayonnaise all down your anorak. You can't go where all the popstars live with mayonnaise all down your anorak. What will all the popstars think about a mom who lets her boy go out like that?"

While my mom eyed the mayonnaise all down my anorak, I circled to the washing machine. "I'll get it cleaned, Mom, I promise—on the plane." Not far now.

"They clean anoraks on planes?"

"It's a special service they do, for all the popstars." Phew! The door at last. I risked a quick peck on her cheek, forcing my way through the bristles. "Gotta go now, Mom."

"But, Markie!"

I raced out through the living room, snatching a couple of cookies as I went.

As I was ferried to the airport, I wondered why my mind had picked Mustique as the setting for my next chapter. I had an idea it was in the same part of the world as Nassau, where Professor Sushing had his headquarters. Could there be a link? Could there be a... Just in time, I stopped myself. I was on the very brink of the trap Herbert had warned me of countless times, the trap of thinking about the plot. I must remain Pollock-like. To distract my mind from my writing, I pondered Mick's idea that the transients in the neutrino scattering could be due to an entangled quantum state involving a tau and a muon. It was a stroke of utter genius, and I was sick in the pit of my stomach that an elderly British rocker, probably stoned out of his brain, had thought of it before I had. There was only one thing to do that was in keeping with the long and noble tradition of science. I'd try to make out I had already thought of it.

LESSON THIRTY

'Herbert, if a reader is to like a book, must they like the lead character?'

'Absolutely, Marco. Suppose the protagonist were a repulsively self-obsessed narcissist with an absurdly high opinion of himself; can you imagine anybody liking such a book?'

'I suppose not. It's lucky I decided to make myself the central character.'

CHAPTER THIRTY

In which Marco is at his unlikeable worst in the run-up to a major twist.

"So I said to Shaughnessy, what did the *nouveaux romans* ever do for us? Ha ha ha ha ha."

"Ha ha ha ha ha."

At Mustique, Mick's party was going with a swing. We were exchanging stories about our dealings with the New York Times, which gave me a chance to insert the pun I'd conceived on the flight while my anorak wasn't being cleaned. Which reminded me of another loose end from the last chapter...

"Mick, Jenn mentioned you'd had an idea about the tau muon being an entangled state of a tau and a muon."

"Just a sec." He asked me to wait while he wiped his eyes after my hilarious wordplay. "You're so quick with those quips. Would be great to have you in the band. Yeah, the tau muon thing was something I kicked round with Keith at the Havana gig while we were setting up. I said it was probably a crazy idea, but he said he'd heard something about entanglement from the guy who does his ear candles, and there might be something in it. Hang on, I've got a word."

Mick put a W and two Os next to a D on the Scrabble board we were sitting around, the word so-formed sparking irreverent merriment among his mischievous bandmates.

"Ha ha ha, Mick's got wood," said Keith.

"First time in thirty years," quipped Ronnie.

"Someone wake his missus!" Charlie played an imaginary drum roll to celebrate his cheap joke.

"Fuck you." Mick cuffed him on the head.

"Eight points—good going." I updated Mick's total score to 32 and took the opportunity offered by the W to lay down all seven of my tiles along the top right edge of the board. "With the double letter score and the two triple word scores, I think you'll find that's three hundred and sixty points."

"Qwizling? Fuck—is that a word?"

"Indeed, Mick; it means a traitor or collaborator. If you doubt it, let's ask Alexa. Alexa, is qwizling a Scrabble word?"

"Yes, the word quisling can be played in Scrabble," said the disembodied voice of the tinny virtual assistant. "Definition of quisling: a traitor who collaborates with an enemy power occupying their country. Quisling is spelled Q..."

"Ooops, sorreee!" I apologized to Mick for accidentally knocking Alexa off the shelf with a kung fu kick and accidentally standing on her and accidentally emptying my glass of wine into her electronic innards before she ruined everything by revealing the correct spelling of quisling. Not that I was cheating, but who's to say what's correct in a mold-breaking book?

"Fuck, I only just got that, you clumsy twat." Mick bent to examine the damage.

"Anyway, your idea about the tau muon being an entangle-ment..." I said to his back as he knelt over the remains of his Amazon Echo. "I had it myself already. Five years ago. Just hadn't got around to publishing it. Been too busy. But I'll probably publish it when I get back, so don't be surprised if you see it in Physics Review soon."

"Whatever."

Piecing together the shards of his Echo, Mick was too pre-occupied to argue, so that was all sorted.

I left him to it, abandoning the Scrabble game in a sensational display of mold-breaking narrative discontinuity. I felt overdressed in cardigan and corduroys while everyone else was in swimwear, but I loosened my tie and my inhibitions and danced among the actresses and models who had been waiting all evening for a chance to talk with me. The DJ was spinning some hot discs, so it wasn't long before I was drenched with sweat. To cool down, I strapped-on one of Keith's guitars, cranked the amp to eleven and jumped on a table.

"Hey, everyone. Everyone, listen."

Once I had the attention of all within sight, I strummed the classic riff from *Smoke on the Water*, knowing Mick and Keith would enjoy its heavy vibe.

Dum dum duuuuh, dum dum...

"Hang on."

I hadn't quite got it right. The third *dum* had been a semitone off. I started again.

Dum dum duuuuh, dum dum du duuuuh...

"Sorry. Must be this stupid plectrum." My seventh strum had missed its mark, producing a feeble *duuuuh* without the power-chord crunch I was aiming for. "One more go."

Dum dum duuuuh, dum...

"Hang on."

Somehow the plectrum had found its way into the f-hole of Keith's vintage Gretsch. I shook it out like a pro after only five goes. "Okay. Let's rock."

Dum dum duuuuh, dum dum du duuuuh, dum dum...

I was just on the point of nailing the riff when my phone rang. I grinned ruefully at all the actresses and models to let them know I was as sad as they were that I had to stop playing to take the call.

I looked at my phone. I recognized the Clarkesville area code but not the rest of the number.

"Soon-to-be publishing legend Marco Ocram speaking. How may I help you?"

"Marco, it's Herbert."

"Herbert. Great to hear from you. I'm at a party with Mick and Keith in Mustique. There are hot actresses waiting to talk to me. It's incredible."

"Don't incredible me, you smug conceited wanker. Of all the people... I never thought it would be you who would stab me in the back."

"Hey, Herbert. What do you mean?"

"You know exactly what I mean. You know you've betrayed me to the press. And now the price you have to pay is that our friendship is over. Do you understand me? Oh-verr."

Herbert hung-up. I tried calling back, but the number wouldn't take incoming calls: Herbert must have been ringing from a payphone in the prison. I wondered what caused his outburst; after all, I'd had no contact with the press other than my interview with Shaughnessy. I asked Mick if he took the evening papers; he said yes, he had all the main US titles delivered daily, and I could see the latest in his study.

I squeezed between the revelers in the corridor to his study, wondering why I'd started to use semicolons. It was a delightful room—the study, that is, not the corridor—paneled throughout in the darkest mahogany, set-off by a mocha carpet, chocolate drapes, chestnut lampshades, tan settees, taupe cushions, walnut architraves, russet rugs and other decorative paraphernalia collectively representing all of the internationally recognized shades of brown. I picked up *The Clarkesville County Evening Gazette*; Herbert's picture was on the front page; the main headline read **'Ocram: Quarry Killed Fifteen-Year-Old Girl.'**

I couldn't believe my eyes—two semicolons in a single sentence. I read on. The story said famous scientist, TV personality and potential Nobel Prize-winner Marco Ocram had been investigating the brutal murder of Lola Kellogg in Clarkesville, he was writing a bestseller about the heinous crime, and his book said Herbert Quarry killed a fifteen-year-old girl.

I scrolled back through my book with finger-strokes of fury. In Chapter Three there were indeed the words '*Herbert Quarry killed a fifteen-year-old girl*', but, as I knew in my heart, they were preceded by eight other hallowed words: '*There was absolutely no way I could believe Herbert Quarry killed a fifteen year old girl*'.

I checked some of the other papers—*The New York Evening Times, The Washington Evening Post, The National Evening Enquirer*—they all had the same story. Hoping the readers would get the joke, I paced about in a brown study, hardly noticing the hot actresses peeking around the door in the hope of catching my interest. I was stung by the way the press had twisted my words. Well, I suppose they hadn't really twisted them, since the words they quoted were exactly the ones I'd used, but you know what I mean.

I decided I couldn't stay any longer. The party had lost its appeal. I took a stretch limo back to the airport for the next flight to New York.

At Terminal Eight of Mustique International Airport—the one reserved for TV personalities and the like—I completed the check-in formalities, had my trunks weighed, and signed copies of *The Tau Muon* for the delighted staff. I had a few minutes to kill before boarding, so I looked back over the chapter thus far. I wasn't sure I had been right to punctuate the *Smoke on the Water* guitar chord sequences with commas between the phrases, but in true Pollock fashion I didn't waste any time fretting about it. Get it?? Fretting—guitar chords? Ha! Eat your heart out, Shakespeare. I also spotted a minor continuity error, which I corrected by unstrapping Keith's Gretsch and arranging for it to be returned to Mick's place by taxi.

Once on board the giant Boeing 797-400, a top-of-the-range model with tinted windows, I changed into a dressing gown and slippers and traipsed to the VIP lounge. Settled in an old armchair, I tried to read for a while, but my Cartland slipped from my fingers and I stared into the roaring log fire as my mind went back to the headlines I had read in Mick's study. How had the papers come by extracts from my novel? The only copy was on my iPad, protected by a special app that locked the device if any face other than mine looked at it. Had someone managed to hack its sophisticated security mechanism? Did I have a doppelganger, who was fiendishly plotting to do away with me and take my place? Had someone assumed a lifelike Marco Ocram facemask to trick the app? Had my secret password—MyBron*MoM—been compromised? None of the possibilities made sense. Even if someone had hacked my iPad, why would they leak to the press the handful of words most damaging to Herbert's fate? I would have to ask Barney about it—he would know how to...

Barney!

It came to me at last. I had left a sample from the book with Barney. It must have been he who leaked it to the press—Herbert's own agent! How could he have breached the agent's code of ethics, the code he would have taken an oath to uphold? I was as outraged as I was bewildered by his treacherous and unprincipled behavior. In a rage, I threw my Cartland into the fire and watched as the flames blackened its edges. I'm kidding—the fire was just an image on a screen. What idiot would think they'd allow naked flames on a plane? I picked up my Cartland from where it had bounced off the fake fire and I traipsed back to my cabin.

At Terminal Eight of New York International Airport—the one reserved for TV personalities and the like—I had to fight my way through a press of press men and women, all yelling for an exclusive.

"Mister Ocram, what can you tell us about the pedophile writer Herbert Quarry?"

"Mister Ocram, did he really slice Lola Kellogg into pieces?"

"Mister Ocram, was she really only fifteen?"

I answered all their questions with the comment "no comment," wondering if any of the headless hacks would have the literary sensitivity to appreciate the irony of it. I supposed I should be thankful the chapters I shared with Barney didn't include the bits about Chief McGee's indiscretions in the woods, otherwise there'd be no end to their impertinent questions.

I spotted a chauffeuse bearing a placard that read *'Soon-to-be publishing legend Marco Ocram'* and sat in the rear of her limo while she loaded my trunks into her trunk. As we headed for the Bronx along the Van Gogh expressway, I answered her question about the background to the sensational book I was writing, strewing here and there the impressive new literary terms I'd heard in my so-called interview with the New York Times. By the time we reached Derrida Boulevard, I had completed a masterful critique of the conventions of the western literary tradition. By 109th Avenue, I had explained to my driver that Barthes's *scriptable/lisible* dichotomy was a false one. Those waiting for the lights at Calvino Avenue might have seen me gesticulate on the back seat as I urged the cultivation of a new literary zeitgeist. Between Eggers Square and Camus Park, I delivered an impassioned attack on the debilitating effect of thought on the creative powers of the author. As we reached the Bronx my explanation culminated with a sentence containing no fewer than four French adjectives too esoteric to repeat on these pages.

When I had finished, she said:

"Did he really cut her up?"

After my luggage had been transferred to my black Range Rover, which miraculously had spent a night on the street without having its tinted windows smashed or its wheels stolen, I went straight to Barney's Seventh Avenue office for a showdown.

"Hey Markie! Twice in two days. Great to see you, Kid."

Barney was getting up from his massive desk, probably to offer me champagne. I stopped him in his tracks.

"Don't you hey Markie me, you conniving bastard."

"Hey Markie, wassamatter? "

"You know precisely wassamatter, so don't pretend you don't. You leaked a sample of my new bestseller to the world's media, and now every newspaper in the country has me saying Herbert slew Lola."

"Yeah, ain't it great! *That's* what you pay a good agent for, Markie. Your book's gonna break all records. The whole world wants to read it now."

"You don't understand. Herbert thinks I've stabbed him in the back. He thinks I wrote those headlines, Barney. He said our friendship was over. Oh-verrr."

"Markie. Markie baby. Listen. You gotta learn something about publishing from your uncle Barney. You say you wanna break the mold of literature, right?"

I nodded, being too emotional to speak.

"So, suppose you break it with your book. What happens if nobody reads it? What happens if nobody sees the mold you broke? Is that what you want, Markie, to break the mold without no one knowin'? The world's full of great books nobody reads—you wanna write another like that? C'mon, Markie, see sense." Barney had his arm over my shoulder and walked me to the window where we could look out across New York. "Look at all those people down there. They all want to read your book. They're gagging for it. We can't deny them what they need, Markie. And when the book hits the stores, everyone will see how you smashed the mold."

As I looked across New York, I thought about the abiding bond of loyalty between fellow writers, the bond that had drawn tighter as

Herbert had coached me to the pinnacles of so many spheres of sport. I thought too of that other loyalty, the loyalty of an artist to their art, the unbending commitment to an artistic principle. Where did my ultimate duty lie—defending Herbert or nurturing the sales of the radical book he himself had urged me to publish to a startled literary world? For a moment I dithered atop the fence dividing my loyalties, like Blondin on a slender wire high above Niagara, until Barney marshalled a new argument to topple me onto the side of my artistic mission...

"Besides, the royalties will make the five-mil advance look like peanuts."

With reluctance and a shrug, I capitulated to the force of his logic. He walked me back to his desk to pop a bottle of Krug.

"Cheers, Kid." We clinked glasses. "Here's to all that lovely dough. And to breaking that mold too," he added to allay the doubt on my face. "Don't worry about pissing off Herbert, Markie. He's made a living out of pissing people off. He's a tough guy; he can take it."

After we'd polished off the bottle and signed some paperwork, I made an excuse and left Barney to whatever it is agents do. I needed time to think, so I left my car and went for a walk, raising the hood of my anorak so I could wander without being pestered by hot actresses and kids wanting answers to their gnawing questions about tau muons. Barney had missed the point: Herbert probably was tough enough to cope with my apparent disloyalty, but I wasn't. I strolled towards the park where the chess players sat. From a distance, I watched my dad with some of his old friends. It was funny, I'd never got into chess, although my Bronx mom said I was bound to have a natural genius for it. I'd played a couple of games with myself, which were interesting enough at the start, but always ending with two kings seemed kind of boring, and I couldn't see what others found so interesting in it.

As I watched my dad, I realized how lucky he was. He didn't have millions, but he could pass his days with his chess-playing chums, with nothing to worry about other than living with my Bronx mom. He didn't have the continual conflict of emotions a great writer wrestles with every day. I mooched back to my car. Everyone I passed seemed to be reading or talking about my involvement in the Herbert Quarry affair. It was already causing a huge stir, and none of the really outrageous twists had happened yet.

LESSON THIRTY-ONE

'Marco, what is that book you are reading?'

'It is 'Virus', Herbert, the latest bestseller by Dan Brown. It's about a deadly virus that is allowed to spread globally because the response of governments everywhere is so slow and inadequate. I've just reached the bit where the President of the United States says the virus can be stopped by injecting people with disinfectant and shining bright lights on them.'

'Marco, it will not help your writing if you fill your head with unbelievable nonsense.'

CHAPTER THIRTY-ONE

In which too much happens to summarize here.

Back in Clarkesville, I sat in Herbert's study, allowing the atmosphere of great literary endeavor to pervade my being. I extracted from my satchel the book I carry everywhere—a first edition of the novel that made Herbert famous. Its title was *Hjumən Raɪts*, a phonetic spelling that could mean *Human Rights*, *Human Writes* or *Human Rites*. Or even *Human Wrights*, now I think about it. I once asked Herbert which meaning he intended; he said my question was unanswerable, as it was based on the false assumption that an author intends meaning. I had no idea what he meant, but I assumed it was very clever.

I looked through the book. Re-reading the glittering prose reinforced my conviction that the author of such a humanistic work could never have committed the crimes of which Herbert was now accused. I replaced my bookmark and closed the book. I smelled smoke. I sniffed a couple of times. Something was on fire.

Before I could decide where to say the smell was coming from, a rock smashed through the window, a message attached.

We warned you, snooper.

I rushed to the smashed window. My black Range Rover was engulfed in flame. Even as I watched in disbelief, its tinted windows exploded into a million fragments in the intense heat. I fumbled for my phone and dialed the emergency number.

A paragraph later, as the fire fighters were rolling away their hoses, Como arrived. He put his arm over my shoulder as we watched the steaming remains of my car.

"Never mind, Writer. The insurance will pay. Anyway, to judge by this, you'll be able to afford any car you like soon."

When he said 'this' Como threw a newspaper onto the garden table beside us. The headlines were about my five mil' advance.

"Nice work if you can get it," he added, cynically. "For cracking the case, I don't even get five thou' a month. You get five mil' as a down-payment."

At first Como's comment seemed like a punch below the belt, but I saw the truth behind his words. What was celebrity after all? Why did I deserve to earn thousands of times more than he, a hard-working lieutenant? Barney would have something to say about that, but I didn't have the answers myself. I looked Como in the eye.

"Como, if *we* crack this case, I promise you that every single cent of the royalties from the book will go the Clarkesville County Police Benevolent Fund."

To underline the emotional intensity of the moment, we had a big man-hug, or, rather, I did. Como stood there with my arms hardly reaching round his sides, and then patted me on the head.

"Let's get to work, Writer."

Energized by the excitement of the fire, we leaped into the Gran Torino. Como gunned the engine.

"Where to now?" I asked.

"Don't ask me—you're the writer."

"Let's go to Elijah Bow's. He's got some questions to answer."

"We're on our way." Como kicked down through the auto-box, the siren and blue lights clearing our path ahead.

On the drive to Bow's ranch, we speculated about who might have been behind the arson attack on my car. Como thought motive was unlikely to be a helpful factor in singling-out suspects, since everyone in Clarkesville hated my guts.

"And not just in Clarkesville," he added.

Piqued by his hurtful comments, I changed the subject to our forthcoming interview with Bow. I suggested we adopt the good-cop bad-cop routine, with me as the bad-cop.

"Aren't you forgetting something?" said Como.

"What?"

"You ain't a cop—you're a writer."

"OK, then let's do the good-cop bad-writer routine, with me as the bad-writer."

"That should work."

At Bow's ranch, Como dry-skidded the Gran Torino to the house. He killed the engine but left the siren shrieking. As a helpful gesture, I reached to switch it off.

"Ow!" He'd slapped my hand. "What was that for?"

He didn't answer, so I reached again.

"Ow!" He'd slapped me even harder.

"We'll keep the siren on for a couple of minutes—it'll soften-up the people in the house. Don't you know anything about police psychology?"

"Apparently not."

"But try and switch it off again if you like—I'm enjoying a chance to slap you. Should have done it when we first met."

I sat in glum silence until the two minutes were up and we walked over to the house. We didn't need to ring the bell—most of Bow's staff were already at the door to see what the drama was about. Como showed his badge and said he wanted to see Bow. We were asked to wait, then shown in by one of the maids. As we neared the vast bronze statue of Lola, I nudged Como. He nodded to confirm he'd clocked the likeness.

When we were shown to Bow's study, the billionaire was far from pleased. He rose from his desk like a missile from a submarine.

"What is the meaning of this disgraceful intrusion?"

"I'm sorry if we've disturbed you, Sir," said Como, "but we are here on official police business."

"You may be here on official police business, Lieutenant, but your snooper friend cannot be."

I wondered if the readers would be smart enough to notice Bow's use of the derogatory title *snooper*, a distinctive word which appeared in all the menacing messages I'd received.

"On the contrary," corrected Como, "Mister Ocram has been made an honorary member of my investigative team, so his presence is as legitimate as my own."

Bow shifted his gaze uneasily between the two of us.

"Then what exactly do you want? I am a busy man, Lieutenant."

"We'd like to speak to your manservant, Bluther Cale," said Como.

"You are welcome to talk to Bluther any time you wish, if you can find him."

"He's not here?"

"He has not been here, Lieutenant, for almost two weeks."

"You know where he is?"

"Bluther comes and goes as he pleases. He is often away for weeks at a stretch."

"Does he have a car?"

"Not of his own, but he has free use of any in my fleet. And if I can anticipate your next question, Lieutenant, he has taken a black Lancia Monte Carlo."

I decided it was time to give Como's good-cop a break and for me to step in as the bad-writer.

"Isn't that a funny way for a manservant to behave? Are you telling me you let him get away with that sort of lack of reliability and punctuality?"

"He is not a normal manservant. My relationship to him is not that of an employer to an employee."

"What exactly is your relationship?" I pounced.

Bow hesitated, reluctant, I imagined, to find himself on the receiving end of any more of my bad writing. Como came in with his good-cop.

"Mister Bow, you can either tell us now, here, or I can drive all the way to police HQ to get a subpoena and drive all the way back and force you to tell us later, and do you know how much gas a '74 Gran Torino guzzles, especially when you floor it? That just isn't sustainable, so for the sake of the planet, Mister Bow, which is the only one we've got, why don't you just tell us the truth?"

"Alright. But this will take some time, so you had better be seated."

We pulled up a couple of chairs and sat attentively in a semicircle around Bow's desk—if two chairs can form a semicircle. Maybe we were more like a chord of a segment or whatever. Anyway, it doesn't really matter, so can we please not get hung up about geometrical trivia. Bow began...

"Go back thirty-five years, gentlemen, to a less sophisticated Clarkesville, in the days when social mores were more rigid than they are today. At that time there was a young man living in Clarkesville, an extraordinary young man. Extraordinary in three ways. One was that he had a genius for every form of artistic expression. He could paint, draw, mold, sculpt, write prose and verse, compose music, choreograph ballet, crochet, play every type of musical instrument, and do all that as if touched with the gift of the angels. The second was that he was extremely shy and diffident, no doubt because of the third of his extraordinary qualities—his cleft palate.

"Yes, I am talking about Bluther Cale, who has lived near Clarkesville for all of his extraordinary and sad life. As you can imagine, Bluther suffered as a consequence of his three extraordinary qualities. Jealous of his artistic talents, the other boys at school picked on him mercilessly for his strange manner of speech. Bluther suffered their taunts and bullying, and, in spite of the encouragement of sympathetic teachers, he grew ever more withdrawn. But one fateful day in his late teens, he was advised by a well-meaning but foolish person that he should overcome his shyness and approach the prom queen to ask if he could be her date for the prom.

"You may readily imagine, gentlemen, the courage Bluther needed to summon in order to overcome the oppressive social forces he had felt every day of his life, in order to realize his dream of taking the prom queen to the school prom. But approach her he did. One June night, more than thirty years ago, he took his courage and a bunch of roses into his hands and knocked tentatively on her door. When she answered he could barely speak, but managed at last to find his voice.

"'*Theve are for you,*' he said, offering the roses. '*Vould you like to go to the prom wiv me?*' She laughed in his face. She took the roses and flung them away in the darkening gloom. '*Go to the prom with you?*' she cackled. '*With you??? Haw, haw, haw, haw, haw, haw, haw...*' She slammed the door in his face and went inside to call her friends and tell them what had happened.

"To the echoes of her laughter, he retrieved the roses and he slunk away. But before he had walked two blocks, he found himself in the path of a gang of boys from the high school, privileged boys from elite backgrounds, boys jealous of Bluther's artistic abilities, boys frequently cruel about his cleft palate. They started to tease and goad him. '*Weave me alone,*' he pleaded, but his strange manner of speech fueled their mischief, and they set about him, beating and kicking him mercilessly, until in the end, their hatred spent, they ran laughing, leaving him a disabled and disfigured wreck, barely able to crawl. He was found prostrate and bleeding by a police patrol, and taken to the local emergency room. After six months of treatment he regained the use of his limbs, albeit in a terribly deformed way. But he never recovered from the psychological wounds inflicted by the prom queen."

I saw where this was going. I barely believed Bow could indulge in such corniness.

"Let me guess," I said. "You were one of the privileged kids who left him disfigured, and you took him on as your manservant out of pity."

I exchanged glances with Como, each of us raising eyebrows to express disbelief.

"No," said Bow. "You are right to suppose pity played a role, but I was not one of those privileged kids."

"What were you, then?" I asked, dreading what was to come next.

"I was... the prom queen," said Bow.

Even I, in bad-writer mode, was taken aback by this latest twist. I didn't know what to say except to ejaculate the words *The prom queen*.

"The prom queen!"

"Yes, gentlemen. I assume this interview is confidential, so I do not mind telling you I live a double life as a gay transvestite. I took pity on Bluther Cale because of a responsibility I felt for his gross deformities. He has lived with me ever since I became able to afford my own domestic establishment. And while the world believes him my manservant, his relationship to me is that of an artist to a wealthy patron. He produces amazing artworks of various forms; his versatility is unmatched, in my experience. For that, and for what I did to him, I allow him whatever freedoms he wishes to take as far as his movements are concerned."

I didn't want to get into the subject of Cale's movements, as we'd had enough shit to deal with, so I nodded to Como to spring one of the questions we'd prepared.

"Mister Bow, when the Writer first met you in this house, you said the murderer of Lola Kellogg had been caught red handed. Can you tell me the approximate time and date of that meeting?"

"I can tell you the exact time and date, Lieutenant, as I am most particular about recording my activities." He scrolled through an iPad or a Rolodex, depending on whether you had imagined him to be a trendy technophile or a traditionalist. "Let me see, it was 2.03pm, on the twelfth."

"Then explain this. You said Herbert Quarry had been caught 'knife-in-hand'. That detail of the arrest has never been released to the media, so how do you account for your knowledge of the fact?"

"A knowledge," I added, "that outside the police could be possessed only by someone who had framed Herbert Quarry!"

Bow smiled.

"You are wrong in your logic, Mister Ocram. You should understand that in a small community such as Clarkesville, where people have few secrets, I, a prominent billionaire, a frequent visitor to City Hall, and an admired figure in the local gay transvestite scene, am taken into the confidence of the most senior law enforcement officials. Officials, I might add, who could bust you down to patrolman, Lieutenant Galahad."

While Como paused to ponder Bow's threat, I took my chance and intervened.

"Mister Bow, could my character and I have a moment alone?"

"My library is at your disposal, gentlemen."

Bow gestured at double doors to the left of his desk. I winked at Como to follow me and closed the library doors behind us.

"Listen," I said, "I think we should end the interview now and go."

"Are you shitting me? We haven't even started. We haven't even got to Cale's death, and the statue, and the taxidermy thing. And he seems to have connections to the City Hall gay scene, so God knows what else Chief McGee has been up to."

"Yes, yes, yes. I know, I know, I know."

And I did know, but I also knew that if we carried on with our questioning, my mold-breaking novel would start to read like a clichéd police procedural. Como was never going to understand or care about my literary concerns, so I thought fast about how I could persuade him to leave. I had an idea. If Como was going to carry on behind my back with Flora Moran, maybe I could turn it to my advantage...

"I've had a text from Flora," I lied. "She says she has something absolutely earth-shattering to tell us."

As I hoped, Como perked up at the mention of the beautiful scientist.

"Okay, Writer, why didn't you say so earlier? Let's get moving."

We made our apologies to Bow, albeit with a stern warning from Como to the effect that we weren't through with him yet, then we leaped into the Gran Torino and left rubber all the way down Bow's drive. I was starting to worry about the state of the tires.

En route, I texted Flora. *On our way to see you. Hope you might have something earth-shattering to tell us.* I kept my fingers crossed for the rest of the drive. Como would have a big sulk if he found I'd been lying.

We found Flora Moran gowned, masked and gloved, examining a spectacularly well-endowed male corpse. Como looked quite put out and got down to business in a cold way.

"Any news about the nightsticks? Have you been able to confirm the microscopic nicks and scratches match those on Cale's body?"

"No. I'm afraid we've encountered an unexpected barrier to progress. A crucial component in my microscope has failed. Ordinarily it would mean a day's delay at most, but I've just discovered there's a statewide shortage of spares. The Swiss manufacturer has been contacted, but an industrial dispute has closed the factory. It might be a matter of hours before the strike is resolved, or it might be weeks. We are in the lap of the gods."

Well, at least my *deus ex machina* ending might be back on the cards.

"But that's nothing," said Flora Moran to my surprise. "I have something far more earth-shattering to tell you..."

She paused to ensure she had our full attention.

"...Lola was two months pregnant when she died."

LESSON THIRTY-TWO

'Tell me, Herbert, which chapter in a bestseller is the most important?'

'All are equally important, Marco. Chapters are like rounds in a boxing match. If you let your guard down in any one of them, you may be knocked out. Even if you are not knocked out, you may lose points. And the match is decided by the points from all of the rounds.'

'I see, Herbert.'

'You must sock your readers mercilessly in every chapter, Marco. Never pull your punches.'

CHAPTER THIRTY-TWO

Which ends with another stunning revelation—
can we take any more?

When I had rallied from the shock of Flora Moran's staggering announcement, I asked the obvious question.

"Was the baby...Herbert's?"

"No."

I punched the air.

"Yes! I knew Herbert was innocent."

Como brought me down to earth.

"What are you talking about, Writer? The parentage doesn't clear Quarry. It could even be a motive. Suppose Lola confessed she was pregnant by another man. That might have tipped Quarry over the edge."

It was a good point, and I instantly felt my elation drain completely away. I asked the next obvious question.

"Can we run some kind of search against some kind of DNA database to identify the father?"

"Yes, but there are procedural difficulties," said Flora Moran.

I'd no idea what she was talking about, so she explained.

"We have to persuade the relevant authorities that identifying the father would be material to determining who murdered poor Lola. And right now, with the local elections due, the mayor won't want to offend the Christian vote, and the DA won't want to offend the mayor, so we're going to have a battle on our hands."

I was beginning to regret choosing crime as the subject for my mold-breaking bestseller—the red tape was fierce.

"Unless…" interjected Como.

We waited for him to continue.

"Unless we can get Lola's next of kin to sanction the search, in which case the DA can't overrule it, election or no election."

I crossed my fingers and hoped none of the readers would be legal experts who'd realize that what I had just typed was pure Pollocks.

"Lola's only known next of kin are dead," I said. "I can't see us getting a statement from either of them soon."

"Point taken, Writer, but we might find a next next-of-kin. Lola must be related to someone."

We made a quick plan with Flora Moran: she would approach the DA via the usual channels, while Como and I would attempt to identify some other living relation of Lola's.

On the way to Police HQ, Como told me the process for finding next of kin.

"Identifying next-of-kin, or NOKs, is routine police business. We'll start with her parents' medical records, which usually identify NOKs for emergencies, and their pension providers, who need to know NOKs for probate purposes. We'll get them in five minutes flat."

After five minutes flat in front of Como's computer we'd got exactly zilch. Lola's mother's NOK was Lola's father, and Lola's father's NOK was Lola's mother. We were obviously dealing with some hard NOKs to identify. We decided to go back to basics and look through Lola's parents' house for clues. Como did the necessary paperwork to legitimize a search, and we drove back to the Kelloggs' place, where the commemorative garlands had all wilted.

Lola's house was a mythical Arabian hollow in the rocks, better known as an Aladdin's cave. I had never seen such an odd mix of artifacts. There were rooms-full of old correspondence between Lola's father and the Catholic Church, correspondence hinting at some form of scandal which Father Kellogg was threatening to expose if he wasn't promoted to bishop, a post he considered his by right. I skimmed the correspondence which had bounced between the parties, letters of increasing acrimony and bitterness.

The earlier correspondence was between Father Kellogg and his local diocese; but as the years passed, Kellogg clearly felt it necessary to raise the stakes: his later correspondence was with the Vatican and some shadowy organization called Dei Profundis. Much of the text was in Latin, which was a relief because it meant I could keep it from Como. The scandal seemed to be about the status of the Holy Virgin herself, although it was difficult to be sure, since the correspondence was couched in euphemistic terms, presumably to avoid the dangers of a leak inherent in plainer language. It was clear enough to my insightful mind, however, that the pillars of Kellogg's argument were the possibility that Christ had a human father, and that the youth of the Blessed Virgin provided biblical legitimacy for a lower age of consent.

What dawned on me as I read the immense trail of correspondence was the parallel with the death of Lola, there being a question of parentage and under-age sex in both.

I decided to sit on my findings, as goodness knew how many readers we might alienate if our investigations got entangled with the Holy See and some shadowy ecosystem of money-laundering Italian powerbrokers. The thought of what Barney might say made me break into a sweat.

I stuffed Father Kellogg's letters into some plastic sacks and looked around the house for other leads.

It was in a filing cabinet labelled W-Z that I found it: a holographic will in Kellogg's neat and distinctive hand. Although signed and dated, it was unwitnessed, which meant the probate lawyers would have a field day arguing for and against its admissibility, so most of the estate would be lost to their fees. The uncertainty about the validity of the will was not really relevant, but I mentioned it in the hope of lending the paragraph a much-needed air of legal credibility. I smoothed the document on the kitchen table to read it.

I, Solomon Nathaniel Obadiah Kellogg, being of sound mind and body, do bequeath all my worldly goods and chattels to my beloved wife Frances Dorothy Kellogg in the event she survives my death by a clear period of six weeks.

In the event Frances Dorothy Kellogg does not survive the six weeks following my death, then my entire estate shall be put into trust for the benefit of my legal daughter Lola Kellogg.

Subject to his decision, the trust shall be administered either by the Diocese of Clarkesville or by Lola Kellogg's natural father, Elijah Bow.

Elijah Bow!!!

LESSON THIRTY-THREE

'Herbert, which is more important, the beginning of a chapter or the end?'

'They are equally important, Marco, although in different ways. At the end of a chapter you want to hit your reader with a knock-out plot twist or punchline if you can, leaving them reeling with surprise. At the start of the next chapter, however, you need to lure them into the ring from their corner. You will find the answer to almost everything in a boxing analogy, Marco.'

'But Herbert, surely it is not possible to deliver a knock-out plot twist or punchline at the end of every chapter?'

'You are right, Marco. It is an ideal to which you should aspire, although like all ideals it may be unattainable. In practice it is rare for an author to achieve a knock-out plot twist in more than one chapter out of every five. If you exceed that, you are doing well.'

'I've just checked, Herbert, and I've had a knock-out plot twist or punchline at the end of nearly all of my chapters.'

'That is truly superb, Marco. I always said you had greatness within you. Clearly you are starting to let it out.'

'I've just had an idea, Herbert.'

'What is that, Marco?'

'How about I take any chapter that doesn't finish with a knock-out plot twist, and simply merge it with the next. Then all of my chapters will end with a knock-out blow, and I will have attained the unattainable.'

'But to do that you would have to edit what you have written. Great writers never go back, Marco.'

CHAPTER THIRTY-THREE

By the end of which, the plot resembles a corkscrew.

I ran outside holding Father Kellogg's will. Where the hell was Como? I spotted him at the door of one of the farther houses along the quiet suburban street, which was a shock because twelve chapters ago I said the Kelloggs lived in an isolated house near a lake. Hoping the readers would consider that to be a deliberate act of mold-breaking, rather than a dumbass mistake, I jogged down the street to show Como the explosive evidence I had uncovered. As I approached, he made a polite gesture of farewell to the householder he had just interviewed. I blurted out the news:

"Como," I panted, "Elijah Bow was Lola's father! It's all here." I pointed at the will.

Como plucked the will from my hand and frowned as he read it. I stood breathing heavily from my run. His next gesture was a massive slap of triumph on my shoulder. It nearly knocked me sprawling into a flowerbed, but its impact was more emotional than physical. At last I had earned his comradeship and respect.

"Good work, Writer. We'll make a cop out of you yet. Come on."

We strode purposefully, like men with a new sense of purpose, to the Gran Torino.

"Where to now?" I said. I knew exactly what his answer would be.

"Where do you think?"

We left rubber along the street and turned right to head for Bow's ranch.

THE AWFUL TRUTH ABOUT THE HERBERT QUARRY AFFAIR

As we drove, Como and I talked through the open leads in our mushrooming case. In no particular order, we had the following questions still to answer:

Was Scoobie McGee's one of the nightsticks used in the attack on Bluther Cale?

Assuming Scoobie McGee had been one of Cale's assailants, who was his accomplice?

How was Cale's death linked to Lola's?

What was Bow's relationship to Herbert?

Who had called the police to trigger Herbert's red-handed arrest?

What were Lola's movements immediately before her death?

What was Chief McGee's role in the conspiracy?

Who had been trying to frighten me off the case?

I was beginning to think my book about the Herbert Quarry affair might never get finished.

Bow wasn't the least bit pleased to see us back in his study.

"Gentlemen, my patience is at an end. If this nuisance is not immediately stopped, it will not just be City Hall on your back, but the White House too. I have indulged your investigations for reasons of my own, but you are abusing my leniency."

"What if we told you," asked Como, "that we knew what those reasons are?"

For the first time Bow looked discomposed. His eyes flitted between us.

"What do you mean, Lieutenant?"

Como leaned across Bow's desk and placed the holographic will in front of the industrialist.

"I suggest you read that, Sir."

Como stood with his hands behind his back as Bow read and re-read the document. At last Bow took off his spectacles and rested them on his desk. He rubbed the corners of his eyes.

"How many people know about this?" he asked.

"Only the three of us," said Como. "We've no desire for anyone else to know, Mister Bow, but unless you cooperate fully with this investigation, we will have no choice but to bring it all out in court."

Como's words hung in the air. We let them do their work and waited for Bow to hit us with another dollop of blatant exposition.

"Very well. I will tell you all I know. I have admitted to you already that I lead a double life as a gay transvestite. You might wonder then why I, with all my wealth, have never taken advantage of modern medical techniques to change my gender completely. The answer is I have retained a deep-rooted desire for fatherhood, a desire which I thought would never find an opportunity for fulfilment, until a chance conversation sixteen years ago.

"In those days the Kelloggs had newly arrived from out of state. Father Kellogg had moved to the prosperous Clarkesville parish from another diocese, some say as a reward, others say as a bribe to end some long-standing dispute with his bishop. Whatever, the truth is long buried. All I know is that in spite of his popularity, and the flourishing state of his wealthy congregation, both he and his young wife harbored a deep sadness.

"One day I was sitting in Clarkesville Central Park when Mrs. Kellogg came by. I could see she had been crying. I was dressed as a woman but unobtrusively so, and I suppose I must have seemed a motherly figure to Father Kellogg's young wife. She shared my bench and we got to speaking. Eventually, the emotions she had been bottling up came pouring out. She was desperate for a child.

"Swearing me to secrecy, she revealed she and her husband had been trying for children since the time they had married. They had sought medical advice, and tests had shown Father Kellogg was infertile. His sperm were deformed and could swim only in figures of eight. The poor young woman was now torn between her vows to her husband and her desire for motherhood.

"To me there seemed a simple way out of her dilemma, and I asked why she had not considered artificial insemination. If it were a matter of cost, surely the rich parishioners would be glad to help such a sad cause.

"At that she cried even more, and it took all my coaxing to get her to speak. She would willingly have succumbed to the treatment, she said, but her husband could not face the embarrassment of admitting to the world that his seed was afflicted. He saw it as a sign from God that he was being punished for some sin, and he was afraid his congregation would take the same view.

"Even as she spoke, an idea formed within me. It seemed crazy at first, but the more I thought the more certain I became. I told her I knew of a man, a very rich and discreet man, who was desperate to pass his genes and his wealth to a son or daughter, but for personal reasons could never be married. Why should you and he suffer, I said, when God had arranged that each of you held the cure to the other's anguish? I was sure this man would donate his seed in the strongest bonds of secrecy in order to achieve his needs. You could have a child after all, ending any possibility that your husband's fertility could be doubted by his flock.

"We do not have the time, gentlemen, for me to describe the anxious weeks that followed, weeks during which arguments raged in the Kellogg household. At times Father Kellogg damned the suggestion as Satan's lure, while at others he imagined the extra respect a complete family would earn from his conservative congregation. And I dare say the thought of inheriting the wealth of my secretive 'friend' might have influenced his feelings.

"A meeting was eventually arranged at which the priest and his wife would be introduced to Elijah Bow. It was a delicate matter, I assure you, for me to appear before them as their anonymous matronly confidante, and to reappear the next moment as the trustworthy industrialist. But it was stage-managed successfully, and a binding legal agreement was later sealed, through which Elijah Bow would provide his seed and commit his estate to its fruits under the strictest possible obligations of secrecy.

"You will forgive me, gentlemen, for skating over the practical details which the scheme entailed, but the happy day came, and a beautiful girl was born. She was eventually christened Lolita, a traditional name for girls in the Kellogg family.

"Lola grew to be a most beautiful and talented young lady. I ensured she wanted for nothing. We found a cover-story, the Kelloggs and I, to explain why a wealthy industrialist should take an interest in the young Lola and have her as a house guest from time to time. I even immortalized her in works of art, and am glad, now, that I did. You might have noticed, gentlemen, the large bronze fountain in my hallway. That is Lola."

Como and I shifted guiltily on our feet. I coughed.

"I'm sorry," I said. "I spotted the statue was her. I thought it was evidence you were having an affair with her. I shouldn't have."

He looked at me with tears in his eyes. "I know your intentions were good, Mister Ocram. And I forgive you."

"Mister Bow," said Como, "I don't wish to compound your grief, but there is one other thing you need to know, and I believe it would be best if I tell you now."

"Yes?" said Bow.

"Bluther Cale is dead."

Bow looked at the huge detective, then crumpled with grief. Como pulled the bell tassel by Bow's desk. A maid appeared.

"Look after him," said Como. And then to me: "Come on."

We walked towards the doors at the far end of Bow's study.

"Wait!"

The command had come from Bow, once more the self-possessed industrialist. Como and I returned to his desk and waited while he dried his eyes with a handkerchief.

"I assume, gentlemen, that in due course you will explain what happened to my manservant. In the meantime, there is something else you should know. Lola was not my only biological child. Someone in Clarkesville is her brother or sister."

LESSON THIRTY-FOUR

'Herbert, I am worried about my book.'

'About which aspect of it, Marco?'

'As you know, Herbert, it has a killer plot-twist at the end of almost every chapter. Is there a danger my readers could become punch-drunk?'

'No, Marco. Never underestimate the resilience and masochism of your readers. They crave a good literary beating.'

CHAPTER THIRTY-FOUR

In which Marco reaches a belated conclusion.

Como and I were staggered by Bow's sensational revelation. I had already been struggling to remember all the strands of the case, and this new twist was the last mental straw.

I pawed at Como's sleeve for him to follow me into the library.

"I'm not sure I can take much more of this, Como."

"How d'you think I feel? At least you got your five mil as an incentive. Look, we just need to do the normal police thing, right? We ask the questions, and we note the answers, and we sift the important facts from the noise at the fastest pace we can. Solving a crime is no different from a boxing match—you have to..."

I put up a hand to stop him. I couldn't take any more boxing analogies. I'd rather lick the dog doo stains off my incinerated car seat.

"Ok, let's get back to Bow."

We returned to the study, where I tried to force my overwhelmed mind to ask some meaningful questions.

"Mister Bow, please tell me what you know about your other child."

"I know very little, Mister Ocram—not even the child's gender. I was unaware the child existed until exactly six months ago, when I received this."

He took from a drawer in his desk a small envelope which he passed to me. The envelope contained a letter. Como and I read it together.

It was a hand-written confession signed by Lola's mother, Frances Kellogg. In it she told how she had shared some of Bow's donated seed with another 'equally deserving woman' in the congregation of the Clarkesville Church. There were no other details to help identify the woman, no other explanation of why Frances Kellogg did what she did. There was only an apology, and a request that Bow forgive her in the sight of God.

"I assure you, gentlemen, I did everything legitimately in my power to persuade Frances Kellogg to identify the mysterious recipient of my donated seed, but she refused to speak, saying she had made a holy vow of secrecy no mortal threat could cause her to break. I could take no legal action for fear my relationship to Lola would be exposed in court as a consequence. But now you know the truth."

It was dark when we left Bow's house and crunched across the gravel to the Gran Torino. I took a deep breath of the cool evening air. I was feeling tired.

As we cruised down the N66 in light traffic, I shared my thoughts with Como. One thing didn't add up.

"Supposing everything Bow has told us is true. Supposing another woman did give birth to a child of Bow's. The woman must have become pregnant around the same time as Frances Kellogg, as the donated sperm wouldn't keep any longer without cryogenics. Which means she must have given birth around the same time as Frances Kellogg. Clarkesville isn't a big county. There can't be more than one birth a day on average. Supposing a spread of ten days either side, there can't be more than twenty kids who might be the other Bow child. Bow must have worked that out. He has billions of dollars and vast resources. Surely he would have tried to track down his other heir."

"Maybe," said Como. "Or maybe he didn't want the pain of it. Or maybe he tried and failed. Or maybe he respected the vow Frances Kellogg had taken."

"All the same, there's a powerful motive hidden there somewhere. With Lola dead, the other child is set to inherit Bow's billions."

"True. But it's a double-edged sword, Writer. You come forward to claim your position as Bow's heir and you immediately come under suspicion in connection with Lola's death."

"No," I said. "Not if Herbert's already gone to the chair for it."

LESSON THIRTY-FIVE

'Marco.'

'Yes, Herbert?'

'I am not sure about this sentence you have written: 'If you can go for a run in the rain, you can write a book'.'

'What is wrong with it, Herbert?'

'I think you might have underestimated what it takes to write a book, Marco.'

CHAPTER THIRTY-FIVE

In which Marco forgets he is not Philip Marlowe.

I spent the night in the guest room at Herbert's, where Como had dropped me after Elijah Bow's explosive exposé. I'd turned in just before ten after reading a Raymond Chandler I'd found in Herbert's bathroom. The next morning, I felt sharp, alert and active.

After sleeping on the idea, I was more convinced than ever that finding Bow's secret offspring would provide the key to decipher the mystery. Another heir provided a perfect motive for killing Lola and framing Herbert, at a stroke removing the original heir to Bow's fortune while diverting the blame for her death. I checked the mental calculations I had performed in Como's car, and confirmed there could at most have been twenty babies born in Clarkesville around the same time as Lola, one of whom must be Bow's other child.

Five minutes on the internet confirmed my next step. The county birth records were held in the public registry office next to Clarkesville City Hall. I would drive there at once.

I almost made the mistake of jumping into my black Range Rover, but I remembered, just in time, that its charred remains were awaiting forensic examination in Flora Moran's lab. Damn.

I went into Herbert's garage and rummaged around. There was a bicycle, but its tires were flat and perished. The only other transport was a sailboard which Herbert often took onto the wild ocean surf to clear his mind for his writing. Hmmm. I found a hand-held anemometer and popped back outside; there was a southerly force four—perfect. Pausing only to tuck my corduroys into my socks and to shorten the strap on my satchel, I dragged the sailboard out and across the sand and headed along the coast.

At Clarkesville, I moored at a pontoon in the marina, paid the extortionate berthing fee, gave instructions for the sailboard to be scraped of barnacles and re-caulked in all joints, then trotted down Main Street to City Hall. The registry office was in a sad, timber-framed building next door. Judging by the cobweb on the door handle, I was its first visitor for some days. There was a bell on the dusty reception counter. I pinged it, flipped a cigarette into my mouth and struck a match on the sole of my shoe. A man came in, a small man wearing last week's shirt and last year's smile.

"What can I do for you, Brother?"

I blew smoke into his face. "If there's no whiskey in the joint then I'll have the birth register."

"Ain't been no whiskey in this joint since '36, Mister."

"And no Hoovers by the look of things," I said, sneezing in the dusty air. "Are you gonna get the register or just stand there looking pretty? On your way, Small-size."

"Ain't no need to get shirty, Mister." He shuffled off to get his ledger while I rolled a nickel between my fingers and stared at the words 'get shirty', hardly an expression an American would use. Doubtless I would receive no end of criticism for the incongruous Briticism I'd intended as a witticism, but such is the lot of the mold-breaker.

Small-size returned with the ledger and heaved it onto the counter. It was a big book, at least six inches thick, with details of every birth in Clarkesville for the last two hundred years. I went over, stubbed my cigarette on the counter and spun the ledger round to read it. Each page listed fifteen births. One line for each birth. The date, the time, the place, mother's name, father's name and occupation, baby's name, boy or girl; each line written in the careful tidy hand of a City Hall scribe. I flicked through to the period I wanted to see. Almost there. Two more pages should do it. I turned to where I expected the relevant entries to be. Nothing. Looking closely, I could see two pages had been cut out, two pages corresponding to the period around Lola's birth. Someone didn't want me on their trail.

I called Small-size back to the counter and swiveled the ledger so he could read it.

"Notice these pages missing before?"

He bent close over the book and peered at the two thin stubs of paper where the pages had been cut away. He looked up at me like I was the man in Candid Camera.

"Are you kidding me, Mister?"

I said nothing, and lit another cigarette, eyeing him through the smoke. He rushed off with his pants on fire and came back with a supervisor. They examined the defaced ledger as if it were the Mona Lisa and someone had drawn a moustache on it. Any minute now, sirens might go off.

"Isn't there a copy?" I asked, just to be sociable.

The supervisor noticed me for the first time.

"Who are you?"

"Someone who wanted to read those missing pages."

I blew more smoke.

"Wait here," the supervisor said, and legged it to the back office.

I leaned on the counter with a twenty in my hand. Small-size eyed it like a trained seal proffered a fish.

"Anyone been here looking at the books?" I asked. "Come on, Small-size. This place is like a ghost town. A visitor sticks out like a tarantula in a bathtub. You know who's been here."

"I don't know that I can say."

I put a second twenty in my hand and puffed more smoke out of the corner of my mouth. Small-size snatched the notes. "It was a dame. A real doll. Came in two weeks ago. One fifty. Five eight. Brunette. Sweet legs. Emerald ring. Asked me to get her a pencil from the back so she could copy something down. Must have snatched the pages when I went to get it."

"Here, Brother." I snaffled another twenty into his hand and sidled out of the door just as the supervisor came back.

I walked to the marina and down onto the pontoon where I'd tied up the sailboard. Taped to the mast was a postcard of Clarkesville with the message 'We're watching you, Snooper.' I put it in my pocket to show Como.

The wind was against me. With all the tacking and jibing, it took me three hours to sail back to Herbert's house on the beach overlooking the ocean.

LESSON THIRTY-SIX

'Herbert, is it important to make one's characters likeable if one is to write a bestseller?'

'No, Marco, it is not important: it is essential. The reader must fall in love with the characters, and especially with the central character. They must idolize and respect the central character, and fall in love with him, and not bear to be away from him.'

'So, if I make my central character a bestselling writer—that should do the trick?'

'Certainly, Marco. No one can resist a successful, self-opinionated narcissist.'

CHAPTER THIRTY-SIX

In which Marco has it taped.

Back in Herbert's house on the beach overlooking the ocean, I explored Herbert's study for more clues the huge team of police forensic experts might have overlooked. I knew it was Herbert's habit to dictate ideas on a tape recorder, and I wondered whether Herbert might have left the machine running, thereby leaving an accidental recording.

Knowing how thorough and methodical Herbert was—like a boxer training for a fight—I imagined he would leave the tapes from his recorder in a cabinet somewhere, labelled with the dates they spanned. I hunted around and discovered a tall cabinet next to his desk, with a label that read *'Dictation tapes—file in date order.'*

I opened the cabinet and selected the most recent tape. It covered the period just before Herbert was arrested. There was a player in Herbert's living room, so I put in the tape, settled down in a chair overlooking the ocean, and pressed 'Play'.

The sounds of Herbert's last days of freedom filled the room.

Herbert's voice: *Ideas for my new novel, 'The Calculus of Evil'. The central character is a bestselling author, a man of tremendous intellectual depth, overpowering charisma, vast emotional resources; a man massively rich, at ease with a-list celebrities, a prodigious sexual athlete, admired by all men, desired by all women; a man of noble brow, eyes of lapis lazuli flecked with grey, thick fine black hair with an intriguing hint of silver at the temples; a man easily moved to wrath or joy.*

THE AWFUL TRUTH ABOUT THE HERBERT QUARRY AFFAIR

Girl's voice from a distance, presumably Lola: *Herbert! It's raining. Please can we go dancing on the beach?*

Herbert: *In a moment, my true love. I am just making some notes about myself for my new book. Tell me, Lola, what is it you find attractive about me?*

Lola: *Oh Herbert—everything! Your lapis lazuli eyes flecked with grey. I love to run my hands through your rich thick black hair, and the way there is just a hint of silver at the temples. I love your athleticism. I love the way you are as lithe as a cat, as strong as an ox, with the eyes of a hawk. I love everything about you.*

Herbert: *But they are all physical qualities. That is why you love the corporeal Herbert, and I can understand all that of course. But why do you love the spiritual Herbert?*

Lola: *Because you are a great writer, Herbert, and writers are all so irresistibly fascinating, especially great writers. But Herbert, why do you look so wistful and sad? You should be so happy with me here.*

Herbert: *Lola, my love, my darling, you are everything to me. You make me the happiest person in the world. But you are so young, Lola.*

Lola: *What does age matter, Herbert? Age is just a measure of the time that has passed since one's birth. The great scientist, Einstein, building upon the ideas of Lorenz and others, has proved time is relative, that there is no absolute time, that only the spacetime metric dS is invariant across reference frames, whether inertial or non-inertial. Experiments with atomic clocks on jumbo jets have proved that if you could be accelerated to 99.999% of the speed of light for two minutes, I would have aged two years and be no longer a minor. Why should we suffer just because technology hasn't yet advanced to the stage at which travel at near-light-speed is possible?*

Herbert: *Yes, but what will people think if they find I have a relationship with a fifteen-year-old girl?*

Lola: *Why do we care what they think? The taboo of age is simply that—a taboo. There are many cultures, Herbert, in which no such taboos exist. Your concerns are an accident of your birth. You find yourself in a blinkered conservative prudish western civilization.*

Had we been born in an enlightened community in Batar Praveesh, our love would now have been celebrated through a Chalankar marriage ceremony.

Herbert: *But think of the effect on my reputation and book sales.*

Lola: *Oh Herbert, are your book sales more important than I in your life?*

Herbert: *No, my beautiful Lola. I am sorry I said that and upset you. Let us go and dance on the beach in the rain.*

I fast forwarded to the next speech on the tape...

Herbert: *Chief McGee! What are you doing here?*

Man's voice, presumably Chief McGee's: *Sorry to disturb you and all, Mister Quarry Sir, but Clarkesville County Police has launched a new crime prevention initiative, and we're offering a free service, particularly to our more prominent citizens, to survey their houses and check for weak spots that could be exploited by felons looking to commit a crime in your house. So, if it's alright by you, Mister Quarry Sir, I'll just take a look around for points of entry and such like.*

Herbert: *By all means, Chief McGee. It is reassuring to know our law enforcement service is working so proactively to protect us from evil felons.*

Chief McGee: *By the way, was that young Lola Kellogg I saw running from your house?*

Herbert: *Yes, she takes things down for me. When I am dictating, that is.*

I fast forwarded.

There is the sound of a telephone ringing, and a receiver being picked up.

Herbert: *Herbert Quarry speaking, the bestselling author. How can I help you? I see...yes...yes...Pregnant?....Are you sure?...But how does Chief McGee come into it?...I certainly will not. I will go to the police. Your threats don't scare me, buster.*

I fast forwarded some more...

Herbert: *Is that Clarkesville County Police? I've got something odd to report. Someone seems to have dumped a manikin in my garage......yes that's right... the sort of figure you might see in a shop window.... No, I haven't seen anyone strange hanging around, although I have seen a black Lancia Monte Carlo parked on the coast road at odd times recently...no I didn't see the number... Thanks.*

Lola: *Who was it, Herbert?*

Herbert: *Just the police, my darling. I was ringing them about the manikin you found in the garage. I've been thinking...*

Lola: *What about, my darling?*

Herbert: *Perhaps I should go and see your father and ask him whether it is really right that he and certain members of his congregation should subject you to exorcistic rituals. I know it is strange that stigmata appear on your back when you are upset, and that you speak in unknown tongues in your sleep, but I am sure modern science can provide an explanation for such phenomena. Besides, it must play havoc with your revision for your exams.*

Lola: *No, please, Herbert. Please don't approach my father. I don't think he will be a problem for much longer anyway.*

I fast forwarded to almost the end of the tape.

Sound of telephone ringing and being picked up.

Herbert: *Oh, darling Lola, lovely to hear from you. What was that? You want me to wait at the beach for you instead of in the house? Yes....yes.. And what else was that? You might be a couple of hours late and I should return to the house and look for you if you have not arrived at the beach by 3pm? OK. See you soon, my darling.*

I had reached the end of the tape.

LESSON THIRTY-SEVEN

'What are povs, Herbert?'

'Povs? I don't understand, Marco—in what context?'

'In connection with writing, Herbert. I keep seeing writers tweet about how many povs they have in their books.'

'POV is shorthand for point of view, Marco. Inexperienced writers are often overly concerned about determining which points of view to consider in their work. You look confused, Marco.'

'Why would writers tweet about how many opinions they have in their books, Herbert? What does it matter?'

'You misunderstand, Marco; in the context we are discussing, a point of view is not an opinion, but the position of a narrator in relation to the story being narrated. Many books are written from varying points of view.'

'Do the best books have the most povs, Herbert?'

'No, Marco—there is no correlation between the literary worth of a book and the point or points of view from which it is written. As I said, only the inexperienced and misguided writer believes that experimenting with point of view will set their work apart somehow.'

CHAPTER THIRTY-SEVEN

In which Marco experiments with a pov.

Extract from the diary of Lieutenant Como Sven Galahad.

Spent most of the morning with my psychotherapist. She says the Quarry case is probably the cause of my depression. She says I should continue to let Ocram think he's helping my investigations, as his comical contributions, brainless gaffes, and hilarious incompetence might help lift my spirits, like watching a Laurel and Hardy movie. I half agreed, but said his narcissistic self-importance made me puke. She gave me Varmazepam for the depression, and Coltenolol for the puking.

Ocram's in all the papers saying Quarry killed Kellogg. It must be just to keep Chief McGee sweet, though it's hard to believe the clown would do anything so logical. McGee says Ocram's a hero and I can spend as much time as I like helping him—that's the last thing I want, but at least it's an excuse for nosing around.

Flora cancelled dinner, so I stayed in to watch TV. Police Squad! was on. After all the nonsense with Ocram, it was good to watch a more serious and realistic detective show to help me get back to normality.

LESSON THIRTY-EIGHT

'Do you prefer coffee or tea, Herbert?'

'I take neither, Marco: they are insipid stimulants for the masses.'

'What is your normal brew, Herbert?'

'I have a blend of rare exotic superfood infusions flown from the Lesser Antilles twice a day. You should try them.'

'Will it help my writing, Herbert?'

'Who knows, Marco? But when you are desperate, anything is worth a try.'

'I meant to ask, Herbert, what is an adverb? I heard someone say that writers shouldn't use too many of them.'

'Broadly, Marco, an adverb is a word that qualifies a word other than a noun.'

'A noun?'

'I suggest, Marco, you forget the technicalities, and just write.'

CHAPTER THIRTY-EIGHT

*In which Marco continues to use too many adverbs and his labor
bears astonishing fruit.*

I woke in Herbert's guest room, feeling refreshed after a good knight's sleep of the sort Sir Galahad himself might have experienced. I made myself a superfood infusion and planned my day. I was convinced that the key to the mystery was to find Bow's second child. The records at the registry office had been destroyed for a purpose, and that purpose could only have been to thwart my investigations, which meant I must be on the right track.

I decided to visit the local hospital to see if they held records of births. Luckily the insurance company had just delivered a replacement black Range Rover with tinted windows, so I was able to drive rather than begging a lift from Como, who had been behaving rather oddly.

At the hospital, I told the receptionist I would like to see the Chief Executive immediately. She immediately agreed and I was immediately shown to the Chief Executive's office, where the Chief Executive immediately greeted me effusively.

"Mister Ocram, it is an incredible pleasure to meet you. My name is Angela. My time and organization are at your service. How can we help you?"

She had warmly held both my hand and gaze throughout her introductory remarks, so I could tell she was a stock character who could be relied upon to conform to the hackneyed conventions of unimaginative genre fiction. I therefore wrote a passage of suitably wooden and unconvincing dialogue...

"As you will know from the local and national media, I am helping the police investigate the Herbert Quarry affair. A key to the mystery may be in your hands."

"Please tell me more. I will help in any way I can."

"I need to identify other children who were born here around the same time as Lola Kellogg. I assume your records cover that period."

"Certainly. We have had a computer system upgrade since then, so the information you require will be in our data archive, but it will be a simple matter to retrieve it. Please come along with me, and we can do it now."

Angela Newman led me through the corridors of her hospital complex, proudly pointing out the new wings and equipment which had been gifted by various wealthy benefactors, presumably hoping I might take the hint and make my own generous contribution in return for her help. I noticed the '*Sushing Maternity Wing*' and asked about its provenance.

"Oh," said Angela. "You must surely have heard of the world-renowned Professor Sushing. He provided a most generous grant, allowing us to completely rebuild the wing after the fire fifteen years ago."

"A fire? Fifteen years ago?"

"Yes."

"That's a coincidence, since it was then Lola Kellogg was born."

Just as we turned a corner, we bumped into a clerk carrying a sheaf of records, knocking her papers over the polished floor. I helped her pick them up, noticing as I bent down that her toenails were exquisitely varnished in an enchanting opalescent shade I had last seen several chapters ago.

When I stood to hand the records to the clerk, I saw who she was.

"Jacqueline!" I said. "I thought you worked in the coffee shop on Tuesdays."

She blushed. "It's Marcia, Mister Ocram, Jacqueline's twin sister," she added, just in case the readers had forgotten.

Marcia—the scorned mad woman who had painted 3,285 pictures of a framed Herbert! What could she be doing here?

"Yes. Anyway, here we are," said Angela Newman.

THE AWFUL TRUTH ABOUT THE HERBERT QUARRY AFFAIR

We had arrived at a door bearing a sign which read *Data Archives from Old Computer System*. Angela rifled through a massive bunch of keys attached by a lanyard to her belt, until she found the one to unlock the door.

"It's already unlocked!" she said after she had inserted the key, the alarm in her voice instantly putting me on my alert.

We went in and switched on the lights. I had no idea what a computer data archive would look like, but I was getting the hang of the Jackson Pollock method, so I typed some technical mumbo jumbo at random. The archive room was a state-of-the-art installation, equipped with the latest uninterruptible power supply—which looked remarkably like a battery—a king-size fire blanket, twin ex-tractor fans (from a John Deere 6080) and a huge modem in fetching beige. Decorated throughout in flame-retardant flock wallpaper, the tape storage area contained bank after bank of shelving constructed from two-by-two cross-sawn Hemlock with exquisite figuring in the grain. Each shelf bore reel after reel of top-quality ferric-magnate tape, the reels kept immaculately clean by a robotic arm equipped with a duster of the finest ostrich feathers.

"They should be in chronological order," said Angela as we worked our way back through the banks of shelving. "So, fifteen years ago should just be about... here." There was a gap in the reels of tape just where she pointed. My mind raced as I realized the implication of what I had just typed—someone had taken the records.

"But that's.... impossible," garbled the self-deluding chief exec.

"Clearly not," I corrected, restoring some much-needed sense of logic to the conversation. "Who else has a key to this room?"

"Only our data archive technician, Alana McGee."

"Alana McGee? Is she related to Chief McGee?"

"Yes, she's his niece. Why do you ask?"

My mind hyperactive, I ignored the question and looked around. A CCTV camera in the corridor pointed directly at the door to the archive room. "Get me the last six months' footage from that camera and get it now!" I thumped my fist on a table to underline my in-patients, sorry, impatience with the hospital's slapdash admin-istration.

I paced up and down the corridor while the frantic chief exec made a series of hurried calls. At last she came to me, a look of complete despair on her tearful face. "The camera. It's been out of action for the last six months. They hadn't noticed until I asked for the recordings."

My face was set in an iron mask of disapproval. I asked the obvious question. "Who is in charge of those cameras?"

An hour later I was driving my new black Range Rover with tinted windows to the nearby town of Assumption Springs. Angela Newman had confirmed that the hospital's head of security was Simpson McGee, another member of Chief McGee's clan. After a hasty staff conference, we established there was no other copy of the computer archive tapes, and the only chance of discovering which other babies had been born at the same time as Lola was to visit the old head midwife, Marge Downberry, who had retired six months ago.

Angela had phoned ahead while I was driving, so when I arrived at Marge Downberry's she was waiting for me.

"Can I get you a coffee, Mister Ocram?"

"You don't happen to have any superfood infusions from the Lesser Antilles?"

"No, only coffee."

"Coffee's fine then, thanks." That was a shame—no chance of the writing getting any better. Speaking of which...

"Did that man Quarry really cut up a fifteen-year-old girl like you said he did in all the newspapers?" asked Marge while she poured us coffees.

"No, he definitely didn't."

I explained how the press had twisted my words to give an entirely misleading impression of my beliefs about the case.

"They're always doing that," said Marge, knowingly. "If I can help clear his name, I'd be glad to. I've no time for the press or the police."

"Why's that?" I asked.

"The reason I retired early is that I used to take photographs of all the new-born babies. You can't believe how useful it is to have pictures. So often, babies get mixed up and mothers can't remember which is which. If you have photographs you can always sort things out. But the crazy PC crowd was going on about it being a violation of the babies' right to privacy. I sent a paper through to the National Congress of the American College of Midwifery condemning the PC brigade as idiots. I put my paper on the internet, with a couple of samples of the photographs. Anyway, turns out some pedophile creep downloaded the pictures, and before I knew it there were headlines in all the papers saying the chief midwife of Clarkesville County Hospital was at the center of a pedophile ring."

"What did you do?"

"I resigned. What else could I do?"

"And presumably the experience has left you with an abiding hatred of the press, and a desire to help anyone falsely accused by them?"

"Yes."

That was lucky. I wondered if my luck was going to be even better... "Tell me, Marge, what happened to your unofficial birth records?"

"I kept them. I figured if they weren't official no one could stop me taking them. I've got them laid out on the table next door."

"Yes!" I punched the air. Here at last would be the answer. Once again, my mighty intellect and detecting prowess had outshone the cream of the Clarkesville County Police.

We walked to Marge's lounge where photograph album after photograph album stacked on her table showed she had prepared for my visit.

"Here they are," said Marge, "memories of happier days. This is the album for the year Lola was born."

We had a look at some of the pictures. There were lots of 'ah isn't he lovely', and 'hasn't she got her mother's eyes?', and 'yes, it's sad, but he had a lovely personality' and such like, before Marge said:

"I understand you're particularly interested in other babies born the same time as Lola."

"Yes. For reasons that would bore the readers to death if we went into them all over again, I am trying to establish whether there was another child born around the same time as Lola who might have shared the same biological father."

"Well for goodness sakes why didn't you say?" said Marge, starting to sound like my Bronx mom. "Look at this. Here's Lola—see the birthmark on the sole of her foot? And just a week later, another baby..." Marge turned over a couple of pages. "See?"

Marge showed me the later baby's picture. It had exactly the same birthmark as Lola.

"Are birthmarks like that genetic?" I asked.

"Mostly," said Marge. "I remember joking with the baby's mom and dad about it. I said we'd had a baby in a week earlier with exactly the same birthmark, and wouldn't it be funny if they had the same father. Of course, the husband wasn't too happy, but I laughed it off. That's the trouble with policemen—they've absolutely no sense of humor."

"Policemen?"

"Yes, didn't I tell you? The little girl with the same birthmark as Lola was Scoobie McGee's daughter."

LESSON THIRTY-NINE

'How should a book end, Herbert?'

'I have told you, Marco—a book never really ends. It is like a boxing match. It lives on in the minds of the spectators, and the coaches, and the referee, and the judges, and the TV commentators, and the girls who walk round the ring with the round cards, and the promotors, and the...'

'Yes, I know all that, Herbert, but how should the actual written part end?'

'Thrice, Marco. Your book should end thrice.'

CHAPTER THIRTY-NINE

In which Marco shares a theory with Como.

At last a pattern was emerging from the tangled threads of the mystery, and I was more convinced than ever that Herbert had been framed for the murder of his young love Lola. Although we had been overwhelmed with the red herrings and false scents I had stupidly typed, a clear hypothesis was forming. I explained my rationale as I stood by the glass wall in the incident room devoted to the Kellogg case. Como watched with unalloyed admiration and respect as I spoke.

"Herbert Quarry is found by the police in his study, surrounded by joints of his beloved Lola, covered in blood, his hand holding the knife that dismembered her. Herbert's story is that he had been waiting at the beach for Lola to meet him and had returned only when she had failed to make the rendezvous. He had found the body and the knife and sunk to his knees in Lola's blood, unable to take in what his eyes had seen. You'll admit, no aspect of the evidence conflicts with his version of events."

"Agreed," agreed Como.

"Indeed, the accidental tape-recording I found on Herbert's dictation machine corroborates his story."

"Agreed, although he could have made it to create an alibi. He might not have been talking on the telephone—just pretending he was."

"True, but unlikely. You must learn to apply Ocram's razor, Como."

"Ocram's razor?"

"Sorry, I meant Occam's razor." I was staggered to find that the surname I had invented for myself at random in Chapter One allowed me to make such a clever pun so many chapters later. "You must learn to apply Occam's razor. In any case, we can check from phone company records whether Herbert was speaking to Lola at the time, so let us assume so for the time being."

"Seems reasonable."

"So, if Herbert is innocent, we must look for another killer, or killers, with the time, motive, and resources to have committed the crime."

"Do you have a theory, Writer?"

"I do, Como. I have a hypothesis."

"Spill."

"Ok. It's this. Herbert Quarry has decided to run away with Lola. Chief and Scoobie McGee get to learn of Herbert's plans. They know that Scoobie's daughter will inherit Bow's fortune only if Lola dies, so Herbert's proposed elopement forces their hands. Chief and Scoobie McGee are in a patrol car together. They see Lola walking through the woods towards Herbert's house, and they chase her on foot. Lola sees them. She assumes the Chief is planning some kind of threesome with his nephew, so she takes off and runs. Lola was being followed at the time by Bluther Cale, who was infatuated with her. Bluther sees Lola being chased by the two policemen, so he chases after them. He arrives too late and sees one of the two men floor Lola with a blow. He roars with rage, betraying his presence. The McGees round on him and kill him with blows from their nightsticks. They then bundle Lola's warm body into their car in an evidence bag, drive to Herbert's house, take one of Herbert's knives and cut up the body on the floor. They wear police-issue gloves, overshoes, and overalls to keep any of their DNA off Lola's body and any of Lola's DNA off theirs. After dismembering Lola's body, they pick up Cale's corpse. One of them drives Cale in Cale's car, the other follows in the prowler. They get to the cliff, move Cale to the driver's side of the seat, and push the car over the edge. And the rest you know."

"I like it," said Como. "It's feasible, and consistent with the known facts. There's a compelling motive. But there are counter arguments the McGees might make, credible ones. The only actual evidence that ties them into the story are the marks on Scoobie's nightstick matching the wounds on Cale. And who's to say someone didn't swap Scoobie's nightstick for another one, just like we did when we picked it out of his locker? And in Clarkesville County Court, who's likely to be believed: two McGees with friends throughout the town, or a pedophile author whose guts are hated by everyone? And there are too many other suspects clouding the case. Professor Sushing who had legal scores to settle with Quarry. The waitress's sister who was scorned by Quarry. The taxidermist whose wife was killed by Quarry. Bow might have had some kind of motive. No, we'll need more than your hypothesis if the McGees are to swap place with Quarry in Clarkesville County Penitentiary."

LESSON FORTY, AT LAST

'Herbert, I was reading a book in which the timeline kept changing. Sometimes the story was set in the present and sometimes it went back in time. Should I do that in my book?'

'No, Marco. Shifts in the temporal setting of a story are a cheap device by means of which a desperate author might try to add interest to an inherently dull and poorly conceived narrative. Flashbacks are not a hallmark of great literature, Marco.'

CHAPTER FORTY

In which Marco tees up his spectacular denouement, and is forced to write a flashback owing to an oversight on the part of his readers.

Back at Herbert's place, I wandered along the beach, throwing moody stones into a strangely calm sea while I brooded upon the frustrating conclusion to the preceding chapter. Como was right—however plausible, my hypothesis alone would never convict the McGees. I needed proof. I decided to rule out the option of finding hard evidence, as I couldn't face writing further chapters about DNA, nightsticks and the like. Besides, the McGees were experienced cops who'd know how to cover their tracks, so we might write thousands of words and get nowhere. Far more promising, to me at least, was the idea of the classic Agatha Christie ending, with yours truly in the Poirot role. You must have seen it a thousand times on corny films and TV shows—the detective confronting the baddies over dinner, compelling them to confess under the combined weight of his remorseless logic and his iron self-possession.

I was clambering over the rocks to round the point into Clarkesville Bay, when an island about a mile offshore caught my eye and imagination. Perched upon it was the Clarkesville Bay Island Hotel, a faded deco edifice surrounded by pine woods and sandy beach. It was one of Herbert's favorite haunts. Its library contained a large Jackson Pollock entitled *The Stag at Bay*, painted, Herbert told me, after the wild stag party Pollock held there before his marriage to Lee Marvin. No, not Lee Marvin—he's that actor, stupid. It was Lee something... Lee Merrick! No, she's another actor...anyway, she was some famous artist called Lee, so let's not get bogged down in trivia—look it up yourself if you're that bothered. Herbert and I once tried to swim to the island, but I got a cramp after twenty yards and had to paddle back. The hotel was closed for the quiet season, but it would form the perfect backdrop for a dinner party with the baddies!

Racing back to Herbert's, I rang my PA in New York, apologized for inventing him so late in the book, and got him to contact the owners of the hotel and arrange for me to rent it for an evening on an exclusive basis. What I had in mind was going to cost money, a lot of money, but it would provide the showcase chapter for my bestseller about the Herbert Quarry affair. Every penny of the cost would be repaid a thousand times by the royalties from my book.

I compiled the guest list to include all of my relevant characters:

Marcia Delgado
Professor Sushing
Lieutenant Como Galahad
Police Chief McGee
Police Sergeant McGee
Elijah Bow
Quimara Tann
Marge Downberry

The invitation I worded as follows:

Marco Ocram requests your company for dinner at the Clarkesville Bay Island Hotel, Thursday, 8pm, to celebrate the announcement of his forthcoming book:
"The Awful Truth about the Herbert Quarry Affair".
White tie. Transport to be provided. Launches to leave Clarkesville Marina from 5pm. Drinks to be served on the Miranda Terrace from 6:30pm. RSVP

Today was Tuesday. That gave me two days to close the remaining gaps in my story. Addressing the envelopes to my guests, it struck me that two days was a ludicrously short time to allow for them to be delivered and for all the RSVPs to be returned—I'd have to invent some story about them all being hand-delivered by a courier company famed for the speediness of its dispatch riders—and its jet pilots too, given that Sushing lived in Nassau. Musing on my mistake, I started to write Quimara Tann's envelope.

Quimara Tann!

For Pete's sake—I never typed what she said when my iPad went flat in Chapter Six!

I cursed myself. Not that it was my fault, mind you—I have the clearest possible memory of tasking the readers to bring it up. *Don't let me forget*, I'd said. Readers! If this were Twitter, I would now be posting a GIF of a writer in an anorak, tearing his hair out. The readers were meant to remind me to use it as entertaining filler if we reached a dull spot. No wonder the book's been full of dull spots. Well, they've only got themselves to blame. To make the whole sorry mess even more messy, Quimara's story was itself a flashback, so I would now have to type a flashback about a flashback, and we all know what Herbert says about flashbacks and great literature. I shuddered to think what the judges in Stockholm would make of it

With a good deal of unease, therefore, I forced my mind back thirty-four chapters to the scene in the coffee shop in order to start Flashback #1. The waitress Jacqueline, I seem to remember, had just slipped out of a chair at my table, and a beautifully made-up woman had just slipped into it...

"You must be Marco Ocram," she said.

"Pleased to meet you, Miss..."

"Mrs. Tann, but you can call me Quimara." She pulled her chair closer and beamed at me. While I felt for my pen, expecting her to ask me to sign her copy of *The Tau Muon*, she said "I understand you're looking to dig up dirt on that sick pedo Herbert Quarry."

I wasn't sure what to say, so to buy time I folded my copy of the *Clarkesville Literary Supplement*, a gesture she took as a cue to continue. Pausing only to check we were being overheard by half of the biggest gossips in Clarkesville, she told me her astonishing story.

Flashback #2. Three months earlier...

THE AWFUL TRUTH ABOUT THE HERBERT QUARRY AFFAIR

Quimara Tann had recently moved to Clarkesville. She lived with her husband Terry and beautiful daughter Esmerelda in a modest house in a leafy suburb. Terry had an ordinary office job in town, and his lack of drive drove Quimara mad with social ambition. She had gone to the coffee shop and was about to take a table, when a waitress said:

"I'm afraid you can't sit there."

"Why not?"

"That table is permanently reserved for the famous writer, Herbert Quarry, who still writes all his bestsellers here even though he is now worth millions of dollars and could afford to write them anywhere."

Famous writer. Millions of dollars. Quimara had hit pay dirt.

"Is Herbert Quarry married?"

"Definitely not. And he prefers beautiful young women."

Wow. Instantly a plan formed in her mind.

"Here's my mobile number and a twenty-dollar tip. Please text me the moment Herbert Quarry is next in the café."

Two days later Quimara was in stirrups at the gynecologist's where she was taking a smear test. The gynecologist was just staring at her cervix when her phone beeped. She grabbed it from her handbag and saw the text 'Herbert Quarry now at table.'

"Sorry, Doc, gotta go," said Quimara, dangling a speculum from her crotch as she ran for the chair where her clothes lay.

In the coffee shop, Quimara walked to the table she had been refused earlier. At it was a man who exuded sophistication, wealth, power, and sex appeal.

"I'm so sorry to interrupt—I bet you are writing another bestseller. Aren't you Herbert Quarry?"

"Yes, that's right. Who are you?"

"I'm Quimara Tann. I've just moved to town with my husband and beautiful daughter. Would you like to come around this evening for a drink and meet my beautiful daughter?"

"That would be lovely."

They agreed on a time and swapped contact details. Quimara hurried home to prepare for her soirée.

As Quimara completed her preparations, she basked in her good fortune. Soon her daughter Esmerelda would become Esmerelda Quarry, beautiful wife of the famous author. Quimara would become famous. She would appear in all the important society magazines. She would invite the press to the wedding, and they would want to photograph every room in her house, and she could wear a different outfit in every photograph, and she could make sure the boob-job she had made Terry pay for would show her figure to its best advantage, and...

She was struck with a nameless fear. What if Herbert Quarry was a Catholic? How could she tell? It was a Tuesday, so serving meat would be no test. Suddenly she had the answer—she ran to the general store and got there just in time before it closed.

Shortly, Herbert Quarry arrived in a black Lancia Monte Carlo, and soon—Quimara could barely believe it—he was in Quimara's living room making small talk with Terry and drinking champagne.

"I see you bought a black Lancia Monte Carlo," said Terry. "I nearly bought one myself."

"You should have," said Herbert Quarry. "They are excellent cars. They reach sixty in under ten seconds, yet they are remarkably frugal. On a trip to Denver last week I managed 38.4 miles per gallon, and you know the price of gas is fierce. The hemispherical voids in the cylinder-head account for the superior fuel economy. It was an innovation first deployed in a production vehicle by Volkswagen, in their 'Blue Efficiency' models, but they licensed the technology to Lancia a couple of years ago. I was reading a really interesting article about the aerosol effects produced by the fuel injection system when the piston is on the downstroke, which results in multiple vortices that distribute the fuel more evenly in the combustion space. I can let you have a photocopy if you like."

"That would be swell," said Terry.

Herbert was so intellectual, thought Quimara. He would make the perfect husband for Esmerelda, but she had to know...

"Herbert," she asked. "Would you be an angel and cut this cake for me?"

"Of course."

Herbert took the knife from Quimara. The cake was what she had rushed to buy from the general store. It was topped with a smiling likeness of Pope Francis, done in colored icing. Without hesitation, Herbert plunged the point of the knife into the benevolent face of the kindly pontiff and cut the cake into slices. Quimara felt a flood of relief.

"Now where's that daughter of mine?" said Quimara. She shouted up the stairs. "Esmerelda, honey, are you coming down? We've a visitor."

Esmerelda was a beautiful young woman, an ex prom queen and head cheerleader. She stepped elegantly down the stairs in a low-cut see-through dress that left little to the imagination.

"Esmerelda, honey, you might have slipped on something a little smarter—we have an important guest. This is Mister Herbert Quarry, the famous writer."

Esmerelda and Herbert shook hands. She instantly fell in love with him and wanted to marry him.

"Terry," said Quimara, "what was it you were suggesting we might do when Mister Quarry came around?"

She gave him a hefty nudge to encourage his memory.

"Oh yeah," said Terry. "I was suggesting we could look at some old family albums, as that would be really interesting for Mister Quarry and nostalgic for us."

"Good idea. Go and get them then."

A moment later, Terry reappeared with a single album in his hands. "For some reason I can't seem to find any of the albums apart from this one."

"Which one is that, honey? Let me see." Quimara took the album and opened it. "Oh, these are the photos of Esmerelda when she was modelling for that men's magazine. I suppose we could look at it with Mister Quarry if you can't find any of the other albums. What do you think of these pictures, Mister Quarry? Esmerelda is very beautiful, isn't she?"

Quimara turned the pages of the album, each successive page showing Esmerelda in progressively fewer clothes and progressively more explicit poses.

"And these are the ones where she's shaved altogether. I think they're so much more elegant. Don't you agree Mister Quarry?"

After they had finished looking at the album, Quimara suggested Herbert and Esmerelda should catch a movie.

The movie theatre was crowded with people queueing for tickets and popcorn. As Herbert and Esmerelda queued to buy their tickets, Herbert saw Lola in the next line. Lola saw Herbert with Esmerelda in her low-cut see-through outfit and went running off.

"Excuse me," said Herbert to Esmerelda. "Please take this money and buy a ticket and popcorn for yourself. I am not feeling well. I hope you enjoy the movie. Here's twenty dollars for a taxi home too."

Herbert left Esmerelda and ran after Lola who had run into a part of the movie theatre closed for refurbishment.

"Oh Herbert," sobbed Lola. "You don't love me after all. You just want to date that tarty slag Esmerelda Tann."

"Lola, it's not true. You are the only tarty slag I want to date. I love you Lola with all my heart and always will. The letters L-O-L-A are engraved on my heart, leaving no room for the letters E-S-M-E-R-E-L-D-A."

"Oh Herbert!" Lola wrapped her arms around him and buried her face in his midriff.

Later that evening, a cab dropped Esmerelda at her parents' house. Quimara, who had been at the curtains all evening, was desperate to know why it was a yellow cab rather than a black Lancia Monte Carlo which had dropped her beautiful daughter at the curbside. Perhaps Esmerelda had gone home with Quarry to make love, leaving him too drained to drive her himself. But her daughter's face, streaked with tears and mascara, told a different story.

"Oh Mom," Esmerelda sobbed. "I've had to watch the movie and eat all the popcorn all by myself. Herbert was sick and had to leave. I think that girl Lola Kellogg was sick at the same time, because she left too."

"There, there," said Quimara, patting her daughter's hair tenderly.

The next day Quimara decided to go to Herbert Quarry's house by the beach overlooking the ocean to leave a card thanking Herbert for attending her soiree, hoping he was feeling better, and inviting him to take Esmerelda out any time he liked. She saw the door was open, so she knocked and entered, hoping she might talk to the famous novelist and impress him with more stories about Esmerelda's beauty and popularity. However, she found the house empty. She was curious to know what Herbert was really like. Seeing his PC had been left switched-on, she stole a glance at the messages on his screen. She couldn't believe her eyes. They were full of selfies of Herbert and Lola embracing and hugging, and 'I love you, Lola's and 'I love you, Herbert's and all kinds of sick messages between a grown man and a young girl. She flung Herbert's PC screen off the desk and stormed out, ripping to shreds the card she had bought.

"I'll get you for this, you sick perverted pedophile bastard," she cursed through her teeth as she slammed the door behind her and stomped back to her car.

LESSON FORTY-ONE

'How, Herbert, is the productivity of a writer measured?'

'In words, Marco, in words.'

'And what is the threshold of productivity beyond which the adjective 'prodigious' might be applied?'

'There is no internationally agreed standard for prodigious literary output, Marco. However, there are several accepted benchmarks. Barbara Cartland, for instance, is reputed to have written 5,000 words per day, and she ranks as one of the world's most prolific writers.'

'And how might a writer achieve such extreme rates of output?'

'There is only one way, Marco, which is to write whatever comes into your head next.'

'But for many people, surely, that would be repetitive meaningless drivel.'

'True, Marco. But remember what I have always told you—if it were easy everyone would do it.'

'You mean...'

'Yes. What separates the great writer from the good is the ability to generate at least 1,000 words per hour consistently, hour after hour and day after day, while presenting some semblance of coherent narrative impetus, however trashy or meaningless. And as I have also often said, you have such greatness within you. You, Marco, can churn it out with the best of them if you put your mind to it.'

CHAPTER FORTY-ONE

In which inappropriate jokes precede a shocking revelation.

Having played a series of rising arpeggios on a harp to signify our return from Flashbacks #1 and #2, I was just dropping the invitations at *ACME Couriers—We Always Deliver*, when Como rang.

"I got a tip-off, Writer. Heading over to check it out. Wanna come along?"

"You bet."

I told him where I was, and within minutes he pulled up outside to collect me.

"Where are we going?"

"The hospital."

"Not the maternity records department?"

"No, the cancer unit."

"Why there?" I asked, hoping Como would give us all an idea of what was going on.

"I got a call from Micky Tropic."

"Micky Tropic?"

"Yeah. His real name's Troppizkawinszki-Jones—Lithuanian Welsh—so Tropic's easier. He's a good guy, another lieutenant in the PD, six months away from retirement. Never had a day sick in five years. Last week he started seeing double, and they find it's a brain tumor."

"Jeez."

"You said it, Writer."

"Can they operate?"

"No—it's terminal."

Now, don't tell me you didn't see it coming...

"You mean," I could hardly bring myself to type it, "they can't cure Tropic of cancer?"

Como shook his head with great sadness, a natural reaction to the appalling pun. Mind you, it could have been worse. Had I been quick enough, I could have named his colleague, Micky 'The Crab' Tropic, and written a sequence in which Como recalled hearing the news of his illness:

'Hey, Como, you heard the news about Micky Tropic?'

'No.'

'He's got a brain tumor.'

'Cancer? The Crab?'

"Why are we going to see him?" I asked.

"They've given him a week to live, so he figures he needs to make peace with his maker. He says he found out that Chief McGee's been up to no good. He's been keeping quiet about it, but now he wants to get it off his chest."

We talked for a while about the cruel vagaries of life, before turning to speculation about the no-good Chief McGee had been up to. Based on comparable cases in thousands of bestselling crime novels, we constructed a shortlist of the more likely revelations, as follows:

A drink problem—two to one.

Embezzlement of Clarkesville County Police funds—three to one.

An affair with a female colleague—five to one.

An affair with a male colleague—twenty to one.

Simultaneous affairs with male and female colleagues—a hundred to one.

Leading a double life with another family in Pasadena—four hundred to one.

At the hospital, we scraped together eighty dollars for the parking fee and headed for the cancer unit. I tried to alleviate Como's melancholic mood by injecting a touch of humor.

"Hey, maybe we've overlooked one."

"What d'you mean?"

"Micky might reveal that Chief McGee's a shape-shifting alien. Haw, haw, haw, haw, haw."

"Haw, haw, haw. Yeah, and maybe he's planting big pods that're gonna steal our bodies. Haw, haw, haw, haw, haw."

"Yeah," I said through my tears. "Or maybe McGee's been up to no-good with Lola Kellogg in his office. Haw, haw, haw, haw, haw, haw, haw, haw, haw, haw, haw, haw..."

"Haw, haw, haw, haw, haw, haw, haw, haw, haw, haw, haw, haw, haw, haw..."

We were still crying at our hilariously improbable jests when we arrived at Micky Tropic's ward.

Thirty minutes later, walking back to the car...

"Wow, so McGee's been up to no-good with Lola Kellogg in his office."

We sat in a stunned silence through the drive back to the coffee shop.

LESSON FORTY-TWO

'Tell me, Herbert.'

'What, Marco?'

'What should I do if I make a mistake when I am writing?'

'A mistake? You are not thinking like a great post-modernist author, Marco. Great post-modernist authors do not recognize the existence of mistakes. The concept of error in literature is an outdated one, important only to the smallminded. Think like a true artist, Marco. If Picasso draws a head with three eyes, is it a mistake? No— it is an act of immense symbolism. To break the mold of literature, Marco, you must rid your mind of the concept of error.'

'Write. Sorry, right.'

CHAPTER FORTY-TWO

*In which a lie is uncovered, and Marco flaunts his technical
knowhow.*

Back at my special table in the coffee shop, Como flicked through the
sports pages while I waited for the next thing to come into my head. It
was Jacqueline, coming for our order.

"Guess what, Mister Ocram," she said with an excited smile, "I've
been on TV too!"

"Really."

"I can't wait to show you." She put down her menus and got her
phone. "Look. My friend emailed it."

It was the exact same clip of the Clarkesville Giants game Marcia
had shown to prove her alibi. One of the Delgado sisters was lying, and
I could guess which.

"Are you sure that's you, and not Marcia?"

"Ha ha ha ha ha ha ha ha ha. Gosh Mister Ocram, that's a good
joke. No, Marcia was working here, covering for my shift."

I looked at Como—he still had his head in the paper. I wasn't sure
I was in the mood to write another trip to the Hacienda Apartments to
confront Marcia with proof of her chicanery. I ordered coffees and
muffins. Maybe I could decide after a caffeine and sugar hit.

I grabbed a napkin and cleaned the screen of my iPad, which had
been horribly besmeared by forty chapters' worth of frantic tapping by
my right forefinger. Jacqueline's mention of an email had tripped a
cog in my mind, so I wasn't surprised when Como put down the paper
and said:

"I been thinking."

That's always a dangerous start with Como.

"What?"

"All this crap kicked off with an email from Quarry. If he hadn't sent it by mistake, we wouldn't be here."

"True, Como, it was a spooky coincidence that I was the recipient. But let's not forget the rich literary tradition of stories that begin with some chance event. If Little Red Riding Hood hadn't visited her granny, there'd be no big bad wolf. Last time I looked at Goodreads, there was no one saying '*just as if*' about Little Red Riding Hood visiting her granny, so I fail to see why you are raising a fuss about my opening hook."

"That's different, Writer. She would have visited her granny every day."

"That, Como, is conjecture. Show me where the Grimms wrote *Once upon a time, Little Red Riding Hood decided to visit her granny,* **like she did every day**. I think not. For all you know, she might have learned of the existence of her granny only through some freak event the day before."

"Bullshit. Everyone knows she was always going to her granny's place."

Our argument about Little Red Riding Hood continued for some minutes, until Como remembered his initial point.

"Anyway, why did Quarry send Lola the email if he'd already agreed to meet her when they talked on the phone?"

"Christ, Como, don't ask me—you're the detective."

"Right. So why have you got me sitting on my ass talking fairy tales? Finish your coffee, Writer—we got some detecting to do."

I gulped the last of my coffee and followed Como out of the coffee shop.

"Where are we going?"

"Quarry's place."

On the drive to Herbert's, Como told me what he had in mind.

"Maybe the email was just a coincidence, like you said, or maybe it wasn't. I'm gonna take another look at Quarry's PC."

My heart sank. Computers were as boring as a box of drill bits. Worse still, I knew nothing about them. And now I'd stupidly let Como talk me into writing about them—a certain recipe for making a complete fool of myself.

In Herbert's study, Como pressed a button which switched-on Herbert's PC. So far so good—faultless technical veracity, no less. I had an idea to allow me to quit while we were ahead...

"Shall I just go and make coffee while you take another look at Herbert's PC?"

"Screw that, Writer. Stick around—you might learn something."

I doubted it—but before I could think of another excuse to skip the PC examination, Como raised the stakes...

"Before I moved into homicide, I was head of cybercrime, so we're gonna let things rip."

Cripes. Now we were for it. Full forensic details about the working of computers, to be made up on the spot, Jackson Pollock fashion, while trying to stay awake. I hoped the readers could stomach the computing equivalent of a face with three eyes—or maybe five. Como flexed his fingers and started to flaunt his prowess with keyboard and mouse.

"On the day of the murder, Quarry sent two emails—one to you, then one to Lola an hour later, which, incidentally, was two minutes after your reply."

"That makes sense," I said, which was a change, given all the other nonsense in the book. "He emails me then realizes his mistake when I reply."

"Wrong. Your email address is nothing like Lola's. Watch what happens when I start typing hers."

I watched. When Como started typing, the computer cleverly anticipated his remaining keystrokes to complete Lola's address.

"See? There's no way to type your address by accident."

"What are you saying, Como? He emailed me deliberately?"

"I've seen this before, Writer. Fraud case, four years ago. Someone getting emails authorizing payments. Thing was, they worked in personnel, nothing to do with payments."

"And?"

"The emails were sent by fucked-up malware. Could be the same here. Okay, let's get serious. We'll do some reverse engineering on the registry..."

I yawned as he reverse engineered the registry.

"...then defrag the disk..."

I pinched myself to fend off sleep.

"...purge the FIFO stacks and...just pass me those pliers... reroute the I/O bus..."

I slapped myself in the face.

"...and intercept the MTA process threads."

Just as I was looking round for a cattle-prod to shock myself awake, Como said:

"Bingo."

"What?"

"Quarry deleted an email contact the morning of the murder."

"So?"

"The contact began with a G."

"So?"

"You're next in his contacts after Lola."

"So?"

"So it's staring you in the face, Writer. Some idiot programmed malware to send an email to Lola, the twenty third name in Quarry's contacts. But Quarry deletes the contact beginning with G. Lola's now twenty second in the list, and you're twenty third. The malware sends the email to you."

I wasn't so sure. It seemed ridiculously implausible, even to me, and I'd invented it. God knows what the readers would think. I'd just have to hope they knew as little about computers as I did. Besides, it was only half the story—I put the point to Como.

"That might account for my receiving the email, Como, but it wouldn't account for the email being resent to Lola after my reply."

"No, that's something else. Whoever made the mistake has also been watching Quarry's email."

"Wow!" I hadn't thought of that. What a brilliant twist. "Can you see who it was?"

"No, but we might get some indications. We'll set up a CSV file..."

I felt sleep returning in waves.

"...dump the IP packet log..."

Zzzzzz.

"...cross-reference the TCP proxy..."

Zzzzzzzzzzzzz.

"...compare that with a DNS whois ping..."

Zzzzzzzzzzzzzzzzzzzzzzzzz.

"Right, whoever's watching Quarry's email has been routing via an IP tunnel from BDP Communications."

"Who are they?"

Como Googled them. They were a telco in Panama, with a network across the Caribbean. Now we were getting somewhere.

"Can we get a warrant to search their HQ? Force them to trace the IP address?"

"Are you shitting me? We can't even trace the calls to police HQ."

I slumped on Herbert's desk. I was losing the will to live. Nearly a thousand words about computers, all for nothing. Or maybe not. An idea came into my head.

LESSON FORTY-THREE

'What is a figure of speech, Herbert?'

'An expression which conveys more than its literal meaning, Marco.'

'What is the point of that?'

'Figures of speech have no purpose other than to impress those who spot them, Marco.'

'Does that mean I need not bother with figures of speech?'

'No, Marco, it does not. If you wish to become a truly great author, you must employ figures of speech continually.'

'Why, Herbert?'

'An author is recognized as truly great only through the collective opinions of other authors and critics. They are precisely the people who are impressed by figures of speech.'

CHAPTER FORTY-THREE

In which a cunning trap is set, and Como's character blossoms.

Dear Mister Quarry. I know you are innocent, and I can prove it. Send someone with $5,000 to Clarkesville amusement park at 5:30pm today. Tell them to go on the Ferris wheel carrying a toy rabbit. I will make contact and hand over the evidence to nail the true killers. Yours truly. A Friend.

"That should do it."

Como pressed *Send* to email the words to Herbert's address, triggering my plan to trick whoever was monitoring his email into thinking they were about to be shafted by an informer, and thus lure them into the open at the fairground. Well, plan might be too strong a word, as the next steps in my brilliant scheme for trapping the eavesdroppers hadn't yet come into my head. However, we still had some hours to kill before crossing that bridge, so to give my mind a break I told Como about Marcia's deception with the Clarkesville Giants footage.

"Why would she do that, Como? What's she trying to hide?"

"Could be she's just friggin' nuts, like everything else in this crazy case. We better have a word with her. Let's go."

Half an hour later, Como rapped for the third time on the door of 1007, Block D, Hacienda Apartments. I didn't mean it was the third time including the last two times we'd visited—I meant it was the third time he'd rapped on this visit, raps one and two having gone unanswered. We looked through the grimy windows of Marcia's apartment.

"It's empty. She's cleared out." Como looked at his watch. "You got her sister's number?"

I shook my head.

"No problem."

Como looked up the number of the coffee shop, then leant against the wall while he made the call. Having asked for Jacqueline, he explained who he was, asked for—and took a note of—Marcia's phone number and new address, told Jacqueline her sister wasn't in trouble but we just needed to make a routine enquiry, thanked her for her time, and hung up.

"Let's go see what Marcia's got to say."

Marcia's new address was in Assumption Springs, and no one was less surprised than I when Como's satnav told us to turn into the exact same housing development I'd visited five chapters ago when I called upon Marge Downberry. It could only mean one of two things in my book—either Marcia and Marge were entangled in the same conspiracy, or their geographic proximity was the product of an incompetent author too lazy to imagine new locations.

Como pulled up on the drive of the house, a sprawling construction in the latest fusion style. Sustainably built from straw and sticks to resemble a giant shoe, it featured fairytale turrets, a Rapunzel tower, a hobbit door, Hansel and Gretel gingerbread bargeboards and fetching green gables. It was within easy reach of the N66 and the top local schools, while line G of the Clarkesville County Metro was a five-minute walk.

"Someone's come into some money," said Como.

We walked to the hobbit door and pressed the buzzer. About five times. No one was in. Evidently a recent delivery driver had encountered the same lack of response, because a huge bouquet had been left by the side of the door. Como picked up the bouquet and looked at the envelope attached to it—on the back was the address of a local florist.

"Let's go see the flower lady and find out who's been sending big bouquets to Delgado," he said, exhibiting the disgraceful sexism that remains a deep-rooted trait within our law enforcement agencies.

"Not all florists are female, Como. Please exhibit less bias when associating role and gender. Remember, there's no place for sexism in a great work of literature."

"Whatever."

We parked in town and sauntered through a mall until we found the florist's. Como seemed not in the least surprised when the flower lady turned out to be a flower man—but he seemed somewhat alarmed when the flower man said:

"What can I do for you, Handsome? A bunch of roses for your lucky friend?"

Como flashed his credentials. "We're investigating a murder in Clarkesville."

The flower man gaped. He grasped Como's arm like a damsel clutching a knight. "A murder! Are we safe?"

"You're quite safe, Sir. We have a suspect in custody. We just need to ask a simple question."

"A question! Exciting—I've never helped the police before. What can I tell you, Lieutenant—my life story? You've such good cheekbones."

Como disentangled himself from the flower man's clutches.

"You delivered a bouquet to a Marcia Delgado here in Assumption Springs."

"Oh, yes! Wasn't it a beauty? An abundance of *thrustinia super-bum*, Lieutenant, with an impressive spray to finish. I bet that took your fancy. I can't get enough of it. And that single red-hot poker at the back—it's a long time since I saw such a glorious stem."

"We need to know who ordered the bouquet," said Como, oblivious to the floral innuendo.

"That was Mrs. DeVere, Sweetness—she's one of my biggest customers. Not as big as you, though." The flower man rubbed his hand over the tight fabric around Como's left bicep. Como swatted the hand away and pulled me by my sleeve to stand as a barrier between him and the florist.

"Do you have contact details for Mrs. DeVere?" he asked over my head.

"No, but I can give you mine."

"Does she live in Assumption Springs?"

"I've never asked—she's not my type. But you—I'd know if you lived in Assumption Springs. We don't have anyone quite as gorgeous as you in town."

I thought Como would press the flower man for more information, but he seemed anxious to leave the shop. On our way out, the flower man reached up a foot to fix a buttonhole to Como's lapel.

"This one's on me, Gorgeous. It's a forget-me-not."

"I'm sorry, Sir, but we can't accept gifts."

"Nonsense, Lieutenant, it's not a gift, just a token. There." Having adjusted the flower to his satisfaction, he stood back to admire either his handiwork or the huge chest it adorned. Lost for words for once, Como gave a slight bow and backed out of the shop.

"Let that be a lesson, Como," I said as we walked to the car. "Had you not displayed a subconscious gender bias, you might have met a charming lady florist, and might now be anticipating a romantic dinner."

"Not the way my luck's been since you turned up. Besides, Writer, if you're so hot about this gender bias shit, what makes you think I wouldn't want a date with that guy? I could be gay for all you know—so who's the biased one now?"

Como's critical question cut me to the quick. He was right—I'd assumed without a second thought, or even a first one, that he was straight, and yet I'd preached to him about gender bias.

Back in the Gran Torino, I fretted about my narrow-mindedness, while Como radioed HQ for a list of people called DeVere in and around Clarkesville. The answer came in three minutes—there were no people called DeVere in or around Clarkesville. I saw an opportunity to test Como's question about my blinkered view of his sexual preferences.

"What now, Como? Back to the florist's, I suppose."

With a look of resentful resignation, Como hauled himself out of the car, slamming the door with what seemed to me to be undue force. We paced in silence back to the shop. Upon our entrance, the flower man dropped the knobweed he was primping, and placed a hand to his cheek in a gesture of surprise to show he was pleased to see us again, or, rather, to see Como.

"It's the lovely Lieutenant, back so soon. Decided to ask for my number after all?"

"Not today, thank you, Sir."

"You big tease."

"According to police records, there's nobody called DeVere with a registered address in Clarkesville County. Do you know anything about Mrs. DeVere that might allow us to trace her?"

"You're so wasting your time, Lieutenant—she's not your type."

"Our interest in Mrs. DeVere is strictly official."

"Oh, I love it when you're strict, Lieutenant." The flower man fingered his weeping cherry. "She drives a Rolls Royce, a blue one, just the color of your friend's eyes. It's the only one like it in town. Will that help?"

"Thank you, yes." Como smiled and put two fingers to his temple as a salute of gratitude.

"You're so gorgeous, I think I'm going to faint."

I was feeling pretty faint myself at all this flirting nonsense. I went to nudge Como out of the shop, but he beat me to it, leaving me to say goodbye to the flower man, who was fanning his face with a large leaf.

"If I'm so biased," I said as we walked back through the mall, "how come you didn't ask him out? He was all over you."

"Maybe I just didn't fancy him."

"C'mon, Como. I've seen you carry on with Flora—no way you can be gay."

"I could be bi. Anyway, it's none of your business either way."

Back in the Gran Torino, I fretted about whether a character's sexual orientation was a writer's business, while Como radioed HQ and spoke with one of the dispatchers.

"Hi Shirl, it's Como. Yeah, good thanks. I need you to look up a car. Ain't got much to go on, just the make and color. Ready? It's a Rolls Royce. The color's...just a minute..." Como leant over, grabbed me by the chin, spun my head to face him and stared into my eyes—a most unnerving experience. "The color's a sort of dingy grey. Ok, we'll wait."

Como flapped the flap of the key fob to let off nervous energy while we waited to hear about dingy grey Rolls Royces. His flapping trebled in intensity when the information came through. There was only one registered owner of a grey Rolls Royce in Clarkesville County—Elijah Bow.

LESSON FORTY-FOUR

'Herbert.'

'Yes, Marco?'

'I saw a book reviewed on Goodreads. Some readers awarded five stars, and some one. How can that be?'

'The quality of a book is a matter of opinion, Marco. What appeals to one reader might repel another.'

'Does that mean I might not be able to write a book that appeals to everyone, Herbert?'

'I've told you before, Marco—you must take more care over your choice of words. You should have written 'anyone' in that sentence, not 'everyone'.'

CHAPTER FORTY-FOUR

In which Marco has a bad hair day.

At 5:23pm I handed Como a candy floss and we wandered to a bench where we could watch the entrance to the amusement park, hoping the trap we set in the previous chapter might soon be sprung. Earlier that afternoon, having completed our research in Assumption Springs, we had returned to Police HQ where we spent the intervening hours following humdrum police procedure of the sort that might have padded out a couple of chapters in a conventional thriller. I find that sort of thing far too boring to write, however, so to spare us all the tedium, I decided instead to summarize it via some utterly unconvincing dialogue to bring the readers up to speed.

"Well, Como, what did you make of this afternoon's discovery that the homes of Marcia Delgado and Marge Downberry are held in trust by a Panamanian law firm?"

"I'd sure like to get to the bottom of that, Writer, especially since we also discovered that the same law firm performs services for several companies owned by Elijah Bow."

"Yes, it's just a shame we didn't manage to find evidence to tie Bow to the houses."

We took bites at our candy floss to give the readers a chance to digest the implications of our discussion.

Having got the blatant exposition out of the way, I wondered whether I ought to build an atmospheric sense of expectation for the ensuing scene, perhaps describing the various rides in the funfair, the many musical sounds, the excited chatter of children hand-in-hand with parents, the thousands of colored lights, the shouts of the ride attendants drumming-up business, the metallic tings from the shooting range, the smells of toffee apples and hot dogs, the teenage girls pretending to ignore the teenage boys, the screams from the daredevils on the scarier rides, the drunks accosting strangers for change, the seagulls wheeling down to gulp discarded food, the nervous-looking woman carrying a toy rabbit, the goldfish that...

The nervous-looking woman carrying a toy rabbit!

I nudged Como.

"Look! Someone with a toy rabbit. Do you think she's our man?"

"Let's go see. Don't get too close."

Cunningly holding our candy floss to obscure our faces—or should that be candy flosses? —we sidled through the crowds to intercept the route of the rabbit-bearing woman, falling into her slipstream about twenty paces behind. From time to time she glanced about, clearly unnerved by her mission, though possibly not as unnerved as I was by the sheer nonsense I found myself typing. As she turned a corner, I gained a clear view of her face—it was Quimara Tann!

"I know her," I hissed to Como. "She was talking to me in the coffee shop, slagging off Herbert."

With huge excitement, on my part at least, we trailed her through the fairground. I wondered whether the readers would be in the least surprised to find she headed straight to the Ferris wheel, as per the instructions we had emailed to Herbert's address. We stood behind her in the line for tickets, Como having coached me to do nothing that might attract her attention.

"A ticket for a lovely lady," said the cheery attendant, helping Quimara into a wobbly gondola. "Two tickets, gentlemen? That'll be ten bucks."

Como preempted any suggestion he might pay.

"Don't look at me, Writer—this was your idea."

"Can't you put it on expenses?"

"Are you shitting me?"

"Hold this."

I gave Como my candy floss while I dug some cash from my stylish corduroys. Payment made, I stepped unsteadily into the next gondola, Como squeezing alongside me.

A bell rang.

"Whoa, sorry folks, that's the overload alarm. Can't have both of you gentlemen in the car, I'm afraid. Begging your pardons, if I could ask the smaller of you gentlemen to come forward and join this lady in the next car. You won't mind will you, Ma'am?"

From behind his candy floss, Como shot me a look loaded with warnings and well-intentioned advice, none of which I understood. Positioning my own candy floss as a visual shield to maintain my incognito status, I climbed in next to Quimara Tann. A big glob of pink goo stuck to the fur on the left ear of her toy rabbit.

"Sorry, sorry."

I tried to wipe it off with one hand, holding my sugary pink mask with the other. The sticky strands went all over my fingers. I juggled the stick of the candy floss to free my clean hand to get a hanky from my satchel, accidentally dropping more sugary gloop onto Quimara's skirt.

"Now look what you've done."

"Sorry, sorry."

I went to wipe it off.

"Don't touch me, you pervert."

"Sorry."

I squeezed as far away from Quimara as I could, while she dabbed at the candy floss deposits on her thigh. Our gondola was approaching the top of its vertical orbit, seemingly a mile above the fairground. I shut my eyes. Ever since a middle-ear infection in my twenties, my balance had been shot and I'd developed an uncontrollable fear of heights. I wanted to clutch the restraining bar with both hands, but I needed to keep my candy floss shield in place to stop her from recognizing me. I almost fell out over the side when Quimara Tann's phone went off, her unfortunate choice of ringtone being the sound of gunshots. Suppressing my panic, I tried to memorize her side of the conversation as she took the call...

"I'm there now...Yes, on the Ferris wheel...Yes, I've got the rabbit with me...No, only some idiot...Half an hour! It's five bucks a go...OK."

We circulated five times before the ride stopped and nudged forward car by car to let off the thrill-seekers. I clambered out in reverse to preserve my anonymity behind my candy floss, half of which had drooped to form a horrible mess all over my forearm. Holding the sticky confection before me, like Liberty brandishing her torch, I reversed from the ride to wait for Como to disembark from the next car. Quimara, meanwhile, had paid another five bucks to stay in her seat. We waited for her to be lifted into the heavens before we spoke.

"Good job you did nothing to attract her attention, Writer."

I ignored his sarcasm and told him about the conversation I'd overheard.

"Sounds like she's taking instructions," said Como. "You've got candy floss in your hair."

I held my iPad where I could see my reflection in the screen. The side of my head was a blur of pink. I angled my neck to view the extent of the mess.

"Does it show much?"

"Like a baboon's ass. You'd better put up your hood, or she'll spot you a mile off."

I pulled the hood of my anorak over my hair, wondering why I hadn't done it earlier instead of trying to hide behind candy floss. We walked to a bench and watched Quimara Tann. She paid for another four rides before she quit. She stuffed the toy rabbit in a bin and stomped off, Como and I tailing. We left the fairground and watched as she hailed a cab. Como flagged the next along, flashed his badge and told our driver not to lose her.

As soon as we'd left the kerb, our driver addressed our reflections in his mirror, unconcerned with what might be happening on the road ahead. "You guys know what's happening with the Quarry case?"

"No comment," said Como.

"I heard he'd murdered that poor girl and cut her to pieces."

"No comment," said Como.

"Let's hope the sick pedo fries in the chair."

"No comment," said Como.

"That's writers for you. They're all sick in the head. They should fry them all in the chair."

"Amen to that," said Como.

To take my mind off the hurtful conversation, I imagined our cab ride as if I were a big-name director making the movie of my mold-breaking book. The film, I supposed, would be mold-breaking too. The famous cab chase scene, as it would come to be known, might be a montage assembled from an eclectic mix of highly original shots, thus...

Shot #1. Two men sit in rear of cab, both Oscar-winning actors. The character to the left, faithfully portrayed by seven-foot tall, 400-pound, black Oscar-winner, glowers through window, while the character to the right—acne-ridden Oscar winner with bad posture—tries to unglue hood of anorak from pink sugary hair.

Shot#2. View from driver's seat. Miscellaneous objects clutter top of dashboard. Rosary beads dangle from mirror. One after another pass the vertical struts of huge suspension bridge over River Clarke.

Shot#3. Aerial view of cabs in tandem on fourteen-lane stretch of Clarkesville expressway, turning off at downtown cloverleaf.

Shot#4. View from camera bolted low on door of cab, showing front wheel bouncing over ruts as the cab drives through columns of steam rising from vents in the road.

Shot#5. View over roof of cab driving through curving section of the Clarke tunnel.

Shot#6. Third vehicle skids to avoid cab#2 which has shot a red light to keep on tail of cab#1.

Shot#7. Cab#2 taking a corner in a tail drift.

Shot#8. In rear of cab#2, both men lean with the g-force of the turn, preferably not in different directions.

Shot#9. View from road surface showing undersides of both cabs passing overhead.

Shot#10. Cab#2 skids into large stack of cardboard boxes to avoid woman pushing pram across the street.

Shot#11. Cab#1 pulls up outside Clarkesville Hilton. Quimara Tann leaves cab and pays driver through window.

Shot#12. Cab#2 is pulled up on opposite side of street, where the actors waste no time springing into action, the action being mainly an argument about which of them should pay the fare.

"I haven't got any cash, Como—besides, I paid for the Ferris wheel. And the candy floss."

"Make your frigging minds up, I can't stop here all night," chipped in the cabby.

Como reluctantly pulled a note from his wallet, and we waited while the driver rooted through old newspapers to find a pen to write a receipt, rather spoiling the tension of the moment.

After Como had recorded the expense in his logbook and stowed the receipt in his wallet, we crossed the street to the hotel.

"What d'you say to that, Writer?" asked Como, nodding at a car in one of the VIP parking slots.

It was a dingy grey Rolls Royce with the registration EB1. Wow!

In the hotel, Quimara Tann had disappeared. We wandered through the public areas, checking the bars and the restaurants—Como even made me check the ladies' restroom, where the appearance of a male intruder with pink blobs in his hair caused a degree of consternation among the toilet goers. Drawing a blank, we went to reception, where Como flashed his badge. Before we could ask a question, the receptionist said:

"You'll be wanting Chief McGee? He's in Meeting Room Five, second floor."

LESSON FORTY-FIVE

'Herbert, what is the purpose of literature?'

'The purpose of literature, Marco, is to entertain, to educate, and to provoke thought and emotion.'

'What about making money, Herbert?'

'Money is a secondary consideration for the truly great author, Marco. You must write for yourself, not for the market. If others like your work, so be it.'

'But what if they don't like it, Herbert?'

'If it is truly great literature, it will be appreciated in time. Remember Moby Dick, Marco. In its day it was a flop, but now it is recognized as a classic.'

'Should I make sure my book includes a whale, then, Herbert?'

CHAPTER FORTY-FIVE

In which, thankfully, Marco decides it's nearly time for the big ending.

We took the backstairs to the second floor and followed signs for the conference suites. Meeting Room 5 was to the left of a communal area where a selection of enticing refreshments had been laid out for conference participants. We stuffed our pockets with muffins and settled down to watch from behind a corner.

About three muffins into our wait, Quimara Tann left the meeting room and walked to the elevator, checking her reflection on the polished surface of its control panel. About five muffins after that, out came Elijah Bow and Chief McGee. Bow looked angry, McGee placatory. They stood by the elevator; as its doors opened, Bow said, "Just make sure you sort it."

We waited for the elevator to go, then sauntered over to the meeting room. Como edged open the door to look inside. The room was empty. Well, not empty exactly—what I meant was there was nobody else in it. Obviously, it wouldn't be empty—what idiot would imagine a police chief and a billionaire would call their accomplice to a meeting in an entirely empty room? *'Mister Bow would like to book Meeting Room 5 for this evening, and can you please ensure all the furniture's removed beforehand.'* I've never heard such nonsense. Anyway, where were we...

The room was a small one, with a central table and six chairs. Pencils and pads of paper, all proudly bearing the Hilton logo, had been placed by each of the chairs to allow their occupants to doodle absently. I was wondering whether the mention of the Hilton logo might lead to some kind of placement deal—room discounts, or free upgrades perhaps—when Como drew my attention to one of the pads, the top sheet of which bore the imprint of words written with a heavy hand on a sheet above it. I shook my head in disbelief—how could he have indulged in such an obvious cliché? Never mind—I'd just have to make the most of it.

"Can you make out what it says?"

Como held the pad at an angle to the light. "Not here—we'll have to take it back to HQ. C'mon."

Como told me to put the pad in my satchel, and we headed downstairs. I wondered what we might find on the pad, and, more urgently, where we'd left our cars. Thankfully I hadn't written anything about how we'd travelled to the amusement park, so I was able to say:

"Gosh, Como, it was a coincidence that we tracked Tann to the Hilton, since you'd left your car right next door earlier this afternoon."

"Did I?"

A bit implausible, perhaps, but it would save another argument about cab fares.

Como drove us to police HQ, where we went to his desk. No, make that his room, as we needed privacy. Como latched his door behind us and pulled down the blinds. From one of the deeper drawers in his desk he pulled some specialist dusting gear from between the empty bourbon bottles.

"Okay, let's see what we got."

He angled his lamp to shine obliquely on the pad and brushed some fine dust onto the surface of the paper.

Like magic, patterns appeared. Round the edge of the sheet were childish doodles with a police theme—handcuffs, a barred cell, nightsticks, guns, bullets, a police car shaped like a Lamborghini—but near the center a single sentence was written in capitals.

GET SUSHING TO TRACE THE EMAIL.

And for those of you who are having trouble keeping up, clearly 'the email' means the one we'd sent to Herbert's address, pretending to have evidence about his innocence.

"Sushing?" Como looked at me as if the appearance of the name was my fault, which I suppose it was. "He's the big shot you saw in Nassau? Looks like he's the one spying on Quarry's email, which would fit the trace we got to a site in the Caribbean."

"But...but..."

"But what?"

But I had no idea what to write next. I remembered Herbert's advice and typed at random, having first taken a sneaky look at Wikipedia...

"But strictly speaking, Nassau isn't in the Caribbean—it's off the coastal shelf in the Atlantic proper."

"Writer, no one's done anything on a strictly speaking basis since Page One, so don't let a little thing like that bother you."

"But Sushing told me all about Marcia and showed me her paintings of Herbert. Why would he do that if he was part of the conspiracy?"

"That's the difference between true crime and fiction, Writer. In true crime there are always things that don't make sense."

"So, what do we do?"

"You can do what the frig you like. I'm going home to eat. Wanna come along?"

I didn't have anything else to do, and I thought the book could do with a scene where the crime fighting duo do some male bonding, so I said I'd go along. Twenty minutes later we were at Como's place—a nice, ordinary house in a nice, ordinary suburban area where nice, ordinary people lived nice, ordinary lives, the kind of place where I'd always wanted to live when I was growing up in a rough part of the Bronx. Como unlocked the door and showed me to the living room.

"Make yourself at home. I'll get some beers."

I flopped on Como's settee and flicked through the channels on his small, old-fashioned TV. The quality of the picture was atrocious, so I switched it off. Como came in wearing an apron, with beers and nuts on a tray.

"Dig in. Cheers."

"Cheers."

We clinked glasses.

"Nice place."

"Ain't so bad. I don't get to spend much time here. You any good at cooking?"

I told Como my Bronx mom was the cook in the family.

"Well you can help anyhow. Bring that through."

I took my beer into the kitchen, where Como looked through his stores to see what ingredients he could throw together for an impromptu feast. When the ingredients turned out to be a yellowing cauliflower, a tin of tuna, a moldy pack of bacon and some peanut butter, Como took off his apron and said let's go to Mario's.

Mario's was a popular pizza place in a rough-looking part of town. There was a line of people waiting for seats, but Como strode past them to be greeted by the doormen, who seemed delighted to see him.

"Hey, Como, how've you been? Sorry, bud," he looked my way. "You gotta join the line there."

"He's with me," said Como.

"Sure thing, Como. In you go, fellas."

Eating pizza, we bonded over a typical alpha-male conversation, an eclectic exploration of girlfriends (mainly Como's, sadly), grooming products, fashion, names for babies, celebrities we fancied, our mums, this year's colors, weight control, favorite cocktails, best locations for honeymoons, and music. Como was a big jazz fan.

"That's a definite plus of being single. Since my girlfriend moved out, I can let rip with the vibraphone any time I like."

"What about the neighbors?"

"They moved out a week after the girlfriend."

We argued about our top fifty lists of great vibraphonists, and the relative merits of the five- and six-mallet style, before Como said:

"How about you—what music gets Ocram's heels tappin'?"

"I'm getting into razz."

"Razz? I ain't never heard of it."

"No, I invented it myself." Two sentences ago, I didn't add. "It's a fusion of jazz and rap. I'm sure it'll catch on once it gets on YouTube."

"Jazz and rap? Shit, that sounds good. You made any razz videos?"

"Not yet. I've been too busy with my writing."

"That's what we'll do when this crazy case is cracked, Writer—a weekend of razz. Yeah, I'm really up for it." Como started to play air vibraphone, hunching his shoulders and screwing his eyes tight shut as he got into some imaginary groove. The other diners looked on as if concerned for his mental health. "Doo be dah dah daah, deee bop a daah daah doohbey. Gimme five!"

I slapped Como's massive hand, mine barely covering his palm. He gulped his last slice of pizza. "We could get some video up. I always wanted to be famous. You finished, or shall we get some more?"

"Honest, Como—I couldn't eat another slice. Let me get these."

Como didn't argue, for once, so I went to pay for our meal. Mario, the proprietor, said his card machine was on strike. I had no money, so he took me to the door and pointed me at an ATM down the street. Como was chatting with a couple of girls at the table next to ours, so I decided to leave him to it and went to get some cash on my own. I'd hardly walked a hundred yards before I regretted my impulsiveness— the street had an edgy, menacing feel I hadn't noticed when I'd promenaded down it with Como by my side. I felt as if predatory eyes were upon me as I withdrew a hundred bucks and furtively stuffed them in my back pocket, instinctively folding the notes to make them appear a smaller prize for a would-be mugger. As I walked back to the pizza place, my hood raised and my head lowered to avoid attention, a group of men ambled towards me from across the street—heavyset types whose garb and accessories were straight out of a props cupboard labelled 'thugs.' I gave my hundred bucks an extra fold and my head an extra droop, aiming to avoid all eye contact. My concern for my cash was misplaced, however—the thugs had other interests, as their leader's next words showed:

"Hey, look here, boys. Guess what I've found. Our snooper friend."

There were ten of them. They looked drunk. I was too scared to describe them, so you'll have to imagine them—typical skanky types found in every similar scene you've seen on TV. The leader strolled toward me with a smug look that became more venomous with every step.

"We warned, you, Snooper. Don't say we didn't warn you."

I backed away, my flight-or-flight instinct kicking in. The other guys fell in behind the lead thug. I didn't have time to check, but I think they were carrying the usual writer-basher gear—baseball bats, lengths of three-by-two with nails sticking out, tire irons, bicycle chains, leather belts coiled around knuckles, flick-knives, and at least one vicious-looking handbag.

I felt vulnerable and afraid. Where was my Bronx mom when I needed her? The head thug started prodding me on the chest.

"What have you got to say for yourself, Snooper?"

It was a good question. I thought of a warning along the lines of *I used to be a boxer*, but I didn't think it would have sufficient effect. I was about to fall to my knees and beg, when a deep, angry voice said:

"Hey, what the fuck?"

It was Como, striding toward us with an outraged glare. Sensing menace, the thugs closed into three ranks behind their leader—two directly behind him, three behind them, and four on the back row.

"He's been helping that pedo," said the leader, presuming to win Como's support for his cause.

I expected Como to flash his badge with instructions to disperse, but he seemed to favor a more direct and pragmatic approach to law enforcement. His timing was perfect. He extended the fist of foe-ship into the face of the lead thug. The lead thug slammed over backwards, taking out the two guys behind him, who took out the three guys behind them, who took out their pals on the back row. Full strike!

"Good thing you came along Como. I might have got myself into trouble for assault if he'd needled me one more time."

Como ignored my shadowboxing and went through pockets looking for ID. At least four of the thugs had pass cards for a meat-packing plant on the edge of town.

"See the logo?" said Como, passing one of the cards to me. It showed the brand of the meat-packing business with the tagline *A Division of EBI*.

"What about it?"

"EBI. Ring any bells?"

I listened. The night air was utterly bell-less. Como replied to my blank look.

"Elijah Bow Industries."

Elijah Bow Industries!

I hoped the readers were imagining me to be near a wall, because at Como's words I slumped against one, unable to face the implications of yet another nonsensical plot twist.

"You okay, Writer?"

"Sorry, Como, I was just struggling to cope with all these new developments."

"You're struggling? How about me? All you have to do is make it up—I'm the one who has his head in a noose if I don't solve this crazy case. And speaking of heads in nooses, how are we going to explain what happened to Father Kellogg? How are we going to explain the Delgado twins both being on TV, and the stuffed bodies and all the other batshit stuff you've written?"

I looked at Como's face, a face I now knew better than my own, a face that radiated the same perplexity and frustration I felt myself at all the ludicrous red herrings I'd written. I knew I wasn't meant to think about my writing, but I had to get it under control for both our sakes. At least Jackson Pollock had a canvass to bound his efforts—there was only so much space to fill with paint. Writing was different—there could be no end to it. For an awful moment, I imagined myself and Como doomed to pursue the eternally spreading branches of an ever more ludicrous plot. The horrific vision made my knees give way—I slid down the wall and sat on the filthy sidewalk, mentally spent. Enough was enough. The lunacy had to stop.

I reached out my hand to Como—he took it and pulled me upright. I wiped the dirt of the street off the seat of my trousers, metaphorically signifying that I was sweeping aside the trivial loose ends of my story. I checked my watch. There were twenty-two hours to kill before the big dénouement. I couldn't face writing any more padding, so I pressed my mental fast-forward button. Skipping quickly through the walk back to Como's, my crashing out on his settee, an unappetizing breakfast with no superfood infusions, a long call from my Bronx mom, two hours wishing I wasn't listening to Como playing his vibraphone, lunch, a snooze, a trip to the dress-hire store, a change of clothes, the drive to Clarkesville Marina, the long argument with Como about which of us was to pay at the car park, and the boat out to the island, I returned to normal speed just as I found myself standing to officiate at the grand dinner.

LESSON FORTY-SIX

'Tell me, Herbert, what should a writer do when he has his readers on the ropes?'

'He should sock it to them mercilessly, Marco.'

CHAPTER FORTY-SIX

In which revelation leads to reversal.

Ting ting ting ting ting ting ting. I tapped a glass until I had the complete attention of my chattering guests. Smoothing the tails of my clawhammer dinner jacket, I glanced at the expectant faces around the table as I waited for the next thing to come into my head. There were the McGees—Chief McGee confident and relaxed, his nephew Scoobie less so—Herbert's spurned lover Marcia, her face beautiful yet brittle, Bow and Sushing, two billionaires at ease in each other's company, Marge Downberry, the kindly ex head of midwifery, and Quimara Tann, the social climber reveling in the glamorous setting of the faux baronial dining hall, her excited eyes reflecting the flames from the huge granite fireplace, over which was hung a splendid painting of a mighty stag beset by hounds—presumably the hotel's famous Pollock.

"Ladies and gentlemen. I trust you are looking forward to the dinner I have arranged to celebrate the launch of my forthcoming book. As is customary on such occasions, the host is obliged to say a few words, but I promise you will not be detained long."

Not by me, that is.

"You might be wondering why I invited you to my modest celebration. The answer, ladies and gentlemen, is that you have all, in some way, helped me discover the truth about the Herbert Quarry affair.

"It is three weeks since the Clarkesville County Police found Herbert Quarry kneeling in a pool of blood by the dismembered body of a young girl. Three weeks since Herbert was arrested and taken to the Clarkesville County Penitentiary to await trial for the murder of

Lola Kellogg. Three weeks, ladies and gentlemen, since he was *framed*."

Until those words my audience had been silent. I had been at the center of every intent gaze. Now various expressions of disgust and dissent animated the features of my characters. It was Elijah Bow, the self-assured industrialist, who voiced the thought shared by all around the dinner table...

"And I suppose, Mister Ocram, you are about to explain how you have brilliantly deduced one of us was responsible for framing your friend."

I waited for the ensuing chorus of chuckles to die out.

"No Mister Bow," I said, mentally twisting the waxed points of my moustache. "I am about to explain how you have *all* been responsible for framing my friend."

The stir caused by my earlier remarks was now intensified tenfold. I saw Chief McGee reaching for a revolver I imagined to be hidden in the pocket of his dinner jacket, but Como had seen it too and had already stood and drawn his own gun.

"Don't anybody move!" commanded Como. "Let's hear what Mister Ocram has to say."

I nodded my thanks and continued my exposé, inventing it on the spot as I spoke.

"It was clear to me that Herbert could not have murdered his tragic young lover. I have known Herbert for many years. I know him as a boxer knows his coach. I know of his Buddhist convictions. I know he is incapable of such a violent crime."

I paused to let the more sophisticated of my readers admire my use of anaphora, and to let the less sophisticated of my readers look up the word to see what it meant, until various grunts and tics of impatience from among my guests prompted me to move on...

"So, I set about discovering who else might possess the combination of opportunity, means, and motive to kill Kellogg and incriminate Quarry. This, ladies and gentlemen, is the story I have uncovered...

"Exactly a year before Lola Kellogg was brutally slain, Marcia Delgado leaves Clarkesville County Lunatic Asylum for the first time in nine years. You, Professor Sushing, take pity on the beautiful young woman whose obsession you have studied for the previous three thousand two hundred and eighty-five days. You use your influence to get her a job at Clarkesville County Hospital, a hospital to which you have been a generous benefactor. You have no specific aim in mind, but a general hope that her return to the community might catalyze some new revelation about Herbert Quarry, some new revelation you might use to your advantage in your long standing vendetta against my friend and mentor.

"Gradually Marcia is re-assimilated into Clarkesville society. Most weeks, she visits the nail bar, a venue as popular for its gossip as for its exquisite nail varnishes. There, one afternoon three months ago..."

I switched to flashback mode to nurture the interest of my yawning readers.

Marcia is waiting for her appointment. She has arrived early, and quickly becomes bored with the tattered magazines she has read on countless visits. She looks at the other clients undergoing treatment. One is an expensively dressed woman whom Marcia recognizes as Mrs. DeVere—a well-known figure in town, but a new visitor to the nail-bar. As Mrs. DeVere is prepared for a pedicure, Marcia sees a birthmark on the sole of her right foot, a birthmark just like one she has seen on Scoobie McGee's young daughter Jenny.

Marcia's thoughts race. Gossip had been flying in Clarkesville for years about Jenny McGee's family and the Kelloggs. Some said Jenny was Kellogg's love child. Others that Lola was the result of a tryst between Scoobie and Mrs. Kellogg. Still others said both children had been born through sperm donation. Marcia knew enough about the gossip to wonder about Mrs. DeVere. Who could she be? She must be related to Jenny McGee in some way, but how?

Determined to know, Marcia decides to follow as Mrs. DeVere leaves the nail-bar. The receptionist shouts 'What about your appointment?' But Marcia has already turned the block in Mrs. DeVere's wake.

Marcia sees Mrs. DeVere get into a Rolls Royce, a distinctive car anywhere, but especially in Clarkesville. Marcia quickly unlocks her own car and follows the Rolls through the lazy Clarkesville traffic. Mrs.

DeVere drives smartly out of town onto the N66 heading north. Marcia checks her mirror, then joins the N66 a couple of cars behind.

After a twenty-minute drive too tedious to relate in detail, the Rolls sweeps majestically through elaborate gates Marcia knows to be the entrance to Elijah Bow's lavish property. Marcia pulls her car into some bushes and follows on foot. She sees the Rolls halt by a block of garages. Mrs. DeVere swings her legs out of the car then climbs out. A man appears from the end of the garage block, squeezing a chamois leather. Mrs. DeVere tosses keys to the man, then heads into the house. Intrigued, Marcia follows as close as she dares, hiding behind the shrubs in the garden. Seeing Mrs. DeVere through a large window, she creeps up to it and peers within.

Mrs. DeVere is by the fireplace at the far side of the room. She kicks off her heels and drops her hat on a table. She removes her earrings and places them in a small box on the mantelpiece. And then... Marcia can hardly believe her eyes... Mrs. DeVere takes off a wig to reveal a short mannish haircut. Now Marcia understands. Mrs. DeVere is Elijah Bow.

Marcia utters a gasp of surprise, a gasp stifled by a huge hand clamped over her mouth while powerful arms enfold her body. Bluther Cale has grabbed her from behind and carries her bodily into the house as if she weighed no more than a beach ball.

Powerless to resist, Marcia finds herself dropped on her feet in the very room into which she had been peering moments earlier. Elijah Bow, still in the dress of Mrs. DeVere, speaks angrily:

"What is the meaning of this?"

"I found her vnooping through the window," says Bluther Cale.

"Snooping," says Bow. "What do you mean by snooping?" he asks of Marcia. "Don't you know I could have trespassers shot?"

"I'm sorry Mister Bow," wails Marcia. "I didn't know it was you. I thought it was Mrs. DeVere."

"Well, now you know I am Mrs. DeVere. What do you have to say for yourself?"

In a panic Marcia blurts out all she knows. About the birthmarks on the feet of Mrs. DeVere and Jenny McGee. About thinking Mrs. DeVere must be related to Jenny McGee. About following Mrs. DeVere to see where she lived. "Honestly, Mister Bow," she wails. "I wouldn't have done it if I had known it was you. I'm sorry. Really, I'm sorry."

"You have no need to be sorry. You have actually done me a favor. However, you must not mention a word of what you have learned to anyone unless I instruct you otherwise. If you fail to be discreet, I have the money and the connections to have you returned to the lunatic asylum. Do I make myself understood?"

"Oh yes, yes, Mister Bow," Marcia kneels and clasps her hands in supplication at the billionaire's feet. "Please don't send me back!"

"Then do as you are told. Return to Clarkesville and act normally until you hear from me again. Go!"

I stared at Marcia Delgado. "That was how it happened, yes?"

She dropped her gaze into her lap, a sure sign of guilt.

"So, ladies and gentlemen, that is how Elijah Bow learns that Jenny McGee is his other love child. Staggering news, you will understand. However, not as staggering as what follows. For Bow had never known about his birthmark. It was on the sole of his foot, by his heel, an area of his body he would never normally see. With the help of a mirror he examines it, and his blood runs cold. For one thing is certain, he has never seen such a birthmark on the foot of his beloved Lola."

I decided to pause at this point to allow Como and the readers to reflect on the momentous importance of the revelation—everyone else around the table already knew about it, of course.

"So, Mister Bow," I looked him in the eye as I spoke, "you now knew that the girl to whom you had left your fortune in a binding contract with the Kelloggs was not your biological daughter after all. It took you three weeks to figure out how it had come about and decide what you were going to do. Three weeks during which you recalled the fire at the County Hospital maternity wing, the fire just after Lola was born. Three weeks during which you examined press records and found that one mother and one baby girl had died in that fire. Three weeks in which you guessed it was your daughter who had perished, and somehow the Kelloggs ended up with another baby, the baby of the woman who had died in the fire. Three weeks in which you and your expensive lawyers confronted Marge Downberry, who admitted she had given the other baby to the Kelloggs..."

"I did, I did, I did," wailed Marge from the other end of the vast dining table. "I did, and I would have done it again too."

There was now a touch of defiance among her tears. I continued her story...

"Yes. You found that Frances Kellogg's daughter by Elijah Bow had perished in the fire, asphyxiated in the deadly fumes. Frances Kellogg, the young woman to whom motherhood had meant everything, had tragically lost her baby girl within hours of giving birth. You couldn't bear to see her suffer, so you switched another baby girl, one born shortly beforehand, one passably alike to the real Kellogg baby, one whose mother had also perished in the fire and would grow up an orphan. At a stroke you were able to fix two ruined lives, and your instinct for good overrode your professional code of midwifery ethics.

"And so it remained your secret, and your secret alone until one day you are visited by Elijah Bow, a man you have known only as one of the two major benefactors to the Clarkesville County Hospital. Bow had guessed the truth, and now with a mixture of bribes and threats he gets it from your own mouth. You show him the photographs of the babies' feet, and he knows for sure: Lola is not his biological daughter. Some weeks later he thanks you for your honesty by buying a house in which you can retire, a house in Assumption Springs, close enough that he can keep an eye on you but far enough to take you out of the Clarkesville gossip machine."

I now turned to Bow.

"Which leaves you, Mister Bow, with a problem. How can you now stop all your wealth being left to Lola Kellogg—a cuckoo in your genetic nest—and instead ensure it is passed to Jenny McGee, your one surviving offspring?

"But a man like Mister Bow never has a problem for long. Mister Bow is resourceful. He has friends at City Hall. Contacts. Backstairs influence. He could not have become a leading industrialist with billions in public contracts without knowing his way around, without buying-off officialdom from time to time. Naturally he knows Chief McGee...

"So, the Chief is invited to Bow's ranch. Over a whiskey or two, Bow is disarmingly frank. The story comes out. McGee's family stands to inherit billions, but for one small problem: Lola.

"Bow doesn't know it at the time, but McGee has his own reasons for wanting rid of Lola. Some weeks earlier, you, Quimara Tann, had gone to see McGee..."

Quimara Tann had barely slept for a week. All she could think about was how that slime-ball Quarry had left her beautiful daughter in the lurch for that young slag Lola Kellogg. Quimara's dreams of celebrity lay in tatters. Pedophiles like Quarry shouldn't be free on the streets; they should be locked up.

Eventually she stoked her indignation to the point where she had to take action. She marched into Clarkesville County Police HQ and told the desk sergeant she needed to see 'whoever is in charge here.' The sergeant went into a back room and phoned Chief McGee. There was a woman in reception demanding to see him. Seemed bananas but was a real looker. Send her up, said his chief.

Quimara Tann was escorted to Chief McGee's office where she found herself confronted by a large, capable-looking man in his early sixties who was appraising her with a bold stare.

"What can I do for you, Mrs...."

"Tann, Quimara Tann." Quimara held out a hand which the Chief shook.

"What can I do for you Mrs. Tann?" asked the Chief, helpfully adding another nineteen words to my book.

"I'm here to report a pedophile."

Quimara Tann told Chief McGee all that had happened, omitting few details, and showed him various incriminating documents she had stolen from Herbert's study. McGee was prepared to believe all she said. Rumors about Quarry and young girls had been rife, and here at last was solid evidence.

He thanked Mrs. Tann and told her he would investigate as a matter of urgency. He shook her hand as she left, holding on to it for a good few seconds more than necessary. Mrs. Tann thought she had found a champion who would help get that bastard Quarry locked up where he belonged.

"But things didn't go as you'd planned, did they Chief? You got Lola in for a chat, and she outfoxed you. Show me what Herbert Quarry makes you do, you said. And she showed you alright—in your own office, then threatened to expose you as a pedophile if you exposed Quarry. When your wits returned you figured it out. You found Lola and told her her threats were empty, there was no concrete proof, it would be her word against yours, the word of a wayward girl against that of a police chief. But that was your first mistake, McGee, telling her there was no proof. Your second mistake was helping her get proof. Over the next few days she was a repeat visitor at police HQ, needing to tell Chief McGee her story. Then the blow falls. Lola tells you she's got proof after all—she's pregnant, and you're the father."

McGee shifted in his chair, his face taut with rage at my accusation.

"There you were, Chief McGee, worrying how to solve your problem with Lola, when the richest man in Clarkesville intimates he wants your help to do away with her, and offering his entire fortune to your family in return.

"Chief McGee breaks the news to Scoobie here. At first Scoobie doesn't want to know. He can't believe he's not Jenny's father. He can't believe Bow is. He can't believe his uncle, the police chief, is serious about killing Lola. But blood, ladies and gentlemen, is thicker than water, and eventually the pact is sealed. Scoobie McGee will help his uncle for the benefit of his daughter, the daughter he now knows to be his by marriage alone. Lola's fate is sealed. All that is missing is a plan.

"And this is where you come in, Professor Sushing. One evening, you and Bow are guests at a charity gala for Clarkesville County Hospital. As the dreary formalities of the evening pass, what is more natural than the two billionaire men-of-the-world drifting together to share cigars on the terrace, to escape the babble of the 'little people' within. Then, quite by chance, Elijah Bow mentions Herbert Quarry. For Professor Sushing, whose inhibitions have been dissolved by a copious intake of wine, the name is a trigger for a venomous outpouring of hatred. Still smarting from the outcome of the court case, you tell Bow how your whole life had been devoted to the cause of literature, how book after book you had written had been rejected by publishers for having insufficient 'market appeal,' how you were sick to your very core to see bestsellers written by illiterate morons, books crammed with cliché, unnatural dialogue, mangled syntax, repellent characters, repetitive flashbacks, nauseating metaphors, redundant words, formatting gimmicks, bizarre and unconvincing plot-twists, books which for all their manifest faults were still feted by the corrupt critics, books typified by the works of Herbert Quarry. It became clear to Bow that you had a manic hatred of Herbert Quarry and all he represented, and you would do anything to see his downfall.

"Here at last was the ally Bow needed to complete his dastardly planning. Professor Sushing was world-renowned as an expert in software techniques, leading the field in the development of quantum computing and sixth-generation programming languages. It would be a trivial matter for the Professor to implant software on the PC of Herbert Quarry, a simple matter for him to eavesdrop on every communication to and from that computer.

"Gradually the eavesdropping revealed a picture of the affairs and intentions of Herbert Quarry and Lola Kellogg. In secret meetings at the Clarkesville Hilton, Bow, Sushing and the two McGees laid their plans. Lola would have to be killed, and to divert all suspicion a patsy must be found, a man who could be so convincingly framed for her murder that there was no possible outcome for him but a trip to the chair. And what better man than Herbert Quarry? A rich and famous author, a person loathed by all right-thinking men, and an alleged pedophile to boot. There would be no jury alive who would fail to convict him if the right trail of evidence were laid.

"So, Professor, from your software labs in Nassau, you planted emails on Herbert's computer, seeming to beg for Lola to meet him.

"On the day of the killing, Chief and Scoobie McGee are in a patrol car together. They see Lola walking through the woods towards Herbert's house, and they chase her on foot. Lola sees them and assumes the Chief is planning some kind of threesome with his nephew, so she takes off and runs. And this is where a complication arises. Bluther Cale. Bluther was in love with Lola and had been following her. Bluther sees Lola chased by the two policemen, so he chases after them. He sees one of the two men floor Lola with a blow. He roars with rage, the noise betraying his presence. The two policemen round on him and kill him with blows from their nightsticks. The McGees bundle Lola's warm body into their car in an evidence bag, drive to Herbert's house, take one of Herbert's knives and cut up the body on the floor. They wear police-issue gloves, overshoes, and overalls to keep any of their DNA off Lola's body and any of Lola's DNA off theirs. After dismembering Lola's body, they pick up Cale's corpse. One of them drives Cale in Cale's car, the other follows in the prowler. They get to the cliff, move Cale to the driver's side of the seat, and push the car over the edge. They make a prearranged call to Delgado, who rings the emergency line from a public phone to report that Herbert is cutting up Lola in his study. And the rest, ladies and gentlemen, we know."

Elijah Bow started a slow ironic clap. "Congratulations, Mister Ocram. You have pieced it together wonderfully. We hadn't counted on having a writer on our case. We assumed we would be dealing with the regular law enforcement agencies, but I see we made a mistake in that regard."

"It wasn't a mistake, Bow, it was just bad luck. Bad luck for you that Herbert had a loyal friend who would move heaven and earth to prove his innocence."

"And what do you plan to do now, young man?" This time it was Professor Sushing who asked the question.

"What do you think? We are going to call for back-up, then have you all taken back to Clarkesville. Herbert Quarry will be freed on the basis of your confession, and you will take his place in the Clarkesville County Penitentiary."

Just as I finished speaking, all the lights went out.

LESSON FORTY-SEVEN

'Herbert.'

'Yes, Marco'?

'What was it you said about credulity?'

'Never mind, Marco. It's too late to be worrying about that now.'

CHAPTER FORTY-SEVEN

In which we wave goodbye to the last traces of realism.

There were sounds of a scuffle.

"Don't nobody move."

It was Chief McGee's voice. Scoobie McGee thumbed a lighter—its feeble glow revealed Como unconscious on the floor. Each McGee held a gun, one of which was pointed at me.

"You, Writer, sit down next to your friend, and no tricky moves or you'll both get it."

I wasn't sure what tricky moves he expected me to write, but I sat on the floor, hoping not to poop in my hired tuxedo. I'd never been so scared. I'd invented Como as a tough giant to keep me out of trouble, and here he was, felled by a cowardly blow from a minor character. I had no idea what to type—the next sentence could be my last. I stared at the proudly defiant stag in the Pollock over the granite mantlepiece of the vast fireplace, a metaphor for my own predicament. I could scarcely believe paint hurled from a tin could have created such a vivid and moving scene. If Pollock could achieve that, surely I could invent some amazing plot twist to save the respective bacons of Como and his young Writer.

Inspired, I let the action flow.

Como stirred beside me. I helped him sit against the wall. About us an argument raged.

"You shouldn't have let him snoop around," said Scoobie.

"Don't look at me," said his uncle, "he said he was investigating Quarry."

"Well you fell for that alright, just as you let that slut Kellogg wind you round her finger." Marcia pointed her own finger in accusation as she spoke.

Tap tap tap tap tap tap tap. As I had done a chapter ago, Sushing called for the attention of the room, hammering the butt of a wine bottle on the polished oak of the dining table.

"Leave the arguments for later. You," he nodded at Scoobie "light the candles, then find some lamps. Keep them covered," he added to Chief McGee, meaning me and Como, obviously, not the lamps.

Sushing and Bow conferred in private murmurs until Bow nodded his agreement to a conclusion Sushing subsequently announced.

"This is what we will do, ladies and gentlemen. We will return to Clarkesville in two boats, one large, one small. We will put our friends here in the smaller boat. They will have an accident and their boat will capsize. A search will find the overturned boat, and they will be presumed lost at sea. When we are asked, we will be shocked—we did not see or hear anything amiss. Ocram and the Lieutenant had drunk much during the celebration. They were unsteady on their feet. Perhaps their intoxicated state contributed to the accident. We should blame ourselves, ladies and gentlemen, for not having insisted they share our safer craft."

"An accident? What kind of accident?" asked McGee, the question being one of interest to all of us, especially me.

"That's your specialty, not mine. Just make sure the bodies are never found."

"Okay, everyone. Down to the boats." Chief McGee waved his gun at me. "You first, Writer."

We filed outside. The complete absence of electrical light showed the island had suffered a power cut, no doubt due to poor maintenance of its diesel generator in the off season, I thought, draping the flimsiest veil of plausibility over the previous scene.

There was a waxing moon, its light sufficient to guide us to the jetty. As we walked—Como and I at gunpoint—Sushing coached the other conspirators: what to say to the police, what not to say, how to act, the importance of sticking to the story, the paramount need for secrecy. He talked with utter confidence in his plan, and utter disregard for its intended victims, as if Como and I were already dead. How could I, a naïve and inexperienced writer, hope to outwit such a cunning and ruthless character?

As we approached the moorings, a tide of panic engulfed me. I cursed Herbert. I was about to die, and it was all his fault. *Break the mold of literature,* he said. *Write as Pollock painted. Don't think ahead. Type the first words that come into your head.* Well I'd tried and look where it had got me—about a page away from an awful death. Why hadn't I written that the Clarkesville Bay Island Hotel was renowned for the reliability of its electricity supply, or even set the dinner in a downtown hotel? Better still, why hadn't I avoided this whole farcical charade by writing a book about being stranded on a luxurious island with a sect of author-worshippers? A tender lump of sadness swelled in my throat as I contemplated my fate. After all I had written, this was how it would end. I thought of my poor Bronx mom, and how sad she would be. I thought of Como's sainted mother, and how sad she would be. I thought of the loss of my huge advance. But most of all, I thought about the millions and millions of bereft readers, denied the pleasure of reading my mold-breaking book. How could I evade that tragic fate?

I was now almost pooping myself with fear. I needed an incredible twist in the next paragraph, or I was a dead man. Trying to walk and cross my legs at the same time, I desperately scanned the skies for some source of salvation—an alien tripod to zap the baddies, a meteorite to squash them, a twister to suck them to Oz, an enraged dragon to blast them with its fiery breath, malevolent birds to peck out their...

Bow's perplexed voice interrupted my frantic speculations.

"Tide's out! It's not meant to be low tide until two oh eight."

Bow had a huge yacht at the Clarkesville marina, I recalled, thus explaining his familiarity with the local tide tables.

I looked for myself. The tide was astonishingly low. The waters had retreated beyond sight, exposing acres of virgin seabed—even the dredged channel for the launches was dry. The boats themselves lay almost on their sides on a slick bank of mud.

The Professor caught my eye. As the two men of science in the party, we were reaching the same conclusion at the same time. There was only one explanation for the extreme tidal phenomenon, an explanation we voiced together in awed, disbelieving tones...

"A tsunami."

Whether I said it first, or Sushing did, doesn't matter, because soon we were all saying it, some of us several times, with varying shades of expression, thus:

"A tsunami?"

"A tsunami."

"A tsunami!"

"A tsunami??"

"A tsuna..."

"A tsunami!!!"

"A tsunami???"

Even Como had a go.

"A tsunami? Are you shitting me? You don't get friggin' tsunamis in Clarkesville."

It was a fair point, but before I could ask him in sarcastic tones whether he preferred death over seismological realism, the tsunami hit. One moment we were standing on the jetty, looking at the vast expanse of seabed eerie in the moonlight; seemingly the next, the waters returned, flooding the jetty, our feet, our knees, our thighs.

Someone screamed. A huge cliff of water loomed out of the night, thundering towards the mainland with the speed of a train.

I will never forget the minute that followed, the mad minute in which I was swept by the irresistible waters in deadly soup of flotsam—baulks of timber, shards of glass, the bodies of countless creatures, small boats, beach balls, airbeds, buckets and spades, sunshades, fishing tackle, lobster pots, sailboards, unexploded WW2 mines, submarine nets, oil rigs; I was buffeted by them all until I was hurled onto the mainland shore, where everything went blank.

I came to in surroundings that became familiar as my mind cleared. I was lying at the top of the high grassy bank that separated Herbert's house from the beach. The spent waters of the tsunami had retreated, leaving mile upon mile of debris all along the coastline around Clarkesville. There was another shape on the bank a few yards away. Could it be? Yes. It was Como. I limped to where he lay. He was breathing but unconscious, no doubt concussed by debris as I had been.

Then I remembered something which seemed more valuable than my own life. I patted my pockets. It was still there—the small portable recorder upon which I had preserved the conversation around the dinner table at the hotel. Its glass display panel was smashed, and, like me, it was completely waterlogged, but would its electronic memory be intact?

I squelched up the path to Herbert's house. I turned on the blessed lights and slopped into the study, a trail of seawater marking my passage. At Herbert's desk, I coaxed the small memory card out of the ruined recorder. I prayed as I inserted it in the slot on Herbert's PC. Yes! The files were there, the files that would free Herbert and earn me the world's largest royalty payments. Taking no chances, I logged in to my account and uploaded the files onto the cloud. There. At last I could relax. I leaned back in Herbert's chair.

Something hit me hard on the back of the head.

LESSON FORTY-EIGHT

'Tell me, Herbert.'
   'Yes, Marco?'
   'Is there anything that is not like a boxing match?'

CHAPTER FORTY-EIGHT

In which Marco imagines more melodramatic mayhem.

I came-to, this time with a hyphen, lying on my side on the floor. My wrists and ankles were bound, my arms behind my back. I heard typing and looked up. There was a bedraggled shape in Herbert's chair. Marcia Delgado. She heard me move. Her face was terrifying. A mask of pure malevolence. She held a knife.

"You snooping bastard. We had it all sorted, but no, the snooping bastard has to come along and interfere where he's not wanted. Well your snooping days are over."

She got behind me and yanked back my head with a handful of hair. I could feel the knife on my throat.

"You're gonna tell me what you've done with those files. Now!"

The now was screeched as if by Satan himself. I summoned an unassailable resolution. I was not going to tell Delgado where I put the files. She could kill me if she liked, but the story would survive. Como would investigate. The truth about the Herbert Quarry affair would come out whether I lived or not.

Something of my resolve must have shown on my face, for she threw me back on the floor.

"Right then," she hissed. "If you won't show me, the computer's going to burn in the fires of hell. And you with it."

I heard her go outside. Lugging a jerrycan from Herbert's garage, she shook diesel over Herbert's desk and computer. Without a word, she doused more over me, then left a trail of fuel into the hall. I heard matches struck.

I was seized with a blind panic. I screeched for help. I couldn't stand but I somehow squirmed to the door. Too late. The hallway was full of flame—the heat seemed to burn my face even at a distance. I squirmed back into the room and tried to shut the door. It was held open by a hook, too high to reach. I tried to get an arm behind the door to wrench off the hook—I didn't have the strength. The flames were moving along the corridor. They would soon be feeding greedily on the diesel-soaked carpet in front of Herbert's desk. I kicked the carpet into folds and pushed it into the hallway. I was only delaying the arrival of the flames, but there was nothing else to do but try to survive.

In desperation I managed to stand and headbutt one of the windows. I almost knocked myself out, falling back on the floor in a daze. The panes were toughened glass, a result of Chief McGee's fake security appraisal of Herbert's property.

The fire was raging in the doorway. Herbert's desk and computer were ablaze. The acrid fumes were choking me. My exposed skin felt on fire. My wet clothes were steaming. I was going to asphyxiate or be burned to death. I wormed across the floor to the corner furthest from the fire and stared at the flames that would soon envelop my body. I felt detached and philosophical. I had written my book without thinking, and this was its end. Was it self-inflicted—a subconscious urge for heroic self-sacrifice—or had the gods of literature wreaked swift revenge for my irreverence? I thought of the characters I had created, good and bad—my Bronx mom and Sushing, to mention just the bad—and especially of the true hero of the book, Lieutenant Como Galahad. My eyes welled with tears as I thought of the companionable times we had spent in the fearless pursuit of Truth. He had been unquestioningly loyal to his Writer—well maybe unquestioningly is going a bit far, but this is the big dramatic scene, don't forget—and now I was to betray him by dying, never more to type a single...

My tragic monologue was cut short as a huge rock crashed through a window in an explosion of glass. The roar of the fire redoubled with the inrush of air. A burly figure stepped over the window ledge, the tail of his damp shirt clamped across his face.

"Hold on, Writer."

Como slung me over his shoulder and dumped me out onto the cool grass.

LESSON FORTY-NINE

'I was thinking, Herbert.'
    'Really, Marco?'
    'I think the last chapter might be the most important.'
    'Why do you say that, Marco?'
    'Because it is the one my readers will read last, Herbert.'
    'Are you sure, Marco? They might not get that far.'

CHAPTER FORTY-NINE

In which the writing of the book proves to be the easy part.

I was the hero of the hour, the face on every front-page and TV channel, the toast of the publishing world. A plague of reporters had descended on Clarkesville. I couldn't move without being mobbed. I had written a book unlike any other. No one could decide which was the biggest story—the tsunami, Herbert's innocence, or my breaking the mold of literature. The combination of the three was a publicist's dream. Barney had been ecstatic on the line from New York.

"Markie baby, this is gonna be the biggest thing ever. And I mean e-verr. There's a bidding war for the movie rights. Cruise is begging for your part, begging for it. Elton's on the phone every five minutes about a musical. *Como go Bro*'s number one on YouTube. I got the contract from Microsoft for the Xbox game. Every talk-show wants our Markie, and the book's not even published yet. So, get yourself up here. We've got a book to finish."

I got myself up to New York. Actually, Barney sent a stretch limo. On the drive I reflected on what had happened since the waters of the tsunami retreated.

Herbert had been released, with all charges dropped; psychologists working for the DA decided Lola had a mental age of 37, so a prosecution wasn't in the public interest.

Como and I spent a weekend making a razz video, he winning a toss to call it *Como go Bro* rather than *Rock'em Ocram*. I promoted him to Police Chief for helping me solve the sensational case—and for saving my life.

Chief McGee had drowned in the tidal wave—a better fate than frying in the chair. The other conspirators drowned too, except for Professor Sushing and Marcia Delgado. Marcia fled from the burning house and disappeared, providing the possibility of a last-minute plot-twist if she came after me with the knife. The Professor escaped to Panama, so I could recycle him as a character in my next book.

Jenny McGee, the innocent object of the conspiracy, had lost her father, but was due to gain all of Elijah Bow's estate, or what was left of it when the lawyers had finished.

My Bronx mom was overjoyed to have her little Markie safe and sound—she threw a party for me with all her friends from the hairdresser's and tried to get me dating their daughters. However, I had no time for that—I had a book to publish.

It was then the real work started. Having written seventy-five thousand mold-breaking words completely off the top of my head, having eschewed all editing—in true Jackson Pollock fashion—and having handed the raw manuscript to my publishers with instructions to change not a single word, I was faced with crafting the blurb for the back cover.

"That stream of consciousness stuff might be OK for the book," said Barney, "but we're not gonna have any of that crap on the cover. We gotta get the backmatter right or we'll kiss goodbye to sales."

It was purgatory. I spent more time on those two-hundred words than I did on the rest of the book. Version after version I sent to the publishers. Never was one right. This was too long. This was too short. That sentence doesn't flow. That phrase will be offensive in Balinese. There was no end to it.

From time to time Barney called with updates. The print run for the first edition had been set to five million—a world record. Everyone wanted to read how Marco Ocram had survived a tsunami to bring the world the truth about the Herbert Quarry affair. According to Barney, hot actresses were queueing round the block to have my babies.

Babies...

I thought of my book. It was going to be my baby. A joyous birth after hours of labor. I thought of all the trauma and grief Frances

Kellogg and Elijah Bow had caused by their own desperate plans for parenthood. Parenthood, I thought—it was like a boxing match...

EPILOGUE

In which a promise is not fully honored.

I was reading a review of my book in *The New York Times*, and wondering what a 'fatuous farrago' was, when my iPad beeped with an email from Barney. An astonished "Wow" burst from my lips as I scanned it. I danced into the kitchen.

"Mom, listen."

"I'm busy, Markie."

"It's about my book."

"His mom's baking and he wants her to listen about his stupid book."

"No, listen. I've made a new world record, Mom."

"A new record? You made a new record? You're a clever boy, Markie. I was telling Mrs. Angelman what a clever boy my Markie was. Her daughter, Josette, Markie, you should see her. She's such a sweet thing."

My mom greased a baking tray on autopilot, imagining me and Josette settled down in a nice place in the Bronx with at least six kids.

"It's the royalties, Mom, for the first year of sales. Listen to this: eight million," I paused to let it sink in, "eight million, six hundred and thirty-two thousand, four hundred and eight dollars, and fifty-seven cents!"

"Royalties? What do you want royalties for? Your poor mom never had no royalties. She brought you up without a single royalty, Markie, and all I hear you talk about is royalties. You got more money than you know what to do with, Markie. You want more?"

"It's not for me, Mom. It's for charity. I'm giving it to the police."

"You're a good boy, Markie, a good boy. When you give it to them, tell them about that bum who's always hanging out by the salon. Tell them he's always dropping bits of sandwich on the sidewalk. For all those royalties they should do something about it."

I wandered back into the lounge, staring at the enormous number on my screen. My mom was right; I didn't need the royalties. I had my income from the spin-offs—the merchandise, the endorsements, the speaking engagements. Honoring the promise I'd made all those chapters ago, I emailed Barney and told him to send every single cent to the Clarkesville County Police Benevolent Fund.

He called me within five minutes.

"Every single cent? Every single cent? Are you out of your mind? And for the police? If you wanna throw your money around, Markie, your uncle Barney knows plenty of places that need it more than the police, for Chrissakes."

"Barney! It's a promise, a promise I made to Como."

"A promise! What's a promise? We make promises all the time, Kiddo. Where'd we be if we all started keeping promises?"

"Barney, I know it's a lot of money, but I'm not going to change my mind. No more arguing—just do it."

"Okay, Kiddo, it's your funeral. But don't say I didn't warn you. One day soon you'll be back to your uncle Barney crying over it and wishing you'd listened to what I said."

About a week later, I was signing books at a promo event when Doris Day sang *Que Sera Sera* in the pocket of my anorak.

"Publishing legend Marco Ocram speaking. How may I help you, Caller?"

"Writer, it's me."

"Como! I wasn't expecting you to call until the first page of *The Sushing Prize*. How're things?"

"I was just ringing on behalf of the Benevolent Fund, to say we'd got the check."

"No problem, Como. A promise is a promise." I thought of the good works that might be done with my bounteous donation. A home for retired police officers, perhaps. An annual prize for the best example of community police work. A bursary scheme to send disadvantaged kids to police college. "Have they decided what they're going to do with all the money?"

"All the money? Are you kidding me? What are we meant to do, with fifty-seven cents?"

"Fifty-seven cents?" For a moment I was too confused to type.

"In the Clarkesville County Gazette, it says author Marco Ocram sets a new record with royalties of eight million, six hundred and thirty-two thousand, four hundred and eight dollars, and fifty-seven cents, and you send us a check for fifty-seven cents. I remember the promise was every single cent, Writer, but I never thought you'd use that as a loophole to keep the dollars. And after everything we went through. I saved your life, Writer, and this is how you thank me, sending a check for fifty-seven cents."

"No, Como, no—I wanted you to have all of it. I told Barney to..." Barney! "Como, it was Barney. I told him to send you the money. He sent the check. I'll sort it, I promise, you'll get a new check. Soon, today, I promise. I just need to sort Barney. I'll call you back."

"Well, we'll see."

He said it with such doubt and disappointment, it broke my heart. I knew he wasn't upset about the money itself, but about the thought that he was no longer important to me—that now I had finished my book I was casting my character aside like a worn sock. I grabbed a cab and headed for Barney's office for a showdown. I'd felt so good about giving all the money to the benevolent fund, righting the injustice that saw an author paid more than a cop, and now Como thought I was a cheap shyster weaseling out of a commitment, that I no longer cared about him. I was devastated by the thought that Como felt betrayed by me, his Writer. I was choked and incoherent when Barney opened his door.

"Hey, Kiddo, wassamatter? You get dumped again?"

He went to put an arm around me. I brushed past him and tried to master my emotions, my face flushed, my eyes wet.

"I've just spoken with Como. I can't believe that you've let this happen, Barney. I've trusted you with everything, and you actually did it. You actually sent him a check for *fifty-seven cents*."

Barney shook his head in sorrow. "You see, Kid—you should always listen to your uncle Barney, especially when it comes to throwing all that money around. I told you you'd regret it."

ACKNOWLEDGEMENTS

Heartfelt thanks are due to the following people who played an important part in bringing Marco to the world...

Galen and the team from Tiny Fox Press, who have encouraged and nurtured whatever it is that passes for talent in Marco's mind.

Literary guru Jonathan Eyers, whose advise, unlike Herbert's, one should always follow.

Minette Walters, who gave Marco his treasured first blurb.

The honorary life members of The Awful Literature Appreciation Society (#ALAS), whose kind comments are a constant source of motivation.

And finally, my lovely wife Leona, without whose ideas and support this book would never have been written.

ABOUT THE AUTHOR

Little is known of Marco Ocram's earliest years. He was adopted at age nine, having been found abandoned in a Detroit shopping mall—a note, taped to his anorak, said the boy was threatening the sanity of his parents. Re-abandoned in the same mall a year later, with a similar note from his foster parents, he was homed with his current Bronx mom—a woman with no sanity left to threaten.

Ocram first gained public attention through his bold theories about a new fundamental particle—the Tao Muon—which he popularized in a best-selling book—The Tao Muon. He was introduced to the controversial literary theorist, Herbert Quarry, who coached Ocram in a radical new approach to fiction, in which the author must write without thinking—a technique to which Ocram was naturally suited. His crime memoir, The Awful Truth about the Herbert Quarry Affair, became the fastest selling book of all time, and made him a household name. It was translated into every known language—and at least three unknown ones—and made into an Oscar-winning film, a Pulitzer-winning play, a Tony-winning musical, and a Golden Joystick-winning computer game.

Ocram excelled at countless sports until a middle-ear problem permanently impaired his balance. He has yet to win a Nobel Prize, but his agent, Barney, has been placing strategic back-handers—announcements from Stockholm are expected imminently (and it might not just be physics and litera-ture). Unmarried, in spite of his Bronx mom's tireless efforts, he still lives near his foster parents in New York.

ABOUT THE PUBLISHER

Tiny Fox Press LLC
5020 Kingsley Road
North Port, FL 34287

www.tinyfoxpress.com

Tiny Fox
PRESS

9 781946 501387